To dear Mr. Benabo,

    With my great admiration, warmest wishes and deep appreciation,

Feb. 19. 2014.

Rethinking an NGO

Rethinking an NGO

Development, Donors and Civil Society in Jordan

Basma bint Talal

I.B. TAURIS

LONDON · NEW YORK

For my husband Walid
and my daughters Farah and Zein al Sharaf
and for Ghazi and Saad my sons

Published in 2004 by I.B. Tauris & Co Ltd
6 Salem Road, London W2 4BU
175 Fifth Avenue, New York NY 10010
www.ibtauris.com

In the United States of America and Canada distributed by
Palgrave Macmillan a division of St. Martin's Press
175 Fifth Avenue, New York NY 10010

ISBN 1 86064 925 4

A full CIP record for this book is available from the British Library
A full CIP record is available from the Library of Congress

Library of Congress Catalog Card Number: available

Typeset in Minion by Philip Armstrong, Sheffield
Printed and bound in Great Britain by MPG Books Ltd, Bodmin

Contents

List of Tables and Maps

Abbreviations

ABA	Alexandria Business Association
AFSC	American Friends Service Committee
AMC	Ahli Microfinancing Company
AMIR	The Access to Microfinance and Improved Implementation Policy Reform
BBME	British Bank of the Middle East
BMEO	British Middle East Office
CAS	Country Assistance Strategy
CDC	Community Development Centre
CDD	Cooperative Development Department
CEDC	Community and Education Development Centre
CERMOC	Centre d'Études et de Recherches sur le Moyen-Orient Contemporain
CGAP	Consultative Group to Assist the Poorest
CIDA	Canadian International Development Agency
DEF	Development and Employment Fund
EEC	European Economic Community
ESCWA	Economic and Social Commission for Western Asia
EU	European Union
GAD	Gender and Development
GCC	Gulf Cooperation Council
GDP	Gross Domestic Product
GNP	Gross National Product
GTZ	German Agency for Technical Co-operation
GUVS	General Union of Voluntary Societies
HDI	Human Development Index
HDR	Human Development Report
IDB	Industrial Development Bank
IDRC	International Development Research Centre (Canada)
ILO	International Labour Organization

IMF	International Monetary Fund
ITDG (UK)	Intermediate Technology Development Group
JD	Jordanian Dinar
JDB	Jordanian Development Board
JETT	Jordanian-European Information, Training and Technical Assistance Office for NGOs
JMCC	Jordan Micro Credit Company
JNCW	Jordanian National Commission for Women
JNFW	Jordanian National Forum for Women
JNPC	Jordanian National Population Commission
JOHUD	Jordanian Hashemite Fund for Human Development
JPA	Jordanian Press Association
JPRC	Jordanian Petroleum Refinery Company
JWDS	Jordanian Women's Development Society
KSSDS	Khsha' al-Slateen Social Development Society
MEED	Middle East Economic Digest
MFI	Microfinance Institution
MOSA	Ministry of Social Affairs
MOSD	Ministry of Social Development
NAF	National Aid Fund
NGO	Non-Governmental Organization
NHF	Noor al-Hussein Foundation
NNGO	Northern Non-Governmental Organization
NORAD	Directorate for Development Aid (Norway)
NOVIB	Netherlands Organization for International Development Cooperation
NPC	National Planning Council
OAPEC	Organisation of Arab Petroleum Exporting Countries
OCSD	Organisation Canadienne pour la Solidarité et le Développment
OECD	Organization for Economic Cooperation and Development
PBWRC	Princess Basma Women's Resource Centre
PLO	Palestinian Liberation Organization
PNA	Palestinian National Authority
PRA	Participatory Rapid Appraisal
PRA	Participatory Rural Appraisal
PRB	Population Reference Bureau
QAF	Queen Alia Jordan Social Welfare Fund
RCTS	Rural Credit and Thrift Societies

RLF	Revolving Loan Fund
SLA	Sustainable Livelihoods Approach
SMI	Sustainable Microfinance Initiative
SNGO	Southern Non-Governmental Organization
SPP	Social Productivity Programme
SSHRC	Social Science and Humanities Research Council
UN	United Nations
UNDP	United Nations Development Programme
UNESCO	United Nations Educational, Scientific and Cultural Organization
UNETAP	United Nations Expanded Technical Assistance Programme
UNFPA	United Nations Population Fund
UNICEF	United Nations Children's Fund
UNIFEM	United Nations Development Fund for Women
UNRWA	United Nations Relief and Works Agency for Palestine Refugees in the Near East
USAID	United States Agency for International Development
WAD	Women and Development
WFP	World Food Programme
WHO	World Health Organization
WID	Women in Development
WPF	World Population Foundation
WWSF	Women's World Summit Foundation
ZENID	The Queen Zein al Sharaf Institute for Development

Preface

My involvement with the social sector in Jordan has evolved through different stages of my life. I was quite unaware of my first introduction to this arena which took place in the 1950s before I was three, when I was sent by my mother, the late Queen Zein al Sharaf, to spend the morning with children at an orphanage which she supported. My mother's guiding principles were a sense of duty and service to her country. As the mother of a young King Hussein, who with the advent of the 1950s had just begun his reign, it was characteristic of Queen Zein al Sharaf to want to instill in her four children, including her only daughter, the values which she upheld.

The early 1950s was a significant period for Jordan during which numerous factors – political, social and cultural – were shaping the country's future. During this period the pioneering initiatives of Jordanian women to carve a space for themselves were to lay the ground for those who followed. In many ways, the public sector was, for women, easier to enter than others. The need for teachers, midwives, social workers or support staff, enabled women to work in the relevant government institutions. Outside the state domain, however, women's activities were limited by social attitudes, except in the area of charity work. Consequently, charitable associations offered a productive outlet, particularly for urban women who wanted to channel their time and energy outside the home. Women's voluntary efforts initially revolved around aiding the poor or the handicapped, supporting orphanages, as well as refugee relief. It was these kinds of activities that led to the establishment of the first women's movements and NGOs. Such activities were not only socially accepted, but after a little while it was expected that women should contribute to society in this way.

These early perceptions were substantially enhanced by the role of Queen Zein al Sharaf. Under her patronage various causes gained recognition and were brought into a more public space. My own association with the social sector was very much due to her influence and example. However, it was not until 1977, when I was asked by His Majesty the late King Hussein to found the Queen Alia Social Welfare Fund (QAF), that social development became a career. I was always aware that it was my family ties that made it possible for me to take on this responsibility. At the same time, the growth of the Fund as a national NGO which fosters development initiatives through a widespread presence in local communities has given me the opportunity to learn about the development sector in ways that might otherwise never have been open to me. It is this experience that, almost twenty years on, motivated me to embark on a comprehensive study of Jordan's development process, and within this framework to examine the role of local NGOs through the work of the Fund, later known as the Jordanian Hashemite Fund for Human Development (JOHUD).

The story of Jordan's development is one of numerous challenges. Situated in what is, perhaps, the world's most volatile region, with few natural resources of its own, human capital has played the greatest part in the country's achievements. Long before it became an internationally acclaimed concept, human development was a principal approach and key to Jordan's progress. Indeed, the cultural value given to education has played a crucial role in social transformation and has been a priority of national policy. However, the achievements wrought through education have been offset by the constraints on development generated by a specific set of internal and external conditions which have placed both state and society under considerable strain. Rapid population increase, coupled with heavy reliance on external aid, have created economic as well as political constraints for national agendas. The combined efforts of state and society, including NGOs, have not always been able to overcome the many problems related to poverty and unemployment, which have intensified since the late 1980s. These diverse factors, which have required mediation by both governmental and non-governmental actors, have largely defined the approaches adopted in response to prevailing conditions.

As the Jordanian Hashemite Fund for Human Development's operational approach has matured, the organization has, by promoting models of sustainable development, become one of the leading NGOs in the social sector. In attempting to deal with the serious issues that have emerged in Jordan, the Fund has had to negotiate conditions at the local, national and international levels and to find a balance between the frequently conflicting demands of community-based partners, government institutions and international donor agencies. The dichotomies thus encountered within the development field have often been difficult to settle. As the Fund's outreach in different communities has spread, it has had to learn that there is no single development model, and that its interventions must take into consideration the specificity of the local context. When development models are primarily imported or defined by external trends, this can prove difficult.

Grappling with such issues during the course of my work with the Fund has made me realize the importance of trying to reach a clearer understanding of the underlying factors which shape development processes and give them their dynamics. The Fund's interactions with other actors, including government agencies, local NGOs and international donors, have shown that different parties operate with varying interests and styles. In some cases, priorities are determined by the interests of a particular party rather than a prevailing need, which can create dissent. By examining the way these various parties act in the development arena, I hope to shed some light on the dynamics of the development process, uncovering areas of tension, while evaluating the impact on the field. In numerous situations, donor conditionality and its effect on development initiatives has been a topic of concern. Organizational sustainability and credibility with local partners can, as the Fund has seen, be undermined by changes in donor priorities and funding commitments. Furthermore, insufficient recognition among donor and development agencies alike of the reality on the ground can all too frequently lead to the failure of projects. The result, inevitable when local knowledge is undervalued and participatory methods are only rhetorically applied, is wasted efforts and resources.

Problems of this kind have created serious dilemmas for both Jordanian policy-makers and practitioners. However, they cannot be separated from the wider context, in which economic, social and political factors all play a major role. It is with this in mind that I have sought to examine the Jordanian development process in order to comprehend the way it has evolved at a level deeper than that of my everyday experiences. In doing so, what has inspired me most is a realization of the tremendous effort which has been required by Jordanians to sustain the development process, despite the critical setbacks which Jordan has witnessed over the last half century.

In this book I attempt to present, in historical sequence, the processes by which Jordan has evolved as a country in response to political and economic events, as well as domestic, regional and international influences, and to view the growth of the Queen Alia Fund against this background. I have conducted substantial research on the development process in Jordan from the 1950s to the 1990s. Much of the existing literature on this subject has been written by non-Jordanians and does not necessarily reflect an indigenous perspective, and most of it has placed greater emphasis on economic rather than social development. I hope, therefore, that my insider's view will go some way to filling the gap, although a comprehensive study has yet to be carried out.

From a different perspective, I hope the book will help to further understanding of the challenges globalization has created for Jordan and many developing countries. International donors, policy-makers and academics alike need to strive for a deeper insight into the specificity of different regions and indeed countries faced with these challenges. While development theory and practice has been informed by examples from Asia, Africa and Latin America, relatively little attention has been paid to the Arab region. Similarly, despite greater recognition by international donors of the role of NGOs, relatively few studies have been devoted to Arab, let alone Jordanian NGOs. Such issues are of relevance in examining the largely Western development agenda in the context of the specific circumstances, current political uncertainties and prevailing needs of Jordanian society.

The book is organized in two parts. Part 1 consists of two chapters which present in sequence an overview of international development policies in the second half of the twentieth century and of the course of Jordan's development over the same period. An attempt is made in these to create a thematic grounding which will enable the reader to link donor agendas, state policies and NGO approaches to the Jordanian development setting. The implications of shifts in donor trends for developing countries are highlighted, including the redefining of the state-centred development model in the early 1980s and the emergence of the New Policy Agenda with donor emphasis on the role of NGOs. The characteristics of international donor policies during the 1990s, and their significance for development processes are also discussed. In Chapter 2 the specific features of the different decades which have defined Jordanian development efforts are explained, revealing the constant mediation entailed by both state and society, between external pressures and internal constraints. The analysis concludes by looking at the implications of Jordan's transitional phase to the end of the 1990s, revolving around structural adjustment and political liberalization.

Part 2 turns to the subject of development efforts in Jordan from the perspective of experience of the Queen Alia Fund (QAF). It begins by setting out in some detail the methodology of the study that was undertaken of the Fund. Chapter 4 describes QAF during the period of its establishment, as it attempted to formulate its national role. In Chapter 5, the second phase of QAF's operations is considered, by looking at the organization's development approach implemented through the network of community development centres (CDCs). The Fund's partnerships and programmes in the field are described, and the methods it adopted to promote local level initiatives are discussed. Chapter 6 focuses on the third phase of the Fund within the context of the 1990s. Parallels are drawn between dilemmas faced by QAF as it embarked on reform, and challenges at the national level brought about by the experience of transition. In its closing pages, the chapter considers future directions for the Fund, as it negotiates the dichotomy of international donor trends and local realities.

With the beginning of a new era for the country and for the Fund, the epilogue draws on the analysis of the Jordanian experience offered in the book to raise questions about the transitional role of different actors promoting development in Jordan, including state, society and NGOs.

Jordan

The Emirate of Transjordan came into being in 1921. In 1946 it was recognized by Britain as a fully independent state. In 1950, with the union of the East and West Banks, it became the Hashemite Kingdom of Jordan.

Jordan is located in the central expanse of the Middle East, bordered by Syria to the north, Iraq to the north-east, Saudi Arabia to the east and south, and by the Palestinian National Authority (PNA) and Israel to the west. Jordan has the longest border with Israel of any Arab country and it lies on the most direct routes between Iraq and the Mediterranean and Red Sea littorals. Eighty per cent of its land area is covered by desert and a good proportion of the remaining 20 per cent is suitable only for agro-pastoralism. Less than 10 per cent is sufficiently humid for cultivation, and even where cultivation is possible in rain-fed uplands wide fluctuations in rainfall can make farming precarious. Three agricultural development regions divide the country longitudinally from north to south: the Jordan valley, the highlands and the semi desert *badia* or steppe. In these areas crops such as cereals, vegetables, citrus fruit and olives are grown.

The geographical distribution of the population is largely determined by rainfall patterns and methods of cultivation, in addition to centres of industry. More than 80 per cent of the population is concentrated in one-eighth of the total land area, mainly in the uplands of the northwest. The rapid growth of towns and cities has resulted in an essentially urban population with 35 per cent of the population living in the capital, Amman and its localities. Shortage of water is one of Jordan's most serious problems and is continuously exacerbated by industrialization strategies, agriculture based on irrigation and rapid population growth.

The country has few natural resources. Phosphates and potash, extracted from the Dead Sea, form the basis of a mining sector. Major manufacturing industries include the production of fertilizers, cement and oil refining. Smaller industries include textiles, aluminium, ceramics, detergents, plastic, pharmaceutical and food products. With its limited agricultural and manufacturing base, as well as the small size of local markets, Jordan's economy has come to rely heavily on services, particularly finance, government services, tourism, transport and trade. During the period from the 1950s to the 1970s, services have counted for some 70 per cent of the GDP, with the bulk concentrated in the state sector. Industry has witnessed a small increase over the same period, from 14.1 to 21.5 per cent of GDP. Major manufacturing industries include the production of fertilizers, cement and oil refining. Smaller industries include textiles, aluminium, ceramics, detergents, plastics, pharmaceutical and food products (BBME, 1986). The percentage contribution of agriculture to GDP has meanwhile declined sharply, from 15.3 per cent in the mid-1960s to 4.4 per cent in the mid-1990s.

The limitations of its natural resource base have led Jordan to rely heavily on its human capital, including its industrialists and businessmen. With the advent of privatization in the 1990s, these economic actors became more vital to the country. The declining role of the state in national economies, and the emergence of the private sector as an alternative to government in the economy at a global level, is reflected in the situation in Jordan (Barham, 2002: 278). But it is too early to judge how this redirection of policies from a mostly state-owned economy to one that is led by the private sector will affect the overall economy and the livelihoods of the population.

Investment and external loan figures from the Ministry of Planning show that, from the 1960s up to the end of the 1990s, more than half of total investment and about 60–88 per cent of external loans went to services and infrastructure. The agricultural and irrigation sector has absorbed around one-quarter of total investment and an average of 12 per cent of external loans. At best, the industry, mining and energy sectors did not exceed 35 per cent of planned investment, and apart from the 1970s, averaged 6 per cent of loans (see tables 2.2 and 2.3, chapter 2).

Jordan's demographic situation has been characterized by rapid changes in population size and one of the highest growth rates in the world (UNFPA, 1997). The total population in 1994 was 4,139,458 – almost double the figure derived from the 1979 census and quadruple that of the 1961 census (Jordan, 1995a: 18). Two factors lie behind the high rate of population growth in Jordan: forced migration, and natural growth as a result of improved economic, social and health conditions (Zaghal, 1984: 53–5). Jordan's natural growth rate for the 1986–1990 period was 3.4 per cent (Jordan, 1995a).

The 1990 Jordan Population and Family Health Survey confirmed a declining rate in fertility levels – from 7.4 children per woman in the mid-1970s to 3.8 in 1999 (JNPC, 2000). Declining fertility rates are attributed to a rise in the age of female marriage from twenty-one to twenty-five years. Also, comparisons between the Jordan Fertility Surveys for 1976 and 1999 indicate an increase in the contraceptive prevalence rate from 23 to 57 per cent (Jordan, 2000b). Although significantly higher than the global average of 2.9, the total fertility rate of 3.8 for Jordan is lower than the regional average of 4.5 (JNPC, 2000). Mortality indicators are generally favourable compared to other countries in the region and to countries with similar incomes. A substantial decline in infant and child mortality occurred between 1960 and the late 1990s from135 per 1,000 live births to between 28 and 30 per 1,000. As a result of high fertility and moderately low infant and child mortality, the age structure shows a young population with over 40 per cent below the age of fifteen (WPF, 1996: 4-6; JNPC, 2000).

Jordanian society is predominantly Sunni Muslim. Christians form a substantial religious minority. Ethnic minorities include Circassians, Kurds, Chechens and Armenians. With the process of modernization and the interaction of different elements, Jordan's society has undergone extensive transformations over a short time span. Urbanization, increased education and communication have all been factors precipitating the change (Day, 1986). It has often been said that Jordan has evolved as a tribal society; but this view is open to debate, for it is quite evident that traditional elements have been significantly modified by the effects of social change generated by the advancement of the modern state (Jureidini and McLaurin, 1984). Jordanians of Palestinian origin have been an important catalyst for change in the country. Their political maturity and enterprising nature have contributed to the transition that has taken place (Abu-Jaber, 1982).

Given its narrow productive base, Jordan has chosen to make its greatest investment in its human resources through education which has played a transformative role both as an agent of social change and an instrument for human betterment. Jordanian society places tremendous cultural value on education. Parents strive to provide the best educational opportunities for their children. White collar, civil service and government jobs are socially preferred and are seen to provide job security; academic education and a university degree are perceived as the most direct route to such employment.

From the beginning of the 1960s, addressing regional as well as domestic labour demand was an important target. Secondary education was diversified to include vocational schools, and the first university, the University of Jordan, was established in 1962. These policies paved the way for the export of educated and skilled workers to other countries in the region up until the 1990s. In turn, economic growth was greatly enhanced through remittances sent home, and domestic competition for employment was reduced. By the early 1970s significant education enrolment rates were achieved, reaching 80 per cent at the primary school level, 50 per cent at the preparatory level, 30 per cent at the secondary level, and 20 per cent for the postsecondary stages including community college and university students (Billeh, 1996).

Awareness of the imbalance between labour supply and demand led to the first attempt at major educational reform in 1973. Despite governmental recognition of the international trend to teach marketable skills and diversify secondary education, reforms were modest and had limited impact (Jordan, 1976a). Problems confronting the educational system continued until the mid-1980s. Consequently, a two-year process of critical review and assessment took place between 1985 and 1987. In the 1990s, reform revolved around the improvement of quality at all levels of the education system. Additional concerns included the need to accommodate increasing numbers of enrolments, as well as to match education supply with labour market demands. However, a central concern of education policy remained one of maintaining a balance between the preservation of traditional cultural values and the needs of a rapidly changing society, in the technological and information-driven global economy (Billeh, 1996: 1–4, 11).

Not only has the information and labour sector undergone major changes. In fact, over a fifty-year period, faced with dynamic internal and external challenges, Jordan has undergone radical transformation in all aspects of society, and yet has managed to maintain its core traditional values. These processes of reform have involved negotiation between diverse, and often conflicting, demands from a wide range of actors each with a vested interest in promoting a particular set of theories and policy priorities. The Government of Jordan has tried to maintain a balanced and stable development path in the interests of the entire nation, and yet is affected by the changing priorities of donor partners on whom it depends for funding and support.

As the Chairperson of the Board of Trustees of the Queen Alia Fund since its inception, I was privileged to experience these fundamental dilemmas of development over a twenty-five year period. For the Fund the obligation to respond to the immediate needs of the poorer and marginalized communities in Jordan added to the complexity. Throughout the book, in describing the phases of organizational growth of the Queen Alia Fund up to its re-naming as the Jordanian Hashemite Fund for Human Development in 1999, I have attempted to draw clear analytical connections between the study of one development NGO and the far broader context of changing development paradigms at a global level.

Acknowledgements

When I first decided to carry out this study, over ten years ago, I was not aware of all it would entail. Looking back today perhaps the hardest challenge was to sustain the effort required, while other aspects of my life pulled me in different directions. I am glad that I did, because the process has been so fulfilling.

The support I received from numerous people who knew what I was attempting can never be forgotten and I am grateful to them all. I am particularly indebted to everyone who was directly involved in seeing me through various stages of this project. During the earlier period of my research at Oxford University, the insight I gained from Dawn Chatty and Eugene Rogan was invaluable and I learnt a great deal from working under their guidance. I am ever grateful to them both for the generous and perceptive nature of their advice and for their steady encouragement throughout this time. I was very fortunate to have had the capabilities and talents of very fine research assistants on which to draw. The commitment and wisdom of Amal Sabbagh and the experience of Salem Ghawi, together with the diligent efforts of Taghrid Abu-Hamdan and Nicholaa Malet de Carteret were an asset. I cannot thank them enough for persevering with me and for the pleasure of working with them. They were an important part of this effort. A special tribute must be paid to Mai Abu-Nowar, not only for her superb technical skills, but for her humour and patience with me all the way through.

While it is not possible to single out all the individual contributions made over the course of this project, I am especially grateful to Professor Alan Jones who I have known for many years and to whom I owe a great deal. Discussions with Ricardo Bocco, James Fairhead and Philip Robins were thought-provoking and I always looked forward to them. The help of Simon Dradri with the literature search in Oxford should also be commended. To everyone who kindly agreed to be interviewed for the study, I express my appreciation. I value their opinions, as well as the time they set aside on my account. The pilot study which was carried out by Riad Mustafa and his research team was an essential contribution to giving voice to the field and I thank them for their skillful efforts.

My understanding about questions of development was also enriched and informed by the knowledge of Farah Daghistani, my daughter. With her own background in development she challenged many of my views and shed light on a variety of issues which underly this study. Professionally as well as personally, she was my mainstay. I am grateful to her for stimulating me with her discerning nature, as I grappled with frequent problems during this work. Ultimately, however, no words can adequately convey the gratitude I feel for everyone at the Fund, and within the Jordanian development field, for allowing me to reflect some of their rich experiences through this endeavour. I am indebted to them all and I simply say thank you from the heart.

The prospect of making a book from my original work found encouragement from Iradj Bagherzade. I thank him for supporting the idea of highlighting development in Jordan through this study. I am also grateful to Winkie Williamson for her knowledgeable advice and suggestions, about assimilating current development debates into the final draft. Finally, I would like to express my great appreciation to Anna Enayat for her efforts in reviewing the entire text. I was indeed fortunate that she agreed to lend her remarkable editorial ability to the study. Without them all, this final stage would not have been achieved.

Initially, as I explored the possibility of pursuing this course, I sought the blessings of those who formed the foundations of my life. From my beloved mother Queen Zein al Sharaf, I learnt what was of true value. In all my recollections, my cherished brother King Hussein was an inspiration like no other. And so it remains. As I honour their memory, they are never far from me.

Throughout this often painful process, my pillars of strength have been my husband Walid, and my children Farah, Ghazi, Saad and Zein al Sharaf. Their faith in me made everything possible. I can never repay them for their loving help which saw me through every step of the way. This book is for them.

Basma bint Talal
June 2003

Part One

1

The Politics and Policies of International Development

Throughout its history, Jordan has had to contend with two overarching challenges: political instability in the broader Middle East region and limited domestic resources. The task of furthering the country's development objectives has, therefore, come with a heavy reliance on external aid, necessitating constant efforts to reconcile its international political environment and internal conditions. Jordan's development process over the past half-century has for this reason been considerably affected by changes, not only in the global economic system, but also in the development policies and discourses of the Western powers and the international institutions largely controlled by them.

The notion of development originated in the concepts of progress and evolution which dominated Western perceptions of history for much of the 19th and 20th centuries; but it was only after the Second World War that it began to assume significance in international relations. The 1944 Bretton Woods assembly believed that in the future depression and global war could be averted through the creation of a 'dynamic world economy in which the peoples of every nation will be able to realise their potentialities in peace' and went on to establish the principles and institutions of the post-war economic order – the International Monetary Fund and the International Bank for Reconstruction and Development, later known as the World Bank (McMichael, 1996: 48). At first the focus of these institutions was the reconstruction of Western Europe. International interest in the development of the 'Third World' was, however, soon added to these concerns and by the early 1950s the notion of three worlds – the free industrialized nations, the communist industrialized nations, and the poor non-industrialized nations, constituting the First, Second and Third World respectively – was firmly in place (Escobar, 1995: 31).

Since then, international development policies, largely directed at the Third World through aid, have moved through different phases, each with its own emphasis and approach. Although each has, in its own way, produced a distinct international arena in which national development policies have been formulated, the latest has been revolutionary. Involving a shift in the emphasis of development theory from state to markets, it has brought a qualitative change in the relationship between donor agencies and nation states largely driven by the power conferred on lenders by debt and rapid change in the global economic system (Mohan, 2000: 75). In addition, international aid has been accompanied by new conditionalities which have had an unprecedented effect on political processes.

The changes in priorities and shifts in strategies which donor policies have undergone, and their implications, are reviewed in this introductory chapter. They form an essential backdrop to the donor agendas, state policies and NGO approaches to the Jordanian development setting discussed in this book.

The State and Development

From state-led development to structural adjustment

During the first three decades following the Second World War it was an axiom of policy that development in the Third World would take place through state planning and intervention (Robertson, 1984 quoted in Leftwich, 2000: 72). The emergence in this period of welfare states in the industrialized countries, the post-war enlargement of the Socialist bloc, and nation building processes in the newly independent countries of Africa and Asia, contributed to a tremendous expansion in the size and scope of government throughout the world. In addition, the strong feelings of economic nationalism fostered by the effects of colonization meant that newly independent countries looked to the state to mobilize resources, initiate rapid economic growth and put an end to social injustice. State-led interventions worldwide emphasized market failures and gave government a major role in correcting them. By the 1960s, states had become increasingly involved in practically every aspect of the economy, including price control and the regulation of labour, foreign exchange and financial markets (World Bank, 1997b). Throughout the 1960s and 1970s, moreover, 'the international community would cooperate in negotiating and integrating various development initiatives designed to strengthen development at the national level' (McMichael, 1996: 45).

The dominant conception of development through much of the period centred on economic growth and the structural changes that would be needed to bring about such growth. This approach was promoted by the new post-war international institutions – the World Bank and the International Monetary Fund – and reflected the views of the major industrial powers which dominated them, as well as thinking in the UN (Leftwich, 2000: 40–1). However, within this basic framework development policies underwent significant changes in emphasis. During the 1960s, economists such as Arthur Lewis and Raul Prebisch argued that the potential of developing countries was constrained by a number of structural factors. These included the structure and composition of domestic output as well as external factors such as patterns of exchange between industrial countries in the developed world and suppliers of primary commodities. Specific forms of intervention were, it was believed, required if developing countries were to achieve a sustained pattern of growth necessary to keep pace with their rapidly increasing populations. Thus, whereas aid in the 1950s was mostly designed to support investment in infrastructure and strengthen national institutional capacities, the focus of development policy during the 1960s was on aid and trade (Benn, 1997; Martinussen, 1997). A second shift occurred towards the end of the decade when the strategies of import-substituting industrialization and community development in rural areas, promoted by many Third World governments and supported by external assistance, were experiencing setbacks. It became evident that sufficient employment had not been created by capital-intensive industrialization. Furthermore, population growth in many such countries surpassed the rate of agricultural growth necessitating increased food imports in order to maintain domestic prices and wages. These considerations meant the introduction of new development policies which emphasized technical change in agriculture, marking the beginning of the Green Revolution (Lele and Nabi, 1991).

By the 1970s, international donor agencies were adopting yet another set of priorities. Studies carried out by the World Bank showed that hundreds of millions of people in developing countries lived in poverty, lacking basic facilities such as safe drinking water, schools or health clinics. It was felt that these conditions stifled productivity and kept earning capacity low, resulting in a cycle of poverty. Moreover, poverty could be linked to insufficient investment in agriculture and in social sectors such as education and health. Although the Green Revolution had revealed that equitable asset distribution was important to ensure that technical change in agriculture would have a broad-based effect on growth, and the World Bank had counted on general economic improvement to reach the poor indirectly, rapidly expanding donor-funded programmes now emphasized a direct assault on poverty. World Bank lending was therefore expanded for rural areas, particularly for agriculture from which most of the income of the poor was derived. The World Bank also began to view population growth as a major development issue, but maintained that population could not be controlled without first giving attention to the provision of basic services such as education and health (Lateef, 1995). Projects financed by international aid during this period were designed to meet 'basic needs' in recipient countries including primary education, health, housing and safe drinking water, with relatively little emphasis on asset distribution in rural areas (Lele and Nabi, 1991; Lateef, 1995).

The final phase of state expansion in the post-war era was signalled by the oil price shock of 1974. In oil-exporting countries the abundant resources which suddenly became available to the state encouraged a further enlargement of its programmes and concealed institutional weaknesses. In oil-importing countries states were kept growing through the heavy borrowing of recycled petrodollars. But underlying trends were ominous: during the second half of the 1970s energy costs increased for most developing countries while food prices were rising due to the world food crisis. In 1979 a second hike in oil prices precipitated a prolonged recession in OECD countries which, in turn, caused the price of primary commodity exports from developing countries to fall. Before long the rising interest rates that resulted from inflation increased the cost of borrowed capital, leading to a debt crisis in the early 1980s (Lele and Nabi, 1991). All at once, government failure seemed patently visible everywhere shattering the dominant post-war state-led and state-planned development paradigm (World Bank, 1997b; Leftwich, 2000: 110).

The debt crisis, combined with the neo-liberal economic theory which by this time ruled in Western policy-making circles, precipitated a radical reconstruction of international development strategies based on 'structural adjustment' and the liberalization of markets. During the 1980s structural adjustment was to international lending agencies, particularly the IMF and World Bank, a straightforward way to help reorder the financial chaos threatened by the debt crisis. Consequently, it was directly translated into a package of measures designed to realign domestic demand in Third World countries with the reduced availability of external resources, while cutting down overgrown governments as part of the process. A standard approach was adopted, focused largely on the need to abolish distorting interventions in market prices and with little consideration for the particular circumstances of individual countries. By the turn of the decade the World Bank believed that, as a result of its measures, 'faith in the ability of the state to direct development has given way to a greater reliance on markets,' and that 'government action should be employed sparingly and only where most needed' (World Bank, 1991 quoted in Leftwich, 2000: 50).

For most developing countries, particularly those with serious economic difficulties, the consequences of structural adjustment policies were severe. In those largely unaccustomed to generating domestic financing for growth, the reversal of transfers, coupled with the burden of overgrown state systems, required extensive changes in established methods of economic operation. In many countries people were dependent on the state as a provider of services and jobs so that ending government subsidies and selling off inefficient public sector enterprises created rising unemployment. Decades of import substitution, together with varying degrees of economic mismanagement, left most developing countries largely unable to meet the competitive demands of the global economy. Meanwhile, the option of deciding on a degree of relative isolation from the world economy was reduced by the scarcity of resources, while the difficulties and political costs of moving towards more open domestic economies were exacerbated.

By the beginning of the 1990s it was clear that the results of structural adjustment programmes had fallen far below the expectations of international donor institutions. Most developing countries had made only limited progress towards economic stabilization, new lending had not come about, and in the recessionary economic environment created by adjustment policies domestic conditions had worsened. Indeed, in some countries political stability was threatened. Consequently, donor agencies which had already committed substantial administrative and financial resources, as well as their credibility, to adjustment, met with increasing resistance as they attempted to impose additional reform packages and more rigid conditions on recipient countries. Gradually, the concept of adjustment itself went through a substantive transformation. Policy literature began to make references to timing, replacing the 'short haul' with the 'long haul.' Meanwhile the main barrier to sustained economic change through adjustment was increasingly identified as the political environment.

The New Policy Agenda

At the end of the 1980s an additional factor entered the state-society equation. The break up of the Soviet Bloc and the fall of the Berlin Wall in 1989 ended the rivalry between East and West in the Third World.

Geopolitical considerations no longer shaped the use of aid and Western politicians were eager to find new ways to further ideas of 'freedom and democracy' and keen to forge ahead with the liberal-democratic model. Making an explicit link between political and economic liberalization, international donors began to argue that concepts such as economic growth, respect for human rights, the market economy, reduced military expenditure, decentralization and democracy were mutually sustaining (Archer, 1994: 10).[1] Consequently donor agencies began to adopt what has come to be known as the 'New Policy Agenda' combining elements of economic liberalism and Western political theory in ways which redefine the roles of and relationships between states, markets and 'third sector' institutions (Robinson, 1994; Whitehead, 1993).

Broad agreement exists between various donors on the overall content of this agenda. It is underpinned by three models: 'the role of competitive markets (the economy), government responsibility to manage (the state), and the importance of private rights and individual initiative (civil society)' (Archer, 1994: 7). Different weight has, however, been given by various countries and agencies to concepts of human rights, popular participation and 'good governance' as opposed to market orientation and a reduced role for the state. In the case of the World Bank, for example, the focus has remained largely economic (Robinson, 1994). Nevertheless, the Bank has, since 1992, largely by consequence of the problems it encountered in implementing policies of structural adjustment and economic liberalization in developing countries, especially in Africa, also promoted good governance which it treats as 'synonymous with sound development management' (Lancaster, 1993; Leftwich, 2000: 121).[2] In the case of other

---

1. The phrase 'good governance' began to catch widespread political attention in 1990, after speeches by President Mitterand and Douglas Hurd voiced new political conditions as an imperative for aid allocations, especially in Africa.

2. The theme of political conditionality was addressed by the United Nations Development Programme (UNDP) in its first Human Development Report (HDR) published in 1990. The report stated that external donors could help protect human development by providing additional resources to ease the pain of adjustment, while making clear that external assistance would be reduced to countries spending more on their military than on their people. The difference between UNDP and the World Bank, as reflected by the HDR, lay in the view that recipient countries had a right, or even an obligation not to cut social expenditures and subsidies benefiting poorer income groups; furthermore, human development programmes should be the last to be reduced in adjustment periods (UNDP, 1990).

donors, including most Western governments and the UNDP, the focus has been more pointedly political.

In the 1990s decisions on aid allocations were increasingly influenced by the commitment of recipient countries to donor priorities such as political pluralism and accountability. International funding agencies began to favour specialized aid programmes to promote good government, human rights and political reform. Refusals by authoritarian or repressive governments to support reforms or improve human rights in their countries have led donors to resort to sanctions, including the reduction, suspension or termination of development aid. The subsequent resumption of aid was made conditional, for instance, upon a clear demonstration of improved human rights, democratic reforms, reduced military spending or greater accountability. These measures have collectively come to be known as political conditionality and are often the subject of heated debate among donors and recipient governments.

The premise of political conditionality is not in itself new, for donors have always used political criteria to arrive at decisions about aid allocations. Throughout the Cold War, Western governments provided aid to counter the spread of communism in developing countries, while the Soviet Union supported governments with similar ideological positions. Both sides regularly gave grants and loans to authoritarian regimes and, in some cases, Western governments supported incompetent and corrupt rulers (Leftwich, 2000: 109). What is different about the political conditionality which developed with the emergence of the New Policy Agenda is the insistence that 'societies characterized by open markets, competent administrations and liberal-democratic politics – essentially capitalist democracies – not only promote growth and development but also secure peace because such societies do not go to war with each other' (ibid.: 107).

The policy emphasis on aid conditionality has met with reservations in many developing countries. Political conditionality is sometimes viewed as an unreasonable intrusion into state sovereignty, tantamount to neo-colonialism. Other reservations stem from scepticism over Western intentions and the perceived dangers of using aid to promote Western models of democracy in developing countries (Robinson, 1994). For one thing, despite the extensive operational autonomy which international lending institutions like the World Bank and IMF enjoy, politically they remain affiliated to members like the USA, Japan, Germany, the UK and France whose constitutional influence over them is overwhelming (Leftwich, 1994). Hence, the World Bank's 'good government' policy reflects the ideologies and interests of its most influential members. This, together with numerous Bank references to limiting state power and strengthening civil society, has contributed to rising concern in developing countries over questions of state sovereignty (Stewart, 1997: 31).

The shift of international donors to NGOs

A striking phenomenon, which coincided with the rolling back of the state in countries throughout the world, was the explosive growth in importance of development NGOs. For almost two decades international donors expanded the nature, range and content of their collaboration with NGOs in an unprecedented fashion. The trend began in 1981 when the United States Congress passed legislation to expand development assistance through NGOs, with the result that US-based NGOs began to receive up to 80 per cent of their funding from their government. In 1994, at the Social Summit in Copenhagen, Vice-President Gore announced that this policy was to be continued and that 'nearly half the aid from ... USAID would within five years be provided to private organizations, not direct to the poor world's governments' (*The Economist*, 1995: 19). Meanwhile, the proportion of total aid from OECD Development Assistance Committee members channelled through international NGOs increased from under 10 per cent in the 1970s to 25 per cent in 1985 (Van der Heijden, 1987). In Britain, the share of total income received from the UK government by developmental NGOs rose significantly from 7 per cent in 1986 to 18 per cent in 1992 for Action Aid; from 15 per cent in 1984 to 24 per cent in 1993 for Oxfam and from 12 per cent in 1984–85 to 37 per cent in 1992–93 for Save the Children (Edwards and Hulme, 1995: 850).

In part the 'quiet revolution'[3] brought about by this shift in donor thinking was due to greater awareness of the financial capacity of NGOs and the difficulty of ignoring the impact of the NGO community on the development scene. During the 1980s, NGO operations expanded significantly as a result of the increased public profile identified with disaster and relief, especially during the 1984–1985 African famine. Equally important was the change of donor attitudes towards the role of government in providing goods and services for basic needs and implementing national development strategies. Multilateral lending programmes were coming under greater scrutiny, partly because donor governments raised

---

3. Fisher (1997) compares the significance of the rise of NGOs to the rise of the modern state in the 19th century.

concerns over aid effectiveness and were sometimes reluctant to endorse requests by international development agencies for increased contributions. Disillusionment with government delivery systems prompted aid agencies to evaluate their operational counterparts and look to other delivery channels. A growing consensus among international donors began to view NGOs as an efficient channel for the delivery of aid programmes, particularly in social areas (Sollis, 1992). In addition, an expanded role for NGOs was directly compatible with the focus of the New Policy Agenda (Moore, 1993, quoted in Edwards and Hulme, 1995: 849). On the economic side, NGOs were viewed as market-based actors able to deliver social welfare services to poor people at lower costs and higher standards of quality than governments (Fowler, 1988; Meyer 1992, quoted in Edwards and Hulme, 1995: 849). On the political side, the desire of Western donor agencies to promote 'democratization' among recipients of aid placed NGOs and grassroots organizations in a central position as components of 'civil society.'

A similar shift has occurred in recipient countries. Donor governments were willing to forego cooperating with inefficient and sometimes recalcitrant official partners in developing countries if NGOs could provide a competent alternative as intermediary or implementing organizations. There may have been other perceived advantages for donor governments in shifting responsibility for projects to NGOs. Donor governments assume that since NGOs are usually grateful for recognition and funding, they are far less likely to criticize their approaches. On the other hand, as representatives of civil society, partnerships with NGOs create a positive impression by which donor governments gain more regard (Post and Preuss, 1997). In addition, both for multilateral donors and international NGOs, local NGOs in developing countries represent an essential component of a flourishing civil society, vehicles for democratization, and a willing channel for promoting the New Policy Agenda (Moore quoted in Hulme and Edwards, 1997: 6; Fisher, 1997).

Development Policies in the 1990s

Preamble: globalization and its implications

From the early 1980s, and with increasing speed in the 1990s, globalization created a radically new international framework for development processes. Globalization involved the integration of national economies into world markets at a level and intensity that is unprecedented, and has led to the emergence of a new kind of global economy driven by information technology. Indeed some have seen structural adjustment and the New Policy Agenda as instruments of this process, used by neo-liberal policy establishments in the West to address delays in the Third World to the ongoing move towards global capitalism (Leftwich, 1994: 370).

While the economic dimension has been central to globalization, most students of the phenomenon have emphasized its multifaceted character. Thus, as Ngaire Woods points out, globalization involves three interconnected elements: 'the expansion of markets; challenges to the state and institutions; and the rise of new social and political movements' (2000: 3). Although there is no consensus on the extent to which globalization is undermining the power of nation states, it is clear that power and authority have been shifting to global institutions and corporations and that national governments have seen their 'sovereignty and control over domestic political and economic affairs rapidly diminish' (Adams et al., 1999: 1).

The complex economic, political and technological changes that drive globalization have, moreover, been linked with changes 'in the way people and groups think and identify themselves, and changes in the way states, firms, and other actors perceive and pursue their interests' (Woods, 2000: 2). Thus the sociologist Roland Robertson has distinguished between two dimensions of globalization. The first is 'compression of the world,' by which is meant the real experience of the way that interdependencies are being created in the economies of the world to such an extent that 'the way people live their lives now on one side of the world has immediate consequences for people on the other side' (Hoogvelt, 2001: 122). The second is the emergence of a 'global consciousness' manifested in the way people throughout the world speak in a 'discourse unified through mass communication.' Hence military-political issues are thought of in terms of 'world order,' people talk about 'world peace' and 'human rights,' while issues pertaining to pollution are viewed in terms of 'saving the planet' (ibid.: 122–3). Other sociological theories of globalization, such as that of Anthony Giddens, emphasize the way in which technological progress has overcome the relationship between time and space, shrinking the world into a 'global village' in which people are able to have 'social relations and even organized community relations regardless of the territory they share' – a trend that has 'enormous consequences, not only for the role of the nation state as a territorially-bounded community, but also for the organization of economic production on a cross-border basis' (ibid.: 125).

While all countries are affected by globalization, its impact has been far from equal. World inequalities and the inequalities which lie within countries have visibly escalated over the past two decades, a trend which, according to some, stems from an 'increasingly inequitable access to consumptive and productive resources within and between countries' (Stewart and Berry, 1999; Scudder, 1999: 356). The main distinction, however, lies between the industrialized nations of the North and the developing nations of the South. According to figures published in the UNDP's 1999 *Human Development Report* the gap in income between the 'richest' and the 'poorest' countries increased from 35:1 in 1950, to 44:1 in 1973 and to 72:1 in 1992 (UNDP, 1999a; Hoogvelt, 2001: 90). According to the same report, in 1997 the richest 20 per cent of the world's population accounted for 86 per cent of world GDP; 60 per cent of middle-income world populations had 13 per cent, while the remaining one per cent of world GDP went to the poorest 20 per cent (UNDP, 1999a: 2). 'Global openness,' as one study has remarked, very clearly 'undermines the already precarious position of *subaltern groups* and intensifies domestic inequalities' (Adams et al., 1999: 6).

The UN General Assembly Special Session on the Beijing Platform for Action pointed to this uneven pattern, noting that 'Benefits of the global economy have been unevenly distributed leading to wider economic disparities, the feminization of poverty, increased gender inequality, including often deteriorating work conditions and unsafe working environments especially in the informal economy and rural areas' (UN, 2000: 14). The UN also pointed out in the same document that the gender impact of changes brought about by globalization have yet to be evaluated in a systematic manner. The same holds true for the effect of globalization on social policy. Social policy issues which were previously the concern of sovereign states have now become supranational and global in character. Yet 'the implications for national, supranational and transnational social policy of this present phase of globalization is an under-theorized and under-researched topic ...' (Deacon, 1999: 212).

The changing meaning of development

The changes that marked development policy in the closing decades of the twentieth century came not only from neo-liberal structural adjustment or the political conditionality that characterizes the New Policy Agenda. Debates over the meaning and purpose of development itself have resulted over the years in important shifts of emphasis from the earlier, purely quantitative approach which equated development with economic growth to more complex notions of social and human development. These see freedom, social justice and the expansion of choice, not just the accumulation of wealth, as central components of the idea of development.

There have also been a series of radical critiques which have challenged the post-war orthodoxy that equated 'development' and 'progress' with 'modernization' and the remaking of the Third World in the image of the West. For example, the dependency theorists, whose work became influential in the 1960s and 1970s, argue that 'underdevelopment' is itself a consequence of Western expansion. Its persistence stems from the unequal relations between rich and poor countries and the inherent logic of international capitalist expansion resulting in distorted economic structures which lack the necessary dynamic to take off into sustained growth (Lewellen, 1995). More recent critiques, such as those of Escobar and Esteva, take their inspiration from the work of Michel Foucault and see the post-world war discourse of development as an instrument of Western domination over the Third World. According to Escobar, the concepts of underdevelopment and the 'Third World' emerged after the war as 'working principles within the process by which the West – and in different ways, the East – redefined itself and the rest of the world' (Escobar, 1995: 31). With the end of colonialism, the assumption was that the underdeveloped world needed only to follow in the footsteps of the modern world: 'Regardless of the diversity of the cultural heritages of Third World nations, the experience of the West became the standard model for their development' (McMichael, 1996: 31). For Escobar, development was an answer to the 'problematization' of the poverty which was 'discovered' after the Second World War rather than a natural process of knowledge which evolved, gradually identifying problems and addressing them. Development, he argues, should therefore be seen as 'a historical construct that provides a space in which poor countries are known, specified, and intervened upon' (Escobar, 1995: 44–5). It is 'not a matter of scientific knowledge, a body of theories and programmes concerned with the achievement of true progress, but rather a series of political technologies intended to manage and give shape to the reality of the Third World' (Escobar, 1984: 384).

Among international donor institutions the post-war definition of development began to broaden in the early 1970s. Growing concerns with social development and social justice, and with the evident failure of 'development' in many Third World countries, culminated in a 1974 UN General Assembly resolution calling for a new international order which, if implemented, 'would have involved a major shift in the balance of world economic and political power' (Leftwich, 2000: 43–4). Simultaneously, thinking in the International Labour Organization began to emphasize the fulfilment of 'basic human needs,' an approach which emerged from the work of the economist Dudley Seers and was underpinned by the idea of development as creating the conditions for 'the realization of the potential of human personality' (Seers, 1979: 10). Proponents of this approach insisted that the systematic and steady provision of basic needs focused on the 'primary redistribution of income, assets and power' and included non-material as well as material needs. For the ILO the operational definition of basic needs focused on five main areas: basic goods for family consumption; basic services including education, water, health and transportation; participation in decision making and the fulfilment of basic human rights; and productive employment (Leftwich, 2000: 46–7).

These issues went into abeyance with the crisis of the state and the imposition of structural adjustment policies but surfaced again in 1990 with the publication of the UNDP's first *Human Development Report*. The report based its concept of 'human development' on the work of economists such as Amartya Sen, Paul Streeten and Mahbub ul-Haq who, during the 1980s, had begun to argue that economic growth should be viewed as a means to improve human welfare, not as an end in itself (Martinussen, 1997: 37). Human development was defined by the UNDP as a process of enlarging people's choices, whether economic, cultural or social. Following this definition, the UNDP Human Development Index (HDI) based its measurement of the state of development of countries around the world on a combination of three indices – life expectancy, educational attainment and purchasing power. Towards the end of the 1990s, the UNDP extended the range of factors taken into consideration in the HDI to aspects of modernization and human rights and the underlying concept itself was changed to 'human sustainable development' in order 'to highlight the importance of sustaining all forms of capital resources – physical, human, financial and environmental – as a precondition for meeting the needs of future generations' (ibid.: 303).

When it was first introduced, the approach of the UNDP's Human Development Index contrasted sharply with the World Bank's annual *World Development Report* which assessed country performances mainly on economic criteria, reflecting the conflicting outlooks in the development community. A year later there were signs that the World Bank itself had begun to move away from a narrow concept of development when its annual report defined economic development as 'a sustainable increase in living standards that encompass material consumption, education, health and environmental protection' (World Bank, 1991: 31). Nevertheless the Bank's approach to the measurement of growth has remained economically based.

Participatory development

The benefits of people's participation in development have, from the late 1970s, been advocated and practised by many NGOs (Oakley, 1991). However, it was not until the 1990s that participatory development became a mainstream concept recognized by international donors, governments and NGOs alike. This trend was driven by the opening up of political systems in Eastern Europe and in several countries in Africa, Asia and Latin America, where whole populations had previously been excluded from direct involvement in political and development processes. Popular demand and outside pressure together initiated change for wider political involvement, greater bureaucratic accountability and more equitable access to national resources and decision-making processes. Within the development community, promoting people's participation was prompted by a recognition of the limitations of the 'top-down' approach to development, the need to ensure a more equitable distribution of development gains and to devise better ways of reaching the lowest income groups (Pratt and Stone, 1994; Oakley, 1995).

Participation rapidly became a key word in the policy papers of donor agencies. For example, in 1993 the UNDP made it a key theme of its *Human Development Report* where it wrote that participation meant 'that people are closely involved in the economic, social, cultural and political processes that affect their lives' (UNDP, 1993: 21). The concept has also been adopted by the World Bank whose 1992 report states that 'the World Bank has learned from its experience that participation is important for the success of projects economically, environmentally and socially' (World Bank, 1992: 27). Since then 'participation' has become a regular feature of the design and implementation of World Bank-sponsored social development projects and the Bank has even published a *Participation Sourcebook* (1996) which presents 'practice pointers in participatory planning and the involvement of the poor, and offers guidance on participatory methods and tools' (Francis, 2001: 78).

As a concept, participation has always encompassed two broadly different threads of discourse. The first is instrumental and looks upon participation as a means of including human resources in development efforts, whereas previously development planners had overlooked the contributions and skills that people could bring to development projects, and which would enhance their chance of success and sustainability. The second thread is more concerned with equity, empowerment and the structural causes of people's poverty. Here, the emphasis lies on improved governance and strengthening civil society whereby, through increased participation in the institutions of state and society, the poor gain influence and access to resources which would help them sustain and improve their standards of life (Oakley, 1995: 1; Pratt and Stone, 1994).

The value of indigenous knowledge
An important source of inspiration for the new emphasis on participatory development has been the work of Robert Chambers. In his *Rural Development: Putting the Last First* (1983), Chambers emphasized the value of indigenous knowledge, arguing that rural peoples' knowledge and modern scientific knowledge are complementary in their strengths and weaknesses. Combined, they may achieve what neither would alone. Centralized urban planners and policy-makers, practitioners of the 'top down approach' to development planning which was dominant in the 1960s and 1970s, often failed to recognize the knowledge of rural people. One of the reasons for this problem, Chambers maintains, was the gap between practitioners and academic cultures. Efforts to experience other cultures from the inside, to learn and understand the values and knowledge of those cultures, were largely undertaken by anthropologists. But neither rural people, nor the small number of researchers with access to and understanding of their rich and detailed systems of knowledge, had any influence on development (Chambers, 1983).

Outsiders' knowledge, which is modern and scientific, and accessible to them in books and information retrieval systems, is easily communicated and taught all over the world. In contrast, the knowledge of rural people exists in innumerable forms and is accessible to outsiders only through learning from rural people themselves or rarely through ethnographic literature (ibid.). To bridge the gap, Chambers contends, reversals are required in order to redress the balance between the two. Ultimately, it is by recognizing the value that local knowledge provides, combined with the contributions of technical expertise, that sustainable development targets can be achieved.

Chambers has gone on since his early critique of the top down approach to rural development to promote participatory learning and planning (known as PRA – Participatory Rural Appraisal) as the key to reversing the domination of outsiders and their knowledge in the development process. 'Outsiders do not dominate and lecture; they facilitate, sit down, listen and learn ... they do not transfer technology; they share methods which people can use for their own appraisal, analysis, planning action, monitoring and evaluation' (Chambers, 1997: 103). PRA has since come to be widely used in the formulation and evaluation of rural development projects by aid agencies, including the World Bank (Francis, 2001: 75).

Some dilemmas of participation

Even though the association between NGOs and the promotion of popular participation is widely acknowledged, the effectiveness of NGO roles has been questioned in the more general debate on participation. Most studies show that, by their very nature, NGOs adopt people-centred approaches easily and are on the whole successful at fostering participation. However, evaluations of the results of NGO participatory approaches in development interventions remain limited and additional evidence is needed to reveal the extent to which participatory methods are in practice used by NGOs. This is partly due to the complexity of the different kinds and levels of NGOs, and the context of their operations. While it is important to demonstrate NGO capability at project level, as well as showing that activities can be sustained, clear indications are also needed which reveal NGO efforts to enhance capacities of local level structures and to build the institutional links necessary for active participation at greater overall policy and decision-making levels (Oakley, 1995).

The view held by international donors, that enhanced participation can be achieved through NGOs, raises certain concerns for NGOs themselves. NGOs have expressed worries that they may be used as 'cheap mechanisms' to help multilateral and other official agencies implement their programmes, and feel the need to ensure that they are not simply being turned into 'private contractors delivering communities to large development programmes' (Pratt and Stone, 1994: 10).

It is also felt that participation is not genuine unless it occurs at the conceptual stages of a development programme, rather than at implementation stages. Donor-NGO cooperation offers advantages such as greater funding prospects and opportunities to manage larger programmes; however, the risk of co-optation is also regarded as a way of depoliticizing development, in addition to undermining the autonomy of NGOs themselves (ibid.).

The way in which development tools such as Participatory Rapid Appraisal (PRA) have been applied in practice is also a cause for concern. They can lead trained professionals on consultancy missions for development agencies to believe that, even as outsiders, they can quickly understand the dynamics and needs of local communities better than local representatives. Furthermore, these techniques often imply that local organizations must fit in with strategic plans prepared in other countries, which are sometimes based on unsuitable project concepts and subject to unchallengeable funding conditions (Powell and Seddon, 1997; Chambers, 1992). Thus, the pursuit of participation by donor agencies is sometimes viewed by local development activists as largely rhetorical, amounting to little more than a restructuring of control and a way to fit new principles into old models of development (Fisher, 1997: 455).

Participation is a multidimensional process which encompasses political, economic and social characteristics. As the direction and outcome of this process is not always predictable or manageable, careful consideration is required in building participation into development projects (Oakley, 1995). Furthermore, the UNDP maintains that ensuring people's participation requires active enabling support from government and a decentralization of decision-making processes on development (UNDP, 1991).

Considering gender roles and relations within development processes

The demand for increased participation of the poor in development processes was driven, to a large extent, by the recognition that top-down approaches failed to ensure equitable distribution of the benefits from development initiatives. One social group who were seen to have been significantly excluded in this process were women. In the 1950s and 1960s, with the drive towards modernization and industrialization, it was assumed that rapid economic growth would bring equality for women. The questioning of the growth model, and especially of its potential to deliver equitable development, also coincided with the emergence, mainly in the developed world, of a women's movement demanding equal rights with men.

For development professionals, this also heralded a new era of development theory where women's roles and interests became a focus for analysis, and women were identified as a distinct target group for development interventions. Spurred by Ester Boserup's evidence in *Woman's Role in Economic Development* (1970), which revealed that many projects not only ignored women's interests but often in fact undermined their economic opportunities and independence, the supposed gender-neutrality of development processes was challenged, and, over time, a well-articulated theory of gender and development evolved. In the 1980s – often referred to as the Women in Development (WID) era – the focus was primarily on women as beneficiaries, and interventions were aimed at improving their social and economic status. Women's units were established in most development agencies leading to a proliferation of projects dealing with 'women's issues' either as stand-alone development initiatives or as 'add-on' components of existing programmes. However, the late 1980s also brought a recognition that the WID approach failed to address the underlying power relations that defined the status of women and men in society. As Anne Marie Goetz notes, policies and projects promoting the interests of women which fail to provide women with institutional survival bases that might be alternatives to dependence on men: 'at best ... improve women's survival at the margins; at worst they reinforce the traditional gender ideologies which contribute to women's disadvantaged position in their efforts to mobilize physical and human capital for self development' (Goetz, 1995: 4).

The complex social relations between men and women, and their ascribed gender roles, came to be recognized as a significant factor either enabling or hindering women from benefiting from development interventions. The call was for fundamental policy and legal reform to ensure that equality of rights between men and women was enshrined in law, and for the removal of obstacles to the exercise of these rights. Under the Gender and Development (GAD) approach of the 1990s, the focus of development theorists and practitioners increasingly moved towards addressing gender bias in the institutional environment in which development initiatives were implemented. Feminist theories of the state, for example, claimed that the state itself is gendered, largely oriented to male interests, and that this is, in part, a result of their longer acquaintance with public citizenship, their literal dominance of decision-making, and the historical embedding of their needs and interests in the structures and practices of public institutions (Goetz, 1995).

In the late 1990s, two issues – participation in decision-making and the nature of institutional structures – became the major focus of efforts to change the gendered outcome of development processes. The inter-linking of these two issues resulted from the recognition that participatory development for women varies widely in developing countries, not only because of differences in the broader economic political and socio-cultural context, but because of differences in the objectives, approaches and structures of implementing agencies. The extent to which institutions are gendered

– in other words promote men or women's interests – varies according to the gendered history and politics embedded in institutional rules and processes. Early interest focused on the role of state bureaucracies, which, argues Goetz (1996), with their status-oriented hierarchical and elitist cultures, are commonly assumed to be resistant to equity-oriented development programmes, in contrast to NGOs which pride themselves on their egalitarian ideologies. However, analysts of gender policy in a range of state and non-governmental settings throughout the world have pointed to common forms of resistance in male-dominant organizations, noting meanwhile that 'male interests' are not entirely coherent, although men do tend to act more cohesively in defence of their gender interest than women.

It cannot be assumed that women are a monolithic category – significant differences exist between women from different classes, age-groups and marital status. Certain categories of women, often leaders in their communities or organizations, such as older or richer women, benefit more than others from the status quo and are sometimes more anxious to preserve their privileges within the system than to dispute them. Many grassroots women's organizations reflect rather than challenge gender and other forms of inequality. Although women's organizations often include women of widely differing views and opinions, in some there is relative consensus about the aims and directions the organization should take. This may, at times, be because cooperation serves the interests of dominant groups (Mayoux, 1995: 244–5).

Cultural factors play an intrinsic part in shaping organizational approaches to programme implementation. Bridging the gap which often exists between local realities and external trends requires recognizing the values and norms which define societal relations in any traditional context. For this reason, institutional initiatives aimed at advancing women's participation in the development process require that particular consideration is given to gender roles and relations (Chatty and Rabo, 1997).

In working to promote women's participation, the experience of NGOs has been that varying perceptions and understandings of the concept prevail amongst both women and men. There are, in addition, differences over the interpretation of women's needs which are reflected in the variations between organizational policies and programmes aimed at addressing women's issues (Moser, 1993; Kabeer, 1994). In practice, the initiatives of NGOs which foster development through community-based participation have revealed that different stages are required for the process to evolve (Pretty et al., 1995). Moreover, key to this process is the need to build intangible, yet vital, elements such as trust and self-reliance, which in essence takes time.

Over the three decades from the 1970s onwards, the gender and development discourse has evolved from an initial focus on women as targets and beneficiaries for development interventions towards a recognition of the need to address complex and interrelated issues of policies, institutions and processes and the promotion of rights-based approaches to gender equity. Gender and development, like participation, is a multidimensional process, in which a more holistic understanding of the inter-connectedness of elements is essential. In many respects, this process of both widening and deepening the levels of analysis also reflected the broader trends in development thinking which were leading to the demand for a greater understanding of sustainable development.

Sustainable human development

The notion of 'sustainable development' was first brought into official discourse by the World Commission on Environment and Development (The Brundtland Commission) in 1987. The Commission highlighted the growing realization among governments and international institutions that 'it is impossible to separate economic development issues from environmental issues' (WCED, 1987: 3) It did not, however, meet the concern for progressive environmental destruction simply by advocating all round constraints on growth. 'Sustainable development,' it argued, would be a process of change in which 'the exploitation of resources, the direction of investments, the orientation of technological development, and institutional change are all in harmony and enhance current and future potential to meet human needs and aspirations' (ibid.: 46).

The ideas and strategies advocated by the Brundtland Commission were discussed and elaborated over the next few years and international attention to sustainable development was heightened by the Earth Summit held in Rio de Janeiro in 1992 (Serageldin, 1994). The 'human' dimension was subsequently added to the concept, emphasizing the people-centred goals of development and the importance of sustaining all forms of capital and resources, whether environmental, human or financial. For example, Michael Cernea, the World Bank's leading social scientist, argued in 1994 that sustainability must be 'socially constructed,' meaning that social and economic arrangements must be formed purposively, and 'be built through a threefold approach which addresses social, economic and ecological domains simultaneously.' 'Putting people first' in policies and investment programmes for inducing development is not, writes Cernea, 'a radical but a realistic call which simply means recognizing the centrality of social actors and their institutions in sustainable development' (1994: 7). Meanwhile, the UNDP included a lengthy chapter on sustainable human development in the 1994 *Human Development Report* where it explored the ethical foundations of what rapidly became a dominant development paradigm. According to the UNDP:

> Universalism of life claims is the common thread that binds the human development today with the exigencies of tomorrow, especially with the need for environmental preservation and regeneration for the future. The strongest argument for protecting the environment is the ethical need to guarantee future generations opportunities similar to the ones previous generations have enjoyed. This guarantee is the foundation for 'sustainable development.' But sustainability makes little sense if it means sustaining life opportunities that are miserable and indigent; the goal cannot be to sustain human deprivation … Human development and sustainability are thus essential components of the same ethic of universalism of life claims (UNDP, 1994: 13).

The *Human Development Report* went on to argue that sustainable human development could only be achieved:

> … through far-reaching changes in both national and global policies … The essence and test of sustainable human development strategies must be to ensure a sustainable livelihood for all. These strategies – especially at the national level – will thus have to focus on three core themes: poverty reduction, employment creation and social integration – in short, participation. At the global level, sustainable human development requires no less than a new global ethic. Universalism in the recognition of life claims and concern for common survival must lead to policies for a more equitable world order … (ibid.: 21)

There was also an emphasis on participation in the policy literature. Thus, according to the report of the United Nations Commission on Sustainable Development to review the status of the Earth Summit agreements and their implementation, national consultations on the subject had revealed consensus over 'the need for participatory processes in which government, civil society organizations … can reach agreement on priorities and actions, including the need for informed participation of different stakeholders in such processes' (UN, 1997a: 2).

Revised approaches to poverty alleviation

The implementation of the 'good government' approach exposed a number of critical drawbacks in the New Policy Agenda. Indeed, by the middle of the 1990s there was a growing realization among international donor agencies that new strategies were needed to address such serious issues as the sharp reduction in the living standards of poor communities brought about by structural reforms. Donors began to recognize that in poor countries market reforms had not only failed to benefit the poorest people, but sometimes harmed them. Moreover in poor countries the reforms at times had such drastic effects that they threatened to destabilize the governments which introduced them (Archer, 1994: 31, 33; Brand, 1994). There were also concerns that decentralization, generally viewed as one of the strengths of the New Policy Agenda, might lead to a transference of authority to local elites, thus further undermining the autonomy of local institutions. In the absence of a strong central mechanism to reallocate resources, inequality between poor and less poor regions might, as a consequence, be increased (Edwards, 1994: 69).

The general framework of the good government agenda is now an established part of international donor approaches and is unlikely to change in its essentials. There is, nevertheless, much to suggest that donor agencies have become acutely aware of the inconsistencies in development policies which have resulted in further marginalizing the poorest groups and have begun to revise them accordingly. A major example of this changed outlook is to be found in the reinforcement of donor commitment to the alleviation of poverty and the recognition of the mutually sustaining roles of the public and private sectors in fulfilling this objective according to country specific circumstances (Archer, 1994; Hurrell and Woods, 1999).

In 1990 the World Bank devoted its *World Development Report* to the issue of poverty, which it admitted was still widespread, and in many countries had even increased. Among the prescriptions of its anti-poverty strategy was social investment to improve poor people's access to, and the 'adequate provision of, social services including private education, basic health care, and family planning services' (World Bank, 1990: 138). A 1997 World Bank report concluded that the challenge to policy lay in creating an appropriate combination of public and private sector interactions that could successfully foster development and specifically reduce poverty, even though the combination would vary according to the socio-economic conditions of each country (Psacharopoulos and Nguyen, 1997: 1–2). The theme of the 1997 *Human Development Report* was also poverty eradication. Like the World Bank, the UNDP took the position that the challenge of alleviating poverty should be undertaken in partnership between government and civil society, including the private sector, although 'the strategy for poverty reduction will naturally differ from country to country' (UNDP, 1997a: 6).

Despite the strong drive to privatize services traditionally delivered by governments, by the middle of the 1990s there was a shift back towards endorsing the state provision of at least 'the core' of basic social services (Edwards, 1994: 68). 'The state,' as the 1997 *Human Development Report* affirms, 'cannot relinquish its responsibilities in providing basic education and health care for all' (UNDP, 1997a: 10). There has been a return, in other words, to the 'basic human needs' strategy of the 1970s (Leftwich, 2000: 123), but at a time when budgetary pressures and anticipated falls in aid flows are prompting governments to examine the effectiveness of aid for basic needs – a subject which raises contention between governments and NGOs.

Microfinance as a new approach to poverty

The role of credit as an instrument to reduce poverty acquired new importance after the 1995 Social Development Summit and the 1997 Microcredit Summit in Washington, where policy-makers and donors committed themselves to campaign for the eradication of poverty by providing one hundred million of the world's poorest families with credit for self-employment by the year 2005 (Grameen Bank, 2000). This was followed in December 1997 by United Nations General Assembly Resolution 52/194 which encouraged all parties involved in poverty eradication programmes 'to consider incorporating microcredit schemes in their strategies and support the development of microcredit institutions and their capacities' (UN, 1997c: 11).

These events coincided with a growing belief amongst a number of donors and policy-makers that subsidized credit programmes were unsustainable, did not reach the poor, and contributed to a distortion of financial markets (USAID, 1995; Von Pischke, 1996). It was argued that borrowers tended to view loans as charity and rarely paid back. Funds were also quickly depleted before a large number of people could be reached (CGAP, 1995). Furthermore, training in health, education, social empowerment or business skills, which was often provided together with credit, was proving to be costly (UNDP, 1999). Certain donors thus began to move away from the traditional enterprise development approach based on providing an integrated package of credit and training (Otero and Rhyne, 1994). This was largely replaced by a 'financial systems approach' which emphasized 'the creation of institutions rather than projects to meet the financial needs of the poor on a sustained basis' (UNDP, 1999: 4–5).

The 'financial systems approach' has been criticized for putting more emphasis on the microfinance institutions (MFIs) providing the services than on the people who benefit from them (Garson, 1996). Nevertheless, because the donor community tends to regard subsidized credit as incompatible with the aim of sustainability, the justification being that donor-subsidized programmes cannot go on forever, the microfinance industry has grown considerably over the last few years. Sustainable MFIs are seen to be in the spirit of entrepreneurship, and, moreover, consistent with the evolving global market economy in which it is envisaged that the entrepreneurial poor also have a part to play (CGAP, 1996). On the other hand, for NGOs embarking on such activities, this approach has raised the question of whether they are being used as 'cheap mechanisms' by donors to promote their programmes in the interest of making anti-poverty strategies more cost-effective (Pratt and Stone, 1994). The dilemmas of this debate, as it relates to the loan programmes of the Queen Alia Fund (QAF), will be discussed in chapter 6.

The sustainable livelihoods approach

The renewed focus on poverty in the world development agenda, coupled with the emphasis in the 1990s on the social and environmental aspects of development, has resulted in attempts to appreciate the multi-dimensionality of poverty and its impact. The most important outcome of these efforts has been the emergence of an alternative approach, known as 'sustainable livelihoods' (SLA), which views poverty eradication as a holistic process.

The International Institute for Sustainable Development defines 'sustainable livelihoods' as an approach that is:

> ... concerned with people's capacities to generate and maintain their means of living, enhance their well-being, and that of future generations. These capacities are contingent upon the availability and accessibility of options which are ecological, socio-cultural, economic, and political and are predicated on equity, ownership of resources and participatory decision making (Singh and Titi, 1994).

'Sustainable livelihoods' thus recognizes that the capacity of the poor to achieve positive livelihood outcomes depends not only on their access to resources, but on the extent to which their fundamental rights and entitlements are respected. It recognizes that the poor are vulnerable to external shocks and trends over which they have little control, but which impact negatively on their fragile asset base. It also places great emphasis on the ways that policies, institutions and processes impact on the lives of the poor (and support or hinder their strategies) and is explicit about the role of powerful political interests in this equation.

In many ways, the sustainable livelihoods approach, with its focus on the poor individual, the household and the community within a local context, represents the only challenge among current development policies to the dominant neo-liberal model of globalized development.

Factors Affecting Development Processes

Context and process in the shaping of state and society roles

The 1990s saw a growing consensus that development processes can only be successfully fostered through an active partnership of the public and private sectors. The New Policy Agenda, through its emphasis on 'good government,' has brought about a change in perceptions of public and private sector roles in the development process. Strong and effective government is now recognized as a prerequisite for successful policy implementation. Rather than the substantial curtailment of state functions advocated by earlier interpretations of neo-liberalism, the New Policy Agenda re-emphasizes the role of government in areas of regulation and accountability. The 'good government' approach acknowledges that markets are not the whole solution. It rehabilitates the state and recognizes its central role and economic responsibilities. Nevertheless, concepts of human rights, democracy and the rule of law are promoted as prerequisites for a modern market economy and a well-administered state. In other words, although essentially more tolerant of the state than the older neo-liberal model, the good government model remains primarily market oriented. Performance judged by this standard largely determines government survival, and even cultural values are at times weighed against market-driven objectives (Archer, 1994).

A new awareness has meanwhile emerged among development specialists that the failure to engage with the history, practice and theory of the state as an agent of development is a major shortcoming of the contemporary concern for governance. The concept of governance, as presented by international donor agencies such as the World Bank, is regarded by some critics as 'naive' and 'simplistic,' presented as if 'governance' were an autonomous administrative structure detached from the turbulence of world politics and the make-up and purpose of the state (Leftwich, 1994: 364). It also ignores the fact that in many developing countries sustained economic growth, at least in its early stages, has been due to state approaches and policies in which political objectives and bureaucratic competence have centred around creating a development momentum in a competitively hostile international environment (Leftwich, 2000: 153–70).

Despite this renewed consciousness of the significance of the state and its environment, international donors have not always been receptive to the fact that 'each national form of democracy takes on its particular character in response to the specific character of the society in which it is embedded and the specific historical conditions under which it emerges' (White, 1995: 31). Nor has there been much consideration of the diversity of linkages and relationships between the public and private sectors in different settings although, 'complex and changing relations between elements of the state, the private sector and civil society underpin both economic growth and enhanced capacities to meet social needs. Contexts and historical timing are of key importance, especially in an area so culturally sensitive as this' (Hulme and Edwards, 1997: 277).

In order to enhance government performance in areas identified by the New Policy Agenda, most donor agencies have tried within their own organizations to improve their capacity for implementing governance programmes by hiring specialists in the fields of political science and public administration (Moore, 1993; Robinson, 1995; Chatty, 1996). However, the ability of donor agencies to evaluate and draft good government interventions is still limited. There are as yet no established methods for studying good government requirements within country or region-specific settings, by which main areas of need can be identified and decisions for aid allocations can be informed. Furthermore, verified procedures for obtaining the opinions of recipient governments and potential partners, as agents of good government initiatives, have not been adequately developed and international consultants suitably qualified to carry out assignments of a politically sensitive nature remain relatively few.

In pushing forward concepts such as democratization as one of the conditionalities of the New Policy Agenda, external agents, whether they are international donor agencies, national institutions, or Northern NGOs, can exert considerable influence on the political as well as the development processes of recipient governments. Yet, for all the emphasis on accountability and transparency in the good government agenda, consultation mechanisms are singularly inadequate. Issues such as transparent and effective policy-making, good financial management, respect for law and international rights, as well as a commitment to democratic accountability and pluralism are of key pertinence to international behaviour. For these issues to be addressed as elements of international governance and to succeed as sustainable objectives, significant changes are needed both in foreign policy conduct and within international aid agencies (Archer, 1994). Above all, a clear recognition among international donors is needed of the magnitude of political change required in many developing countries for them to apply good governance. For those countries struggling with problems of poverty, ignorance and disease, the conditionality of good governance creates its own complexities and is often difficult to sustain (Leftwich, 1994).

In carrying out long-term reforms in democratizing societies it must also be recognized that policy implementation is as much a question of process as content. Traditionally, officials in developing countries and international donor agencies have concentrated mainly on policy content while paying little attention to process. Because process is as political as it is technical, as well as highly interactive and complex, it requires elements such as consensus-building, contingency planning and adaptation. Moreover, new policies often entail readapting roles, structures and incentives. These, and many other problematic aspects of policy implementation, mean that no amount of external donor pressure or resources can, by itself, produce sustained reform. Participation is key to the state-society realignments associated with democratization and good government, as these changes influence the political and bureaucratic context within which policy implementers operate. It is therefore important that action plans are the result of the combined efforts of those who have a direct interest in policy outcomes and those who play instrumental roles in the implementation process: collaboration between state and civil society is, in other words, a major requirement for the process of implementing policy (Brinkerhoff, 1996).

The relevance of setting to state-NGO relationships

To better understand the range of considerations that shape development interventions, it is necessary to recognize that the factors determining state-NGO relationships, and the policy instruments which governments may use to influence the operational space of NGOs, are primarily country specific. They depend on the make-up of the NGO sector itself, as well as diverse governmental and societal considerations. In countries where state-NGO relationships are based on mutual objectives and comparable priorities, cooperation between the two sides is naturally enhanced. Even in situations where friction does arise out of differences in objectives this does not necessarily mean incompatibility, for collaboration is achieved through complementarity rather than competition. But in countries where, for example, government does not regard a commitment to poverty alleviation as a strong priority, then initiating dialogue and collaboration becomes a more difficult task for NGOs (Clark, 1995).

Official aid agencies can play a constructive role in influencing state-NGO relationships. Just as they are able to directly affect the NGO sector by providing or withholding funding, they are also able to influence state-NGO relationships through their project and policy dialogue and possibly reinforce the political will for productive interaction (Clark, 1995; Stewart, 1997). However, since there are no set rules for any given situation, greater awareness by donors that contexts are specific is needed in order to enhance the positive interaction of all sides involved in development activities.

NGOs are sometimes viewed as organizations which offer 'development alternatives.' This is, however, misleading because people do not actually have a choice between the development model tendered by their government and a model or models represented by NGOs. The role of NGOs in areas such as filling gaps in state services or advocating change in national development strategies is essential; but this does not necessarily constitute providing alternative approaches. Although NGO innovations offer a means of testing out new approaches, these only become sustainable or significant if they influence national development, in which case they become mainstream rather than alternative (Clark, 1995). Furthermore, weakened state capacity can undermine NGO performance. For if the basic planning and policy functions of the state are reduced to a bare minimum, NGOs may, in the absence of adequate policy coordination provided by government, get caught up in competing over limited resources (Robinson, 1994).

Most Arab countries have been carrying out structural adjustment programmes since the beginning of the 1980s. Throughout the region this has necessitated cutbacks in the public sector and the liberalization of markets to encourage private sector initiative. State roles have generally diminished in areas such as healthcare, education and social services for poor income groups. Simultaneously, there has been a marked increase in the number of Arab NGOs, largely due to liberalization processes and structural reforms, giving them a greater role in gap-filling activities and areas of social development traditionally carried out by the state. Many Arab states are now so weakened that they are becoming unable to effectively provide services to their populations. At the same time, while non-state players in Arab transitional societies are continuing to evolve, the problems which they are trying to take on are far greater than their present capacities can handle (Marzouk, 1997: 201). Because neither in the public nor in the private sector are systems strong enough to provide adequate solutions, the dilemmas of dealing with issues such as poverty and unemployment have become more intense in the region.

In many transitional societies in the developing world 'NGOs are very new and huge areas of state-society relations are being rapidly redefined, under great pressure from outside interests, to conform to Western models' (Hulme and Edwards, 1997: 277). The question that arises in such circumstances is whether the New Policy Agenda is 'really strengthening civil society, or merely an attempt to shape civil society in ways that external actors believe is desirable?' (ibid.) Most transitional societies, including Jordan, are having to handle different dilemmas while simultaneously staying on the course which they need to follow. For the Jordanian state and society, this mainly means coping with the negative effects of economic reform on many segments of the population, especially the poor, while maintaining stability in the face of the political complications of the Middle East peace process. For both state and society undergoing processes of transition, the prospect of change holds both opportunity and threat; how to maintain the momentum for change where it needs to happen, and how to guard against it when it is harmful.

The effect of conditionality on the nature of NGO relationships

For NGOs the New Policy Agenda has held considerable promise, both in terms of finance and opportunities for greater recognition (Hulme and Edwards, 1997). Yet at the same time their reliance on outside aid has created new vulnerabilities especially for the national NGOs of the South. As Hulme and Edwards point out, 'he who pays the piper calls the tune' (ibid: 8). The new dependency, they argue, has the potential to alter drastically the very nature of NGOs and can compromise their autonomy.

With the shift in development policies from geopolitical control to market competition and maintaining political stability and economic growth in the developing countries, aid has become progressively geared to creating the right international environment for fostering these objectives. It is also becoming more evident that the pace of global change, an expanded range of aid conditions and growing tax-based finance for NGOs from the North, are affecting the nature of relationships and the authenticity of partnerships between them and the NGOs of the developing countries. Studies conducted to examine perceptions among NGOs from the South of both Northern government and NGO behaviour reveal that the gap between rhetoric and practice over North-South interdependence appears to be growing wider as the basis for aid leans towards the values and practice of the business sector (Fowler, 1998).

The acceptance of increasing volumes of foreign aid involves NGOs entering into agreements about what is done, and how it is to be reported and accounted for. It fosters emphasis on certain forms of activity at the expense of others, on upward accountability (rather than downward accountability to members and beneficiaries), and on particular techniques and donor definitions of 'achievement' throughout the organization (Edwards and Hulme, 1995). Unit costs, quantifiable outputs, logical frameworks and detailed specifications of what 'partners' are to do become organizational norms (Hulme and Edwards, 1997). As a result, most major donors are ill-equipped to provide the sustained, yet flexible, capacity building assistance which NGOs require if they are to improve their operations. This results in a substantial gap between the stated policy objectives of donors and what they are actually pressured to do by their own political and bureaucratic imperatives (Korten, 1980).

Donor conditionality has raised a whole range of questions for NGOs. Donors are sometimes criticized for being inconsistent in applying conditionality and for using double standards. Reservations over economic conditionality are usually shared by development NGOs from both the North and the South who feel that a more focused conditionality, which aims at benefiting the poor, is needed. It is also generally felt that greater transparency and consistency by donors is required. However, there are also differences of views among NGOs themselves, depending on whether they are from the North or from the South. This flows from the fact that NGOs from the North themselves apply conditions to their Southern partners for the receipt of funding. In this regard, both Northern governments and NGOs apply the New Policy Agenda with similar approaches, and conditionality depicts the uneven power relations between them and the Southern organizations which they fund (Clayton, 1994; Dias, 1994).

The vulnerability of Southern NGOs to donor conditionality has been vividly illustrated by the experience of the Sarvodaya movement in Sri Lanka analysed by Jehan Perera (1995). Sarvodaya started in the late

1950s in a single village with volunteers working to evoke self-reliance and build community participation. Its approach was based on fostering innovation, adapting to new technologies and fulfilling basic human needs through planned action, while upholding value systems and encouraging progressive traditional norms. Programmes included early childhood development, as well as promoting rural technical services and economic enterprises. Gradually, the movement expanded to cover several thousand villages. In 1985, donors offered to support Sarvodaya's programmes through a consortium of international development agencies working in Sri Lanka. The proposal was initially welcomed by the movement, as it presented the opportunity of long term planning, the commitment to a three-year budget and capacity-building initiatives. However, when the consortium concept became operational the potential advantages gave way to manifold impediments. The approaches of evaluators and donors who took over the policy and decision-making functions were geared to promoting a delivery mechanism, rather than the alternative approaches to sustainable development fostered by Sarvodaya. Highlighting these conflicting approaches was a statement made by the project director of NOVIB (the Netherlands Organization for International Development Cooperation), Sarvodaya's main donor partner, in response to various proposals made by the organization: 'We are not interested in philosophy. For NOVIB development is a business. There is nothing idealistic about it. Sarvodaya should conform to a businesslike relationship with NOVIB' (Perera, 1995: 874).

During this time, the executive director and other senior officials at Sarvodaya became preoccupied with implementing proposals and recommendations made by donors, as well as accompanying various monitoring and evaluation missions and consultants on almost a daily basis. Consequently they had little time left to see what was happening in the villages. In a period of less than two years, 123 recommendations were made which were virtually impossible to implement. Donor consortium meetings were gradually converted into business forums where humanitarian considerations were given little attention. Subsequently, donor representatives imposed 'sanctions' on Sarvodaya for its inability to meet their expectations. What started off as a partnership based on dialogue had by the mid-1990s become a sub-contractorship based on commands and sanctions (ibid.: 877). Finally, the donor consortium decided to approve only half the budget for Sarvodaya's programmes and made the condition that the 8,600 villages which Sarvodaya had reached should be reduced to 3,000 in 1992 and 2,000 by 1994. The contributions that donors initially made to help Sarvodaya expand its network were lost in the clash of cultures and donor inconsistencies.

A parallel can be drawn between the Sarvodaya story and certain Jordanian NGO-donor experiences. Even with the best intentions, the conditions which donors have been known to place on their partners can sometimes have a negative effect on the outcome of projects. Yet as funding opportunities decrease, local NGOs sometimes have few options but to accommodate the priorities of their donors. As in microfinance schemes, a major donor trend in Jordan in the late 1990s, the success of a project is increasingly measured by business criteria and NGO efforts are often diverted from other, more integrated, development approaches.

Another situation affecting interactions with donors is the issue of transparency. When one side feels that it is required to act with transparency but has limited knowledge about the workings of the other, relationships are unlikely to evolve on equal terms. It is, for example, generally the case that the information available to a Jordanian NGO about the internal workings of its foreign partner is inadequate. On the other hand, foreign consultants working on behalf of their organization with a Jordanian NGO have ready access to information about its methods of operation. Other pressures on local NGOs derive from trying to administer projects while catering to the conditions of their external partners as well as considerations arising from the domestic context.

Social capital

Sarvodaya provides a good example of how Southern NGOs can emerge, grow organically, and fit with their environment. They reflect local cultures and they promote the idea that the well-being of the community (which encompasses diversities of gender, age, physical ability, and poverty) is as important as individual well-being. They draw strength from people's sense of community and belonging, and their willingness to give 'of themselves,' without calculating the returns on their investment, to movements which bond them more tightly to their fellow human beings.

NGOs, in other words, rest on, and in their turn generate, 'social capital' – a term first introduced by a sociologist, James S. Coleman, in the late 1980s which has since found its way into economic analysis and the discourse of development. For Coleman 'social capital is defined by its function. It is not a single entity but a variety of different entities with two elements in common: they all consist of some aspect of social structures, and they facilitate certain actions of actors – whether persons or corporate actors – within the structure' (Coleman, 1988: 98). Social capital, by contrast to human capital, inheres in relations between individuals and groups, and not in individuals per se and it may be found in 'features of social organization such as trust, norms, and networks, that can improve the efficiency of society by facilitating coordinated actions' (Putnam, 1993: 167).

External development actors often see only the more tangible forms of capital created by NGOs – their physical assets, financial reserves or human staff – which they treat as 'cost-effective' systems which can be utilized to deliver messages, goods and services that serve their interests effectively. The urgent need among donors to disburse aid through NGOs on ever larger scales, and to meet measurable targets and standards of efficiency, has to be achieved through a standardization of products and economies of scale. As a result, the organic structures which underpin so many Southern NGOs are replaced by a hybrid of the business-government bureaucracy model. In the process, NGOs are co-opted, depoliticized and their autonomy is undermined.

However, it must also be recognized that social capital is not necessarily neutral or benign. On the contrary it can be valuable for some actions and harmful for others (Coleman, 1988). The complexity of understanding social capital reflects the underlying cultural dynamics and tensions within all communities. An understanding of these factors can reveal that social inequalities may sometimes be embedded in social capital. Affiliations through norms and networks may obstruct some groups while serving others, particularly if the norms are discriminatory or the networks are socially segregated. Recognizing the importance of social capital in sustaining community life does not discount the need to be aware of how that community is defined, who benefits from social capital by being inside, and who is outside and does not (Putnam, 1993).

It is perhaps significant that theories of social capital emerged and captured the interest of development theorists just as the impact of globalization began to be felt even at the community and household levels. Social capital builds on reciprocity and trust, but also, by definition, implies that certain people are excluded from the benefits. Analysis of the role of social capital in development requires a recognition that the interests and expectations of certain social groups may change as external influences are brought to bear, and new opportunities open up. This in turn leads to changes in the balances of power and emergence of new forms of social relations, often articulated through transformation of development institutions.

Questions of culture

The global restructuring of capital has necessitated a changing relationship between the North and the South and an emphasis on new partnerships for the more effective implementation of development programmes and projects. This has involved not only new relationships between donors and beneficiaries, but also new forms of organization to administer the transfer of resources from bilateral and multilateral donors.

This changing reality has required the evaluation of local-level development projects which aim at qualitative change in people's lives. Although the emphasis in such projects now centres on 'appropriateness' and 'sustainability,' as David Marsden (1994) has rightly asked, to whom are they appropriate and in what contexts are they sustainable? Central to these issues is a fundamental concern with the problem of cultural specificity and the 'space' to be given to the elaboration of local development strategies in the face of trans-cultural preoccupations which suggest that certain sets of values – such as those underpinning structural adjustment, environmental sustainability, enhancement of the role of women and 'good governance' – are not negotiable.

In the course of the 1990s it was widely acknowledged that the failure of many development projects lay in not fully recognizing the role of the human factor within the local setting. However, this heightened awareness of the need to focus on the development of appropriate organizational forms within their culture-specific settings requires a reassessment of aid relationships themselves. Here, consideration should be given to the fact that different approaches based on divergent value systems will lead to the development of various organizational forms. While recognizing that organizational culture must be taken into account in assessing whether development objectives are being achieved, more effective partnerships in development processes can be enhanced by building on elements which provide opportunities for positive change (ibid.).

In the Arab region, for instance, the considerable politicization of social institutions prior to the reorientation of state roles and the political reforms undertaken by some governments was clearly reflected in organizational forms. Similar authoritarian structures to those governing Arab political and social life in general were reproduced within the organizational cultures of Arab NGOs. However, as the need for social and political democratization was increasingly felt within the region, at popular as well as state levels, opportunities for new forms of social or community representation began to emerge (Marzouk, 1997). As change continues in both the external and indigenous environment, the culture of organizational forms will respond to external factors and gradually undergo simultaneous processes of change.

The domination of the ideological goals of 'modernization' has been contested in the Third World by new priorities based on different approaches. These aim at increasing autonomy and self-reliant development which breaks relations of dependency in worldwide structures of capitalism (Buller and Wright, 1990). The failure of development efforts is often attributed to the incompatibility between models derived from the experience of the North and Southern realities, and sometimes to factors such as patronage networks, institutionalized corruption and extended kinship connections which are believed to inhibit the rational development of effective organizational forms in the South. Whatever the case, the focus needs to shift to the 'values that underpin "Southern" realities in the eyes of the people themselves,' in order 'to build from where people actually are, rather than where we think they are' (Marsden, 1994: 38).

Development interests

Development processes are shaped by a range of social forces which, besides culture, include social classes, national governments, international donors and NGOs (Ferguson, 1994: 16). Different interests in development policies often exist between national governments and international agencies and are sometimes not easy to reconcile, for national governments must respond to the interests of various local groups which may conflict with the policies and requirements of international agencies (Heyer, Roberts and Williams, 1981). Furthermore, different interests operate mostly through a complex set of social and cultural structures that are usually deeply embedded and ill-perceived. Consequently, even when various interests are accommodated, the outcomes of planned policies are often far removed from their original intention (Ferguson, 1994: 17).

Philip Van Ufford (1988) has introduced yet another dimension to the equation by questioning the extent to which policy-making processes are determined either by cultural factors or by dominant economic and political interests. The implication of his argument is that development goals and strategies reflect the power balances between different elites and economic interest groups. Moreover, development policy-making becomes the arena in which each tries to assert itself, and where the interests and contradictions of the development scene are reproduced.

There is an increasing awareness in developing countries that the adoption of externally defined development models has the potential to undermine a nation's fundamental right to self-determination. Even those countries which want to pursue the path to 'modernization' need to manage it at their own pace, through their indigenous institutions and in a way that is consonant with local values and cultures. At the same time, arguments about the cultural and political factors which shape the development process underline the fact that the 'national interest' versus 'foreign interest' is not a simple differentiation – within developing countries, there are certain social actors which in fact identify with the interests and expectation of 'outsiders'.

Conclusion

The constant shifts in international development policies pose many questions. A principle issue is whether the pace of change has been driven by the need to further development in general, or the need to keep finding ways to serve the interests of the developed world at the expense of the developing countries? The rapid changes in international development policies cannot be considered to have adequately addressed the problems of developing countries. Not long after agricultural development became a priority (with Third World countries providing a market for the agricultural technologies of Western nations), donor strategies shifted to a focus on basic needs. In effect, it was largely through international donor financing for this new approach, that government spending in many developing countries increased and state services expanded.

The geopolitical control of Third World countries by developed nations has been replaced by the economic control of a global economy which is largely based on the ideologies of the West. Originally, state expansion in the developing world was propelled by aspirations of nation-building, as well as economic nationalism in many newly independent countries after the end of colonial rule. The shift from state-centred development to market economies that took place during the 1980s redefined development strategies, providing ways of reasserting economic and political control over Third World countries and reorganizing their systems according to Western criteria. One may question the extent to which the New Policy Agenda and the good government approach aim to advance the process of development in the Third World or instead to adapt development processes in the Third World to suit Western policy agendas. The other alternative, that Western paradigms may be considered to be promoting true development, is equally problematic.

The conditionality of international aid may have indeed strengthened civil society and the liberalization process in many parts of the developing world. However, it has come with a high price for state sovereignty. When power relations between countries are uneven, conditionality remains conveniently one sided. The imbalances of power between developed and underdeveloped countries, and the ensuing inequalities that shape their relations, are mirrored in the relations between Northern NGOs and their Third World partners. As advocates of liberalization and democratization processes, how democratically do Northern NGOs apply these concepts to their NGO partners in developing countries, when they themselves impose conditions for project support?

Multilateral donors advocate 'participation' as a major issue. But even at the highest levels this is not applied since governments in Third World countries often have no part in formulating the international development policies which they must subsequently adopt. While attention to context and setting is now part of development discourse, concrete evidence of how international donor policies are accommodating these considerations remains to be seen. As factors such as state and NGO roles are now recognized to be context-specific, it must also be recognized that they cannot be refashioned purely on Western development models. Furthermore, within context-specific settings, culture-specific values which reinforce development objectives already exist. Social solidarity and the concept of 'community' have been inherent values in Arab and Muslim societies, long before social or community development.

While civil society has grown stronger in many developing countries, largely due to liberalization processes and aid conditionality, governments have grown weaker. The New Policy Agenda re-emphasizes the role of state and the good government approach redefines the role of government. Undoubtedly, a well ordered state is vital to the well-being of any country. Moreover, experience has shown international policy makers that a weakened government cannot create the necessary environment for entering into the global economy. Political and economic stability, both priorities of the New Policy Agenda, cannot be achieved by promoting market economies at the expense of vulnerable groups; for through neglect, the poor become a political and economic liability which only delays progress. Consequently, the shift back to endorsing government provision of basic needs, reflects a realization by donors that the role of state remains a prerequisite for maintaining social stability. Ultimately, despite all the accepted shortcomings, the state is primarily capable of sustaining basic service distribution, especially to the poor, on a continuous and equitable basis. The complementarity of government and private sector partnerships, including the participation of NGOs, now strongly advocated by international development agencies, may represent a plausible combination for promoting development objectives. However, it is also necessary to be critical and discerning, as to how, within this framework of 'complementarity,' the changing nature of the state and the role of NGOs may be manipulated to further the agendas of international aid.

2

The Development Process in Jordan

For Jordan, reliant on external assistance to compensate for regional and domestic vulnerability, the changes in donor policies and priorities over the last fifty years, reviewed in the introductory chapter, have significantly affected the context in which it has been able to pursue its own national development path. This chapter traces the process of that development over four distinct periods: the 1950s–1960s, the 1960s–1973, 1973 to the end of the 1980s and 1990–1999. The discussion seeks to address the following questions: Did Jordanian development policy follow or coincide with international donor agendas? Or did the specific political and socio-economic context of the country set the criteria for addressing national development priorities? The dilemma which trying to balance these two factors has posed for different actors in the development field is a significant theme.

Setting the Scene in the 1950s

Although the historical context of early development efforts in Jordan during the 1950s differs from present day circumstances, parallels can be drawn between the actions of both local and external agents. Politically, the first six years of King Hussein's rule, from 1951 to 1957 (sometimes called 'Jordan's first transitional period'), were critical. During this phase, the need to ensure the security of the young state was the main priority for the country's leaders; consequently, promoting economic development was, for them, a secondary concern (Satloff, 1994). Against this background, the threefold population increase which followed the 1948 Arab-Israeli War created additional burdens for the newly established country's already meagre resource base and limited development structures. For these reasons Jordan was heavily reliant on external funding and development programmes were primarily in the hands of foreign donors whose agendas were largely based on their own political and economic interests.

Table 2.1
Population Increase in Jordan, 1928–1998

Year	Population size (in thousands)	Average annual growth rate %[1]
1928[2]	300.0	–
1947	400.0	1.5
1952[2]	586.2	7.6[3]
1961[2]	900.8	4.8
1965	1028.2	3.3
1970	1508.2	7.7[4]
1975	1810.5	3.7
1979[2]	2133.0	4.1
1980	2233.0	4.6
1985	2700.0	3.8
1990	3700.0	5.0[5]
1991	3701.0	6.5[5]
1994[2]	4139.4	3.7
1998	4755.8	3.5

Source: Statistics are compiled from different sources of the Department of Statistics for the years 1928–1998.
1. Population growth rate was estimated by employing the exponential growth equation.
2. Years in which a population census was conducted. Figures for other years are estimates.
3. Result of the Arab-Israeli War 1948.
4. Result of the Arab-Israeli War 1967.
5. Result of the Gulf War 1990–1991.

A comparison of early donor policies

A study by Paul Kingston has analysed the approaches of foreign donors promoting development in Jordan in the 1950s: the British Middle East Office (BMEO), the US Point Four Programme, and the United Nations Expanded Technical Assistance Programme (UNETAP) (Kingston, 1994). While the collective ideology of these agencies lay in the post-war model of centralized development there were contrasting views on how the model should be applied: 'While the British were aware of the need to build up the administrative and technical capacity of the Jordanian state in the long run, the Americans were more resistant if not at times oblivious to this need' (ibid.: 205). To the Americans the most effective way of promoting development was through the use of modern technology. To the British, who until the late 1950s played the dominant role in Jordanian development processes, the first priority was political and financial stability. The British approach called for gradual development based on institutional capacity building, particularly in the agricultural sector. Far from taking the capacity of the state for granted, the British model advocated building it to the point where the state could assume the role of a supportive framework for larger-scale social and economic development. In contrast, Point Four's approach, which revolved around the transfer and demonstration of technology, assumed that, once they had proved successful, projects would eventually be turned over to the government. However, in Jordan, as in many developing countries, this did not work. Even in successful cases, projects with a large technical component often incurred high recruitment costs, were expensive to run, and often required more experience than existing technical capabilities could provide. By the mid-1950s, when the demonstration phase of many of the original Point Four projects came to an end, rather than take them over the Jordanian government went back on many of the project agreements. 'Not only did the US approach overstretch the limited capacity of Jordan's administration,' Kingston observes, 'it also tended to weaken it.' Point Four created what was almost a parallel bureaucracy which in 1954, for example, employed over 'forty US experts and more than 1500 Jordanians' (ibid.: 206).

British development aid in the 1950s, although more limited than American aid, was far more effective in helping to build capable state institutions. The gradual model of development advocated by the British was also reflected in the report of a World Bank mission to Jordan in 1955, which stated that 'Care must be taken to maintain a balance between efforts in the various sectors of the economy and to coordinate the pace of development in related sectors' (World Bank, 1957: 35). The American approach, on the other hand, which was based on importing the latest technology and creating a large bureaucratic structure to correspond, 'tended to promote the emergence of a neo-patrimonial administrative apparatus, especially given the aversion of the Americans to delegate any authority to the field or to local institutions' (Kingston, 1994: 215).

The differences between American and British development models were not simply related to programme models. Behind them lay a fundamental struggle by foreign donors for dominance and control of Jordanian development policy. However, such attempts to gain decisive influence over the development setting cannot be viewed in isolation from the domestic struggles for control which were simultaneously taking place. The rise of Arab nationalism throughout the region had a considerable effect at the local level and served to intensify problems facing the already fragmented centre of political power at this transitional time. External pressures from regional forces created further difficulties for the process of state formation and the maintenance of internal security (ibid.: 214). Nevertheless, political parties were able to operate and efforts were made to allow greater press freedoms despite the sensitive climate (Dallas, 1999). Indeed, the general political trend in the country during this time has been described as Jordan's first real attempt to further political liberalization (Brand, 1998).

Largely due to the political vacuum created by the fragmented process of state formation, the 1950s saw attempts by Jordanian nationalists to contest the ever-increasing control of the development field by foreign donors. Demands for economic reform came mainly from a number of young East Bank Jordanian technocrats working in the Ministry of Economy. They advocated a more centralized and dynamic programme of economic and social development aimed at reducing Jordan's dependence on external sources of funding and breaking the top-down style of the Mandate period (Kingston, 1994: 192).

The approaches of foreign donors, including their strengths and weaknesses, had varied effects on the development process in Jordan during the 1950s. However, the general unwillingness of Britain and the US to coordinate efforts in their respective bids to gain control meant that development interventions generally lacked cohesion and were not properly integrated into the young country's system of administration.

Institutionalizing the social sector

In 1949 a Department of Social Affairs had been established within the Ministry of Health. However, as the demand for social services grew, in 1951 the department was turned into a fully fledged ministry. In 1956 the Law of the Ministry of Social Affairs No. 14 was passed by parliament. This law remains in force until the present day (Jordan, 1998a). The mission statement of the Ministry of Social Affairs (MOSA), as contained in its Law, was 'to provide comprehensive social security, productive sufficiency and to coordinate social services to citizens of all ages, that represent the human capital of the state' (Jordan, 1992a: 1). All associations within civil society came under the Social Affairs Law including NGOs, cooperatives and unions. The ministry was assigned fifteen tasks through legislation, including the supervision of local, foreign and international associations and organizations, both public and private, which offered cash or in-kind assistance or which were engaged in social work. It was also legally responsible for registering such organizations, guiding their work and financially supporting their efforts to serve society. Consequently, at the institutional and legislative levels the period from 1951–1956 is generally described as the organizational phase of social work in Jordan (Jordan, 1998a).

The voluntary movement of Jordanian NGOs

Early voluntary efforts in Jordan through the non-governmental sector may be divided into three categories: political (in solidarity with Arab revolutionary movements in neighbouring countries), religious (mainly of Christian denomination, especially with support from the Greek Orthodox Church) and ethnic or regional (such as community work carried out by Circassian or Hijazi groups). With the influx of Palestinian refugees in 1948 and the tremendous socio-economic changes that resulted, new priorities emerged which shifted voluntary work to a focus on humanitarian efforts and refugee relief services. A connection has been drawn between the growth of the voluntary movement and the establishment of the Ministry of Social Affairs (MOSA) in 1951 based on the complementarity reflected in the ministry's organizational structure with the evolving role of the voluntary movement at the beginning of the 1950s (Khatib et al., 1977: 134).

This period witnessed several organizational measures taken by the government to formalize the work of 'voluntary societies' (for the purposes of this study, referred to as NGOs). For instance, in 1953, Law No. 36 made the registration of societies a function of MOSA. However, with the rapid change in the nature of work carried out by NGOs, the ministry drafted a new law which was passed in 1956. This further identified the types of NGOs doing voluntary work and defined regulation and registration procedures. During this time, NGO activities revolved around providing assistance to needy families, education, relief to Palestinian refugees, orphanages and shelters for the disabled, hospitals for the poor, care for those who were handicapped as a result of the Palestinian struggle, literacy programmes and in-kind assistance (Jordan, 1957: 35).

Among the Jordanian NGOs registered in the 1950s (and still in existence at the end of the 1990s) were the Circassian Charitable Society, the Islamic Cultural Society, several new branches of the Young Women's Christian Association as well as additional branches of the Red Crescent

Society (previously registered in 1948). In 1953 and 1954 there were fifty-six registered local NGOs and twenty foreign NGOs (Jordan, 1957: 44–50). In early 1959 the number rose to 107 local NGOs and nineteen foreign NGOs (Jordan, 1959). These were supported by MOSA with financial assistance or customs exemptions.

Throughout the 1950s, MOSA held annual symposia to review the work of the voluntary movement. By the late 1950s, it had defined voluntary work as: 'service to others, especially those who could not help themselves, without discrimination between ethnic or religious groups of the population.' Democracy was seen as a basic tenet of voluntary work, and NGOs were viewed as democratic organizations that relied on democratic processes through elections and the distribution of responsibilities among all members. Cooperation and participation between NGOs themselves, and between NGOs and the government, were considered by the ministry to be two basic factors underpinning the voluntary movement (ibid.: 17).

The Cooperative Movement

In 1952 the Jordanian government took steps to activate and promote cooperative societies, first started in the West Bank in 1933. Subsequently, the Cooperative Development Department (CDD) was set up within the Ministry of National Economy with its own Law No. 39 of 1952 (Qutaina, 1963). Because the aim of cooperative societies was to enhance the social and economic status of their members, they were viewed by the government as an important channel through which development could be promoted. As an international trend, they had seemingly demonstrated positive results. During the 1950s around 75 per cent of Jordan's population was engaged in various forms of agricultural activity; consequently, the mobilization of grassroots initiatives supplemented government efforts to advance this sector (Jordan, 1959).

In order to assist in enhancing the technical capacity of cooperative societies, the CDD enlisted the support of foreign experts such as the American Friends Service Committee (AFSC). The aim of the project was 'to promote the organization of credit and thrift societies in the project villages, and to demonstrate the value of supplementing a credit programme with technical assistance' (AFSC, 1958: 19). The cooperation seems to have been successful since, according to AFSC, 'one of the most satisfactory and fruitful relationships established between the project and a government department, was that with the Department of Cooperative Societies' (ibid.).

In this situation, relationships between local and foreign development agents were by partnership. There was no 'top-down' approach and this seems to have contributed to the success of village development in the early 1950s. The recognition by foreign donors at that time of the importance of supplementing credit programmes in particular with technical assistance must also be pointed out. Forty years later, discontinuities within the development scene in Jordan resulted partially from the difference between these early approaches and the attitudes prevailing at the end of the 1990s.

Altogether, the 1950s represent a distinctive period in the evolution of the Jordanian development scene; in the midst of a pivotal political transition the foundations for subsequent development efforts were laid. While substantial energy was spent to ensure the political security of the state, significant efforts were also devoted to building the institutional foundations that would consolidate the state's role. Although political and economic circumstances appeared to give foreign donors great leeway within the development arena, there is nevertheless some evidence that simultaneously the state was able to focus attention on strengthening the organizational functions of development-related domains.

By the end of 1957, the period of political transition within Jordan had come to an end. Internal and regional challenges to the stability of the Kingdom had been overcome by King Hussein (Satloff, 1994). As the decade drew to a close, the process of state formation had made considerable headway in setting institutional and legal frameworks for different sectors of government activity. Less preoccupied with the country's political security, and better placed on an operative level, with the advent of the 1960s the state was more able to focus its attention on economic development and planning.

Advancement and Disruption: 1960–1973

The beginning of state planning in Jordan

By the 1960s, planning had, throughout the world, become an increasingly technical and standardized affair. While aiming to systematize their own approaches, planners also sought to reorganize the economies and societies in which they worked. Consequently, the power to achieve these objectives made planning primarily dependent on, as well as an embodiment of, centralized political authority (Robertson, 1984: 26, 36). Like many other developing countries, Jordan adopted national planning at the beginning of the 1960s as its most important method of advancing development knowing that if it had plans it would have a better chance of attracting foreign assistance (Waterston cited in Robertson, 1984: 38). Given the country's limited resources, Jordanian development plans were essentially geared to acquiring external funding. Moreover, they were primarily project-driven and sectorial, centering around infrastructure and service provision to cater for the country's rapid population growth.

The first development plan for Jordan was the Five Year Plan for 1962–1967 produced by the Jordanian Development Board (JDB). Partly due to a lack of aggregate economic data the plan consisted mainly of proposals for government investment projects and fiscal and administrative reforms. Little attention was given to preparing an overall strategy or making projections for the economy as a whole. The main aim was to ensure consistency between estimated development expenditure and projected estimates of the funding that would be available. The Plan also assumed a sustained level of budgetary support throughout the period of implementation. Less than two years after the Five Year Plan was published in 1961, it was revised by the JDB due to reductions in the level of budget support, mainly on the part of the USA. As a result, a completely new plan document was formulated, namely the Seven Year Plan for 1964–1970. This was the first to use national accounts data and to present integrated aggregative forecasts for the plan period (Mazur, 1979: 243).

Although both the Five Year Plan and the Seven Year Plan aimed at improving living standards through increasing per capita income, the Five Year Plan was designed to achieve this objective through concessional aid including grants, whereas the Seven Year Plan depended more on development loans and grants. Greater attention was also given in the Seven Year Plan to export-oriented and import-substitution projects in order to increase income, as well as to reduce the balance of trade deficit (QAF, 1998a). The aims set out in the Seven Year Plan included reducing dependence upon foreign budget support, reducing the balance of trade deficit, increasing per capita income and reducing the level of unemployment. Priority was given to services and infrastructure, followed by agriculture and the irrigation sector. Investment and external loan figures from the Ministry of Planning show that more than half the total investment and about 88 per cent of external loans went to services and infrastructure. Agriculture and irrigation absorbed more than one quarter of total investment and about 12 per cent of external loans compared to no more than a fifth of total investment and very few loans to the industry, mining and energy sectors (as shown in tables 2.2 and 2.3).

Table 2.2
Planned Investment (JD Million)

Sectors	1964–1970[1]		1973–1980[2]		1981–1990[3]		1993–1997[4]	
	Total	%	Total	%	Total	%	Total	%
Agriculture and Irrigation	70.6	27	165.2	18	1330.4	21	475.9	26
Industry, Mining and Energy	56.7	22	333.1	35	1708.8	27	356.5	20
Services and Infrastructure	132.8	51	446.0	47	3376.1	52	967.9	54
Total	260.1	100	944.3	100	6415.5	100	1800	100

Sources:
1. Jordan, 1964: 37–8.
2. Jordan, 1973: 40; Jordan, 1981a: 59.
3. Jordan, 1981a: 59; Jordan, 1986a: 95.
4. Public Investment only; Jordan, 1993a: 201–3.

Table 2.3
Loans Extended 1960s–1990s (US$ Million)

Sectors	1960s		1970s		1980s		1990s	
	Total	%	Total	%	Total	%	Total	%
Agriculture and Irrigation	14.6	12	193.3	14	439.2	16	274.1	8
Industry, Mining and Energy	–	–	344.7	26	171.0	6	210.7	6
Services and Infrastructure	104.9	88	446.0	60	2089.0	78	3019.7	86
Total	119.5	100	1331.9	100	2699.2	100	3504.5	100

Source: Ministry of Planning.

Compared to international donor policy, which in the 1960s emphasized industrialization over agriculture and service provision, the priorities reflected by Jordanian trends in investment and loans at this time were related to internal factors which shaped the country's socio-economic structure. Such factors, including the sudden population increase with the influx of refugees in 1948 and 1967, and Jordan's own high population growth, placed severe demands on state services such as compulsory education and health. Education statistics in the Seven Year Plan (1964–1970) prior to the 1967 refugee influx, show that 79 per cent of students were expected to enrol in state schools, compared to approximately 9 per cent in private schools and 12 per cent in UNRWA schools (QAF, 1998a). Although the private sector played a greater role in healthcare, the government still provided the majority of health services. Almost two-thirds of all hospital beds were part of the government health sector (Jordan, 1964: 293–4). Beyond the provision of basic services, the state also recognized that a fundamental requirement for dealing with rapid population growth was to promote the country's manpower resources. As a result, the National Council for Human Resource Planning was established in 1966, under Provisional Law No. 101, with the aim of identifying relevant strategies to cater for national manpower needs (The Official Gazette, 1966: 2445–7).

During the 1960s the economy witnessed a high investment in infrastructure, mainly in transport and communications. Investment in these two sub-sectors was in keeping with the government's aim to develop infrastructure facilities throughout the country in order to expedite the movement of goods and services, promote tourism and provide necessary facilities to support the private sector (table 2.2). Such facilities included the building of roads, highways, an airport, a seaport, telephone networks and other telegraphic and postal services.

Substantial efforts were also made to advance the agricultural sector. The focus of attention was the construction of the East Ghawr Canal in the Jordan Valley which began in 1962. The aim of the project was to enhance the Jordan Valley's considerable capacity for agricultural production by introducing an extensive irrigation system which would break the pattern of subsistence farming and increase areas of cultivated land. An equally significant dimension of the plan was to resettle large numbers of Palestinian refugees in the valley within a stable socio-economic framework (Khouri, 1981: 68–70, 73). From a political point of view, the promotion of social and economic stability through intensive investment in this strategic geographic location was seen both locally and internationally as a means of enhancing security in the region as a whole.

The major source of finance for the Jordan Valley development scheme was the USA. According to a USAID publication marking thirty-five years of work in Jordan, the project was 'One of the most ambitious attempts at multi-sector development ever undertaken by USAID worldwide' (USAID, 1988: 10). The report relates that, before 1948, the Jordan Valley was mostly 'a sparsely populated area of subsistence farmers who relied on animal herds and cereal crops for their livelihood. With the influx of hundreds of thousands of war refugees in that year, Jordan was desperate for an agricultural area where these new citizens, who were mainly farmers, could support themselves ... the Jordan Valley's potential was so great that in comparison with other areas it presented the most feasible solution to the resettlement problem' (ibid.). In 1960, the East Ghawr Canal Authority was established with US management assistance. A process of land redistribution was started in the valley in 1962 by which land was divided into units which could be adequately irrigated 'with each settling family receiving approximately thirty dunums (three hectares)' (ibid.: 12).

The construction of the East Ghawr Canal transformed the Jordan Valley 'from subsistence-level farming by a few nomads to a vibrant agricultural and marketing centre with the necessary social and economic infrastructure to attract and keep dedicated workers.' It was, according to USAID, one of the greatest success stories of its 'economic partnership' worldwide (ibid.: 13). The introduction of new irrigation techniques led to an unprecedented increase in the yield of marketable fruits and vegetables. Furthermore, the technology of sprinkler and drip irrigation systems which were introduced for the first time in the valley quickly spread to other areas of the country (Jordan, 1987).

NGO activity in the 1960s

Among foreign NGOs operating in Jordan during the 1960s, the American had the largest presence. These included CARE US, the World Christian Council, Lutheran Relief Services, Catholic Relief Services and the Central Mennonite Committee. Their initial efforts centred primarily on relief work with the population of front line villages and Bedu tribes. Activities were later expanded to include nutritional programmes, and 'employment projects' which provided job opportunities for local communities through the building of roads, canals and other similar efforts (Jordan, 1963: 30). UNICEF and the British Save the Children Fund were operating in Jordan during this period as well. Their programmes also revolved around relief work and food distribution in addition to healthcare.

At the beginning of the 1960s steps were taken by Jordanian NGOs to formalize their representational structure. Initially, local NGOs coordinated their work regionally. It was eventually felt, however, that a general union was needed to represent all NGOs at the national level. The General Union of Voluntary Societies (GUVS) was officially established in April 1961. Its role was to coordinate, plan and draw up social policy for the non-governmental sector in cooperation with MOSA (Jordan, 1961: 22). Relationships between the ministry and local NGOs seem to have been particularly friendly and co-operative during this period. In its early annual reports, MOSA frequently refers to the serious funding problems faced by local NGOs and its willingness to support them. 'Although NGOs are autonomous civil associations, yet in reality they are complementary to the Ministry of Social Affairs which is entrusted with the comprehensive social security of citizens. Cooperation between the ministry and NGOs is not restricted to guidance and moral support, but goes beyond that to offering cash and in-kind assistance to NGOs to enable them to continue offering their humanitarian services' (Jordan, 1960: 18). During this time, efforts by the ministry as well as local NGOs centred mainly on implementing supplementary food programmes for vulnerable groups who were severely affected by drought conditions. However, following the 1967 War, MOSA led government relief operations, until a Higher Ministerial Committee for the Displaced was established (Jordan, 1967: 7).

By the end of the 1960s, there were 304 Jordanian registered NGOs, 175 of which were in the East Bank (Jordan, 1969: 60). These included various Islamic organizations of which the largest was the Islamic Centre Society registered in 1963. The membership of this society was, and still is, drawn mainly from the Muslim Brotherhood. Other Islamic NGOs, including branches of the Islamic Centre Society, were spread throughout larger towns in the country such as al-Zarqa, Irbid, Salt and al-'Aqaba (Dabbas, 1997).

Several of the NGOs founded in this period chose names with a religious connotation but are not necessarily related to any Islamic movement or group, directly or indirectly. Even in cases where certain NGOs are known to be linked to an Islamic group, the relationship usually stems from a common membership rather than any official organizational link (Hammad, 1997). As generally seen in other Arab countries, Islamic NGOs focus on social work in three major areas: health, education and poverty alleviation, in addition to awareness-raising from an Islamic perspective (al-Osbou' al-'Arabi, 1992: 33). In Jordan, these achievements have basically been promoted through a cooperative relationship with the state.

During this period MOSA began to object to the fact that not all local NGOs were registered under its umbrella. These objections were raised in relation to both religious and other organizations that were registered through the cabinet of ministers and supervised by local governors. The ministry responded by drafting a new law for local NGOs to bring their registration and supervision under its mandate which was passed in 1965.

Soon afterwards, however, a new draft law was put forward because the ministry wanted to distinguish between the different types of organizations. The reason behind this was 'to discourage family, ethnic and religious organizations in order to ensure internal unity' (Jordan, 1966: 67). As a result, the Law on Voluntary Societies and Organizations Number 33 for 1966, was passed (Jordan, 1992a: 4–18). This same law is still in effect.

For the purposes of this study, reference made to Jordanian NGOs is based on the official definition used in Law No. 33, which applies to NGOs registered by this law under the present MOSD. Exceptions such as the Queen Alia Fund and the Noor al-Hussein Foundation, are governed by special laws or decrees and therefore do not fall under this category. Law No. 33 for 1966 initially recognized three types of NGOs: charitable societies, social organizations and ordinary societies or organizations. In a later amendment, the registration of ordinary organizations was transferred to the Ministry of Interior (Jordan, 1992a: 19). These included family, clan and tribal organizations that extended services primarily to blood relations (Jordan, 1960: 19). Essentially, GUVS forms the main body of Jordanian NGOs which are registered with the MOSD and which are referred to as charitable societies and social organizations. A charitable society is defined as an organization of seven or more persons. Its basic objectives are to provide social services to citizens through coordinated efforts, without financial returns or self-interest. A social organization is based on the same principles and includes the establishment of centres to carry out social services, as well as other academic and training programmes (Jordan, 1992a: 4).

The impact of the events of 1967–1970

The 1967 Arab-Israeli War resulted in the loss of the West Bank and the Holy Places. As a consequence of the war, 350,000 refugees were added to the population of the East Bank. It has been argued by some that the loss of the West Bank did not significantly affect Jordan's economy because before 1967 the main concentration of industry and investment was on the East Bank, which provided affluent Palestinian West-Bankers with a more secure investment base (Kanovsky, 1989: 5). Moreover, after the war Palestinians who set themselves up in the East Bank brought a further increase in investment. As well as strengthening the economy, areas such as trade and commerce were particularly enhanced by Palestinian human resources.

However, others have argued that Jordan's economy, which before 1967 was moving ahead according to specific plans and objectives, was completely disrupted (Salibi, 1993: 222; Mazur, 1972: 227, 237). With the loss of the West Bank, Jordan forfeited its most developed territory in terms of arable land, antiquities and cultural heritage. The loss of the Holy Places deprived the country of its most important tourist sites and revenues. Although the human and financial resources of wealthy and educated Palestinian elements were a major asset to Jordan after the war, waves of impoverished and destitute refugees placed a great burden on the country. Without the West Bank, the immediate border area became the Jordan Valley; as a result, what was previously one of Jordan's most productive agricultural areas turned into a war zone that harboured large numbers of refugees waiting to return.

Either way, the destabilizing effect of losing half the country, including the Holy Places with their deep symbolic significance, coupled with the highly charged emotions of the large numbers of refugees added to the population of the East Bank, had far-reaching political, demographic and economic implications. Although the grave consequences of these events could not be quantified in a systematic way, they had a serious bearing on the future.

The 1967 war in fact created both substantial setbacks and new considerations for the course of development in Jordan. A period of notable and sustained economic growth had been interrupted, and immediately after the war the East Bank economy fell into a sharp recession (Mazur, 1972). At the development level, the emergency situation created by the aftermath of 1967 had various repercussions. The influx of refugees from the West Bank caused severe bottlenecks in all socio-economic sectors, especially in the supply of production and services (QAF, 1998a). The Seven Year Plan was interrupted and plan resources were redirected from development projects to reinforce the country's defence.

Although the economy of the East Bank seemed to make a marked recovery in 1968 and 1969, the improvement was superficial because it was primarily due to large grants from Arab oil states. After the Khartoum Agreement in 1967, Saudi Arabia, Kuwait and Libya committed themselves to provide aid to Jordan on an annual basis in order to strengthen its defences as a confrontation state. Aid from Arab countries amounted to US$ 105 million in 1967 and US$ 130 million in 1968 (Mazur, 1972: 238).

The greatest loss of development momentum was in the Jordan Valley. People were obliged to flee as a result of the hostilities, and from a population of 60,000 only an estimated 4,000–5,000 remained (Khouri, 1981: 99). Following 1967 and 'for four frustrating years, the Jordan Valley languished, a helpless victim of regional hostilities.' Between 1967 and 1971, the main East Ghawr Canal was hit and knocked out of service on four separate occasions by Israeli bombing raids against the Jordanian army and Palestinian forces. Furthermore, maintaining the irrigation system in the face of frequent shelling was a dangerous exercise (ibid.: 102).

The case of the Jordan Valley clearly illustrates the interrelation between Jordan's development and regional instability. Before 1967 the Jordan Valley, by virtue of its geo-strategic position, had seemed to offer a viable means of enhancing political stability; yet this same factor became part of the intensive turmoil which occurred there in the subsequent four years. Also discernible, however, was the basic resilience that has been fostered among Jordanians for coping with these conditions as, immediately following the troubled period in the Jordan Valley, efforts to resume the development process were mobilized on a major scale.

Before 1967, the country was always having to readjust and adapt in order to cope with the outcomes of political developments frequently beyond its control, as well as rapid and often negative changes. Regional instability, as well as Jordan's own limited resources and vulnerable position, required it to pursue whatever options were available to enable it to fulfil its needs (al-Zu'bi, 1991). In this context, Jordan was heavily reliant on relations with its neighbours and other Arab countries to address its economic requirements and provide markets for its products.

After 1967, Jordan was obliged to embark on the process of putting its own house in order and to readjust its relations with Arab states in order to adapt to new realities. A period of civil strife ensued, culminating in the conflicts of 1970 between the Jordanian state and the Palestinian Liberation Organization (PLO). The instability created by these events ended only when the situation of a state within a state was firmly resolved by the Jordanian authorities. However, as a result of the conflicts of 1970, the country suffered a period of isolation; the Syrian embargo on Jordanian goods meant that for two years the country was cut off from its natural markets and its economy suffered severe damage (Kanovsky, 1995: 30).

Equally significant was the considerable influence which the volatile circumstances governing the Arab political scene exerted on donor states. This was a decisive factor when, in reaction to the civil conflicts, political conditionality was imposed on Jordan by Arab donors. As a result of the effort to contain Palestinian armed activity in the country, Kuwait suspended financial assistance in 1971 and Libya cut off aid completely.

Given the country's heavy reliance on external support, the withdrawal of donor funding took a heavy toll (Wilson, 1991). After these events, Jordan set about reorganizing itself and finding the most appropriate way forward. With growing Arab recognition of the need for Palestinian self-representation, the PLO was subsequently declared the sole legal representative of the Palestinian people by the Rabat Summit resolution in 1974. Rabat marked the end of a period of adjustment to an East Bank Jordan.

For nearly five years after 1967, there was no systematic development policy; indeed, whatever measures that were taken at this time were ad hoc improvizations, probably all that could be achieved in view of the immense political uncertainties. After the war, economic decisions were delegated to an Economic Security Council under the auspices of the prime minister, the governor of the Central Bank and the ministers of Finance and National Economy. In 1971, Law No. 68 was passed establishing the National Planning Council (NPC) which officially replaced the Jordanian Development Board (JDB) as the state planning mechanism.[1] One of the earliest tasks assigned to the NPC was the preparation of a short-term plan to oversee economic recovery during the post-war period and to lay the ground for longer term development planning (Jordan, 1971). Accordingly, the Three Year Plan for 1973–1975 consisted of an interim programme to bridge the gap between the phase of improvization and the return to systematic development planning (Mazur, 1979).

Essentially, the Three Year Plan achieved its transitional purpose, as well as setting priorities to address the problems with which the country was left by the earlier period of instability.

Growth and Change in the 1970s and 1980s

The 1970s and the 1980s represent the dynamic phase of economic development in Jordan. This period is characterized by tremendous economic growth manifested in rapid social change, a complete transformation in the structure of the labour market and marked state expansion. Underpinning this singular phase of economic development was a favourable combination of both internal and external economic and political factors. At the political level, Jordan enjoyed strong ties with other Arab countries and at the same time maintained good relations

---

1. In the mid-1980s the NPC became the Ministry of Planning which still operates under the same law.

with the West. On the socio-economic level, the four development plans implemented over these years played a significant part in enhancing political stability by extending services and infrastructure and expanding industrial, mineral and agricultural production.

The boom years: 1973 to the mid-1980s

The Middle East oil boom marked the beginning of a ten-year period of economic prosperity for Jordan (Day, 1986). From 1974 the Arab oil states entered a period of unprecedented wealth due to the rise of oil prices. Consequently, their influence both on world markets and regional politics was considerable. Saudi Arabia provided substantial aid including grants and development loans, assistance for military purchases and subsidized oil supplies. In exchange, Jordan played a key security role for Saudi Arabia by serving as a buffer between the Saudis on the one hand and the Arab-Israeli conflict and radical forces for change in the region on the other; it also provided training for Saudi army officers. Kuwaiti aid payments to Jordan consisted of annual contributions towards the budget and to reinforce the security and military apparatus. Jordan, in turn, trained members of the Kuwaiti military and worked closely with Kuwaiti security systems. Kuwait also provided a major market for Jordanian goods. Jordan's relations with other Gulf countries such as the United Arab Emirates, Qatar and Oman were based on similar arrangements (Brand, 1994). A great number of Jordanians were employed by the Arab oil states in high-salaried jobs, mainly as white-collar professionals – educators, doctors, contractors and engineers (Sayigh, 1978).

Remittances sent home by expatriates working in Saudi Arabia and the Gulf states raised living standards, particularly in urban areas. As a result, a consumer society was rapidly created and standards of living began to resemble those of an oil economy, but an oil economy without the oil.

In 1977 President Sadat made his trip to Jerusalem, paving the way for the Egyptian-Israeli Peace Treaty which was concluded at Camp David in March 1979. In order to keep other confrontation states from following Egypt's course and making peace with Israel, resolutions were taken by Arab countries at the Baghdad Summit in 1979 to provide states neighbouring Israel with financial aid. Jordan has the longest border with Israel and substantial financial support was pledged to meet the economic and defence needs required by the political situation. Consequently, the country became heavily dependent on Arab aid and relations with Arab oil countries were a major consideration in Jordanian policy. Heavily subsidized by oil revenues from rentier states, which were redistributed to non-producing countries, Jordan itself became an indirect rentier state, living far above its means and largely subsidizing its own domestic needs with revenues received from Arab oil producers (Chatelus, 1987).

New perceptions unfold

With the mending of regional relations in the aftermath of 1970 and during the 1980s, the Jordanian state was able to gain substantially in definition and form. Its central role as a procurer and distributor of financial resources and of socio-economic development brought about changes in both societal relations and state-society relations. The Palestinian community benefited considerably as economic opportunities were augmented through labour migration, professional jobs and commerce, largely due to Jordan's good relations with Arab countries. Government regulation of private sector activity further increased the interdependence between state and society, which in turn helped to reinforce the state during this period of economic prosperity (Sayigh, 1991).

Another sign of the process of transformation taking place within Jordanian society was social change among the tribes. From the time the Kingdom was established, the major tribes had formed the bedrock on which the government was built and the core of the Jordan Arab Army which ensured the continuity and stability of the country. It has been argued that as urbanization, government settlement policies and education advanced, the role of tribes in Jordanian life began to decline (Jureidini and McLaurin, 1984). During the 1950s and 1960s, state policies encouraged nomadic settlement through schooling, health services and the development of water resources. The expansion of education and mass communications had marked effects on tribal traditions. Military service was another influence for social change among the tribes because it provided secure and steady income in the face of the great insecurity of the pastoral economy.

However, another view contends that despite the economic diversification induced by these factors tribal identity was reinforced, not weakened. The basis for this argument is the influence of the Jordanian political system on the 'reproduction' of Bedu identity. From the establishment of the Emirate to the present day, Jordanian electoral laws have maintained exclusive constituencies for the tribes and have acted as a state mechanism to guarantee the cohesion of Bedu groups and to mitigate the effects of intra-tribal rivalries. Although the objective of reinforcing tribal solidarity has not always been achieved, these provisions have at the very least helped to preserve tribal identity and protect it from being dismantled by external political forces (Bocco, 1989: 281–2).

Some maintain that 'tribal identity has become politicized as it continues to be the basic channel for the allocation of resources by central government' (Shami cited in Bocco, 1989: 283). Others argue that during the 1980s a process of detribalization was taking place and that the individual's sense of identity was less and less associated with tribal affiliation; instead, smaller groups such as the extended family and clan gradually replaced the tribe as principal reference groups. Particularly in the urban sector, professional qualifications as well as positions in the civil service, academia and other fields increasingly reshaped perceptions of social capital and prestige (Jureidini and McLaurin, 1984). Nevertheless, it has also been noted that a rise in publications on 'tribal literature' occurred in the 1970s and further increased in the 1980s. Moreover, monographs on folklore, genealogy, Bedu poetry and tribal law were, as one writer notes, welcomed by the Jordanian press as a new form of patriotism (Shryock, 1995).

Arab aid and Jordanian state expansion

State expansion in Jordan reached its peak during the 1970s and 1980s. This phenomenon was not only precipitated by prosperous regional conditions, but by the Arab pledges to Jordan at the Baghdad Summit, mentioned earlier, which amounted to US$ 1.2 billion annually for the period 1979–1989. At this time, external aid shifted primarily from funding for development projects from bilateral and multilateral donors such as the USA, Germany and Japan, to Arab aid mainly in the form of budget support (QAF, 1998a: 13).

Loans were also taken to finance the country's ambitious development programmes, including loans from Arab Development Funds (el-Mallakh and Khadhim, 1976). Until the early 1980s, Jordan experienced a real growth in GNP of over 10 per cent annually, one of the highest in the world, and an over-valued currency was maintained (Jordan, 1994a: 71). The general shift from project-oriented Western donor aid to Arab budgetary support had both immediate and long-term effects on the Jordanian development process. Western funding, which at this time was closely linked to the economic interests of donors, tended to foster a methodical approach to development based on project implementation. Less restrictive in nature, Arab budgetary aid allowed Jordan greater leeway

Table 2.4

GDP and Percentage Contribution to GDP by Kind of Economic Activity at Current Factor Cost for Selected Years

Economic Activity	1955 Million JDs	1955 %[1]	1965 Million JDs	1965 %	1975 Million JDs	1975 %	1985 Million JDs	1985 %	1995 Million JDs	1995 %
Agriculture, Hunting, Forestry & Fishing	10.6	10.5	30.3	15.3	30.2	7.9	98.4	5.5	171.8	4.4
Industrial	8.6	8.5	27.6	14.1	54.0	14.1	311.1	17.4	835.5	21.5
Mining and quarrying	(0.4)		(2.6)		(16.9)		(65.6)		(157.7)	
Manufacturing	(7.8)		(23.3)		(34)		(205.4)		(579.7)	
Utilities (Electricity and Water)	(0.4)		(1.7)		(3.1)		(40.1)		(98.1)	
Construction	4.8	4.8	10.3	5.2	36.5	9.5	148.7	8.3	297.5	7.7
Services	166.9	76.5	129.4	65.8	264.6	69.3	1260.6	70.6	2649.9	68.4
Wholesale & Retail Trade, Restaurants & Hotels	(12.4)		(27.1)		(47.9)		(289.4)		(414.6)	
Transport, Storage & Communications	(7.9)		(17.9)		(42.8)		(265.4)		(572.3)	
Finance, Insurance, Real Estate & Bus. Services	(41.3)		(52.8)		(84.7)		(314.4)		(721.7)	
Government Services	(99.3)		(23.6)		(77.4)		(328.3)		(756.4)	
Others[2]	(6)		(8)		(11.8)		(63.1)		(184.9)	
Total	190.9	100.3	197.6	100.4	385.3	100.8	1818.8	101.8	3954.7	101.9
Less: Imputed Bank Service Charges	0.3	0.3	1.3	0.7	3.1	0.8	36.3	2.0	75.0	1.9
Gross Domestic Product at Factor Cost	190.6	100.0	196.3	99.7	382.2	100.0	1782.5	99.8	3879.7	100.0

Source: Derived from website of the Department of Statistics (Jordan, 2000a).

1. Percentages are rounded and do not total 100.

2. Includes: community, social and personal services; private non-profit services to households; domestic services to households.

in spending; however, the continuity of this support depended primarily on congenial political relations between Jordan and Arab donors which in later years could not be assured.

Following the shift to Arab aid government expenditure rose dramatically, accompanied by a marked expansion in the size of the civil service. The most pronounced rises were in budget allocations to defence, education and health. The current military and security budget increased from JD 55 million in 1975 to JD 206 million in 1985, compared to a total current expenditure increase from JD 120 million to JD 488 million for the same period. Also during this period, non-military expenditure increased by 180 per cent. The government became the largest single employer, which meant it had to shoulder the enormous long-term financial burden of salaries and pension payments (Jordan, 1975a; Jordan, 1985).

The other visible aspect of expansion was rapid urbanization, most notably the growth of Amman. Private capital, mainly from the remittances of expatriates, poured into land and housing and sent prices soaring. This also prompted speculative investment as well as investment in housing as a kind of long-term security (Dejong, 1996: 272). The 1975 Lebanese civil war gave the construction industry a further boost from an influx of Lebanese and Palestinian businesses and the relocation of various international institutions like the UN from Beirut to Amman.

However, high rents, together with Jordanian policy restrictions on foreign banks and firms, created disadvantages for many of the enterprises which settled in Amman. Eventually, most departed to other more congenial bases, leaving a depressed construction sector as well as local inhabitants with acute housing problems (Biegel, 1996: 385). 'The construction boom of the 1970s left Amman with thousands of empty luxury apartments ... yet at the same time 80 per cent of the city's population receive such low incomes that they cannot even afford the minimum desirable housing standards' (Findlay cited in Dejong, 1996: 274).

There were also large disparities in population density between East and West Amman, from 100 people per dunum in the poorest neighbourhoods to less than 10 in the wealthiest (Ameri cited in Dejong, 1996: 274). As the value of land went up in wealthy residential districts, urban settlement began to encroach on agricultural areas surrounding the city. Encouraged by rising prices, landowners took to selling prime agricultural land for building purposes which in turn made them huge profits. At the same time, because the remittances of expatriates came mainly to Jordanians of Palestinian origin living in Amman and other major cities, rural areas did not experience similar rapid economic change. Indeed, as people sought better opportunities in urban areas, the rate of rural to urban migration rose sharply.

Revising development priorities

For the greater part of the 1970s and 1980s, development planning continued to focus on infrastructure and services. A brief overview of trends in state policies follows, highlighting the main features of Jordan's development plans. It also shows how in certain circumstances these plans were unable to achieve their objectives.

The main objective of the Three Year Plan 1973–1975 was to overcome the setbacks created by the previous period of political instability and to restore the economy (Jordan, 1973: 25). The first Five Year Plan (1976–1980) came during the period of the country's economic prosperity. However, there was insufficient awareness of the importance of using favourable economic conditions to generate further opportunities and promote sustainable efforts. Self-reliance was not actively fostered and dependency on the state continued (Jordan, 1976a: 26). The aim of the second Five Year Plan (1981–1985) was to achieve high growth rates and increase the share of the commodity producing sectors. Emphasis was also placed on the private sector's contribution, social welfare and regional development (Shakhatreh, 1990: 21). However, the results fell well below the targets that had been set. Unfavourable conditions, including the fall in oil prices, resulted in a progressive decline in foreign transfers and a negative growth rate (Jordan, 1981a: 33). The third Five Year Plan (1986–1990) aimed to reduce unemployment and achieve a balanced distribution of development projects throughout the country (Jordan, 1986a: 80).

However, deteriorating economic conditions forced the government to cancel or postpone many projects. The acute economic crisis eventually led to the suspension of the plan in late 1988 and the launch in 1989 of an economic adjustment programme which was to continue until 1993. The programme was interrupted by the Gulf crisis and subsequently resumed with an amended programme covering the period 1992–1998 (Jordan, 1993a: 1). The impact of the economic crisis and its implications for the nature of subsequent development plans (1993–1997 and 1999–2003), will be examined at greater length later in this chapter.

In the early 1970s, development policies centred on addressing high levels of unemployment, deteriorating rates of growth and a large deficit in trade (Jordan, 1973: 6). At this time, a shift in external financing was made from the agricultural sector to industry, mining and energy. Whereas in the 1960s, 12 per cent of external loans went to projects in the agricultural and irrigation sector and very few to industry and mining, in the 1970s this sector absorbed 26 per cent of all external funding compared to 14 per cent for agriculture and irrigation; moreover, funding for the agricultural sector was allocated mainly to projects in the Jordan Valley (QAF, 1998a: 9–10; see table 2.3). Because of its highly capital intensive nature, investment in industry and mining grew faster than in the agricultural sector which was limited by the scarcity of water and cultivatable land. Moreover, not only did investment in the production sector achieve faster growth rates and better returns, it also provided more job opportunities and improved the balance of trade by increasing Jordanian exports.

The phosphate, potash and chemical fertilizer industries formed the backbone of Jordan's export trade and were the principle source of its foreign exchange earnings. From 1973 through to 1980, planned investment in infrastructure and services, together with industry and mining, accounted for more than 80 per cent of total investment (table 2.2) and absorbed more than 84 per cent of development loans (table 2.3). Although the focus of Jordanian development policy on industrialization was inconsistent with international trends, it nevertheless helped to solve unemployment problems in the early 1970s and later contributed to economic growth. Hence it was consistent with national priorities and trends. In the area of service delivery, however, Jordanian policy in the 1970s was in keeping with international donor priorities which centred on basic needs.

The structure of the labour market was totally transformed in the mid-1970s. The shift from unemployment in the early 1970s to full employment by the end of the decade, a result of the demand for skilled labour from Arab oil states, left the domestic labour market with serious shortages. A reverse migration was witnessed, mainly of Egyptians and South East Asians who replaced expatriates who left for the Gulf and compensated for labour shortages in the rural sector resulting from the sharp increase in rural-urban migration. Besides the mounting demand from Gulf countries for vocational skills, the scarcity of skilled labour in Jordan stemmed from increased investment and the limited training capacity of trade and secondary vocational training schools. Consequently, government spending on training and education increased substantially to compensate for both domestic deficiencies and the brain drain (Jordan, 1978a: 46).

For most of the 1970s and the 1980s, as this analysis has tried to show, Jordanian state policies centred primarily on matching internal resources with external demands. However, despite the opportunity presented by this singular phase, keeping up with the pace of change was not always conducive to an adequate evaluation of the impact of short-term policies and the development of strategies for the longer term. Largely based on regional priorities, national development policies were at the mercy of regional changes. At the local level, where some areas were overextended by catering to evolving demands, at times standards of performance could not be maintained and goals were not always achieved.

The beginning of regional planning

A decentralized approach to Jordanian development policy was first introduced by the 1976–1980 Five Year Plan which paved the way for the adoption of regional planning during the 1980s. This approach was prompted by increased state awareness that the benefits of economic growth should be more evenly distributed nationwide. Regional development strategies centred on achieving a better balance in population distribution by increasing economic opportunities in rural areas through a greater spread of development projects, and in addition improving linkages between different regions by strengthening the network of basic services (Jordan, 1976a). The process of regional planning began with the preparation of a master plan for the Municipality of Amman. This was followed by the implementation of a comprehensive regional planning study for the rest of the country. The aim of this effort was to determine population distribution and available human and natural resources in order to establish suitable projects for each governorate (ibid.).

Decentralization, democratization and local councils: early attempts

As state policy moved towards promoting regional development, local councils began to assume a more prominent role. Local authorities were viewed as a vehicle for encouraging people's participation in the development process and municipal and village councils were asked by the government to participate in regional planning and in identifying local priorities. It was also envisaged that attention to development needs within communities would increase financial resources at the local level, through the establishment of income-generating projects (ibid.). As an indication of political support at the highest decision-making level, during a meeting with members of municipal and village councils in 1977, King Hussein referred to three main areas for achieving comprehensive national development. These included local participation in the development process, moving from a service provider to a productive country, and promoting cooperation between government and civil organizations working within local communities (Jordan, 1977a). On the whole, however, throughout the process of regional planning which started in the mid-1970s and continued in the 1980s, local councils did not play an active role (Arabiat interview).

Although during this period the effect of local authorities' participation in regional planning was not particularly significant, they had a greater impact in promoting democratization. Local councils raised people's awareness within communities about participation in municipal elections, and by the end of the 1970s popular interest in local elections had increased substantially (al-Rabi, 1992). In many areas the outcome of elections was affected by tribal allegiances, especially in village councils where people tended to vote for their tribal relatives. However, the population of the more urbanized areas showed greater political awareness; on two occasions, in 1977 and 1985, voters rejected the candidates' list, which resulted in the postponement of the election day (*Baladi*, 1988). Although village councils continued to be elected on a tribal basis, municipal councils began to attract candidates based on merit, in addition to political parties. Given the absence of a parliamentary life in Jordan at this time, the role of local authorities contributed to the process of political participation and democratization. At times of regional political tension this provided an outlet through which nationalist feelings at the local level could be expressed. For instance, a national conference of municipal and village mayors denounced the Israeli invasion of Lebanon in 1982 (*Baladi*, 1982). Moreover, raising political awareness through the process of political participation within communities, which culminated in local elections, helped build experience for parliamentary elections in the late 1980s.

Modifications to the social sector

The early 1970s saw the beginning of a shift in interest by MOSA from welfare to development. In 1971, a development department was established within the ministry. This progression was largely due to the thrust of community development programmes implemented by various foreign NGOs in close cooperation with MOSA. Policy discourse also began to move in new directions. Statements by the ministry alluded to cancelling in-kind assistance and replacing it with rehabilitation projects as a means of improving living standards amongst the needy. Generally, however, no significant changes were made despite these articulations, and up to the mid-1970s the ministry continued to carry out relief programmes.

During this time MOSA began to lose some of the ground it had gained through the powerful legislation it had drawn up in the 1960s. Its declining role can be traced through budget allocations. For instance, in 1964–1965 MOSA was allocated 0.66 per cent of the total state budget; during the problematic year of 1970, its share went down to 0.36 per cent and in 1975 it was given only a slight rise to 0.38 per cent, despite the expansion of the state budget and MOSA's attempts to promote a developmental dimension in its working approach (Jordan, 1970; Jordan, 1975b).

On the institutional level a notable change took place in 1976 when MOSA was downgraded to a general department and attached to the newly formed Ministry of Labour. This was a complete institutional reversal, as beforehand the labour department was part of MOSA. It is likely that prevailing conditions were behind the change. With the country's prospering economy and the substantial emphasis on basic services, MOSA's work may have seemed less necessary. Also due to growing regional demand, the issue of labour probably gained ascendancy as a government concern. Nevertheless, although it could not fulfil its goals as a ministry, subsequent policy statements by the Department of Social Affairs repeatedly maintained that without due consideration to human and social dimensions, development could not be achieved (Jordan, 1976b: 7).

A major concern which began to emerge at this time was the lack of coordination within the social field. Most unclear was what approach should be adopted by different players, including the government and NGO sector, in order to move from social welfare to social development. Despite various committees which were specifically set up to define the roles and directions which these actors should take, a coordinated approach to social work could not be formulated. In the words of Minister Issam al-'Ajlouni:

> Although we can consider 1976 to be a year of consolidating social work, both governmental and non-governmental, we still cannot view on the horizon any indicators that predict that social work is taking the path of social development. Not one single issue or aspect of social work has been left without forming, at various levels, a committee or a council or a commission to make revisions. However these bodies have worked independently of each other and even sometimes without knowing that the others existed. The net result has been duplication and squandering of efforts (ibid.: 7).

Compounding these frustrations may also have been the fact that by this time it was no longer financial constraints that hindered the work of local NGOs. In 1972, the government had passed the Charitable Lottery Regulations, giving the General Union of Voluntary Societies the right to hold a national lottery on a monthly basis. The revenues went to support the activities of GUVS and member societies, as decided by its executive board (Jordan, 1992a: 71). It was expected that the substantial revenue generated would relieve the funding problem of local NGOs, raise the level of their services, and relieve the pressure on government to allocate funding to local NGOs. The inauguration of the National Lottery had another important outcome. Until then, GUVS did not carry much weight, whether with MOSA or with its member societies. However, once it could generate its own income through the lottery, dependency on the ministry lessened and GUVS was increasingly able to assert its presence as a significant entity in the social field. '… starting in the 1970s our financial contribution was more. People were starting to realize that the NGOs were becoming an important movement. And so people were recruiting into it' (al-Khatib interview).

As in other spheres during the 1970s, a climate of transformation was emerging within the social sector. A shift in thinking from a welfare approach to the concept of development was, for the first time, articulated at different levels 'by the intelligentsia, intellectuals and people in the government and the newspapers etc' (Abu-Jaber interview). Although not a full ministry, policy statements coming from the Department of Social Affairs repeatedly pointed to the need for new directions based on developmental concepts. Public discourse was mirrored by a similar awareness amongst others in the field. According to Khatib, previously people working in the NGO movement 'were coming from a charity concept, from a religious concept … In the 1970s, there was a shift in the meaning of social work, a shift to the social development process. It wasn't just a question of aiding, but of going into how we could change the environment – realizing a quality of life in the villages was one of the themes which we were behind' (al-Khatib interview).

Echoing the same sentiment, Sari Nassir considers that:

… from the mid-1970s things began to change. The first half of the 1970s was a continuation of the 1960s in terms of handouts etc. In the second half of the 1970s we started seeing an awareness that social work should not only be about the poor and underprivileged, nor should it only centre in the hands of wealthy women. It should be done more publicly in the sense that young people should be involved; social work should be studied, produced in universities, community colleges, institutes. We started with the concept that you must not help people as such, but help them to help themselves …

Our work didn't start in 1977 in developing centres. I took my students out (of the classroom) in 1974 and they built bus shelters, and this was involving them in development. At that time development, and I'm not saying social development, development in general became popular in Jordan. That was due in part to our work, plus the encouragement from the world community that there should be development plans etc (Nassir interview).

However, despite various signs of a shift towards a more developmental orientation during this time, numerous problems continued to beset overall efforts within the social sector:

I think social work has developed in Jordan along two lines – the official area and the NGO area ... Each can enhance and reinforce the achievements of the other, although they sometimes compete ... the nature of that competition comes from who is providing better services and a better system of service delivery to citizens, or who is going to gain the acceptance of the beneficiaries as well as state officials. And sometimes within the NGO sector, you find people who are doing the work, more out of religious beliefs and religious motivation, both Christians and Muslims (al-Saqour interview).

While the positive aspect of such considerations was that they created the motivation for different efforts, at the operational level they did not offer solutions to the many difficulties which prevailed:

There were many NGOs, about 160–170, and they lacked a lot of funding, they lacked capacity-building, they lacked some sort of management, they lacked so many things that the government wasn't able to cover. The Department of Social Affairs at that time couldn't cope with that and couldn't provide for that (al-Saqour interview).

Against this paradoxical backdrop, it was quite feasible that a new kind of organization should emerge, forming a bridge between government and non-governmental efforts. The advent of such an establishment was in itself part of the process of change which was evolving within the arena of social work: 'I would say that there were different issues which so many ministries and other authorities were trying to introduce. At the same time, some of the NGOs took that initiative and tried to push further and the first step was the establishment of the Queen Alia Fund in 1977, and there was a need for them at that time' (al-Saqour interview). The Queen Alia Fund will be discussed in greater detail in the second part of the book. However, this early reference reflects a significant outcome of the climate of transformation which was building within the social sector during the latter half of the 1970s.

In conclusion, the boom years were characterized by a set of favourable factors which had a significant effect on socio-economic and political conditions in Jordan. Nevertheless, as this period of economic prosperity was largely based on external resources, it did not develop internal resources adequately. Moreover, the increase in economic activity by certain sectors of society did not spread to other areas, where traditional activities remained (Owen, 1983). As the boom years drew to a close, a growing concern for both state and society had become the widening gap within different sectors, and the dilemmas posed by the problems which consequently emerged.

Meeting the Tide of Transition in the 1990s

The chain of events which began in the mid-1980s, and continued through the 1990s, played an instrumental role in shaping the economic and political transition of Jordan. The nature of Jordan's evolving transition has implied a major redefinition of directions by both state and society. A reaction to this process has sometimes been resistance to change. This section lays out the circumstances which precipitated this transitional phase and attempts to shed light on the complexities of interconnected factors which characterized the decade of the 1990s, and which underpin the process of development as it stands today. A central dilemma posed by investigating this particular period is that the issues concerned are for the most part still with us or remain unresolved. Hence the analysis is unable to draw on the benefit of hindsight.

A reversal of fortunes: 1986–1989

Given the unpredictable nature of regional politics during the 1980s, Jordanian state efforts to compensate for limited political options were understandable. In the absence of political solutions to the Arab-Israeli problem, considerable emphasis was placed on promoting tangible goals such as national infrastructure, and subsidizing welfare and other services. However, by assuming the role of the patron state Jordan had increased its dependency on external sources for expanding and maintaining subsidized services while reducing self-sufficiency and internal productivity (Harik, 1992). These directions generated specific problems for the country when the oil boom came to an end.

The collapse of oil prices in the second half of the 1980s precipitated a slump in the economies of the oil states. As local professionals in the Gulf were capable of taking up jobs previously held by expatriates, the demand for Jordanians decreased and lower salaries were offered. Alternative jobs were generally in sectors which Jordanians regarded as beneath their professional level. Consequently, expatriates began to return to Jordan in numbers which the labour market could not absorb and unemployment began to rise (Jordan, 1991: 81). In macro-economic terms, the vulnerability of the Jordanian economy and the price of its reliance on certain states became apparent. Meanwhile, Jordan's special economic relationship with Iraq had also become a liability. This relationship was to have a fundamental impact on Jordan's political and economic situation in the early 1990s.

Economic ties with Iraq

From the beginning of the 1980s, economic and political expediency had significantly increased ties between Jordan and Iraq. During the 1980–88 Iran-Iraq war, al-'Aqaba became strategically important to Iraq as a major cargo link and for the import of military supplies. Iraqi government loans and grants went largely to expand facilities at the port and to improve the highway between al-'Aqaba and the Iraqi border. By the late 1980s the relationship, established through a series of commercial protocols, accounted for almost one-third of Jordan's exports and 10 per cent of its GNP (JPRC, 1996: 17). In 1989, more than 160 Jordanian firms were commercially connected to Iraq; by the beginning of 1990, three-quarters of Jordanian industry was working primarily for export to Iraq (Baram, 1991: 56–8). A whole range of products from fruit and vegetables, to foods, medicines and textiles were exported to the Iraqi market (MEED, 1980a). Jordanian contractors also expected a big share of Iraq's post-war reconstruction contracts (MEED, 1980b).

By the late 1980s, Jordan had gradually shifted from the import of Saudi oil by pipeline from Saudi Arabia, to the import of Iraqi oil by tankers for most of its supplies (ad-Dustour, 1996: 34). Jordan became dependent on the Iraqi market for its exports to the extent that these exceeded imports of Iraqi oil, particularly after 1990 when Iraq reduced the price of the oil it sold to Jordan by almost half (Jordan, 1993b: 20–1). During the war with Iran, Iraq made increased Jordanian imports conditional upon credit to Baghdad (Jordan, 1996: 38–9). By the end of 1989 Iraq's debt to Jordan was reported to be no less than US$ 835 million, almost twice Jordan's foreign reserves. It was, it has been argued, Iraq's debt that largely caused the country's economic crisis (Baram, 1991: 58).

The pressure on Jordan's already fragile economy from the Iraqi failure to settle letters of credit was too great. After a collapse in foreign currency reserves, a precipitous fall in the value of the Jordanian dinar occurred in 1988 (Jordan, 1989: 1).[2]

The beginning of structural adjustment

The rapid deterioration of the Jordanian economy between 1986 and 1988 was in fact caused by several factors. These included Iraq's debts, depressed economic conditions in the Gulf due to the fall in oil prices, Jordan's own overspending and the fact that, with the exception of Saudi Arabia, the Arab states did not fully honour the pledges of financial support made at the Baghdad Summit in 1979. The severe deficit which developed both in the government budget and the balance of payments led to a further increase in the country's external debt (Jordan, 1996: 21, 25, 31). 'In October 1988, the country faced a severe shortage of foreign currency. This financial crisis forced a set of austerity measures on the economy, including import bans, devaluation of the dinar and a rise in several administered prices. Government wages and salaries were frozen, and a further loss in real income per capita was inevitable' (Buhbe, 1990: 197). The recession called for immediate action to restore the economy, and negotiations on debt rescheduling between the IMF and the government opened in 1989 (ESCWA, 1990: 4–6).

The IMF structural adjustment programme for the period 1989–1993 aimed at 'correcting the main structural imbalances in both the balance of payments and the general budget while maintaining a reasonable growth rate' (Jordan 1993a: 8). This was translated into economic policies geared towards curbing public expenditure and reducing the budget deficit: encouraging investment, increased production and exports, as well as a more aggressive drive to find new markets (ibid.).

The government began to address the prospective impact of deteriorating economic conditions on the population even before the financial crisis reached its peak. For the first time, the Economic and Social Development Plan 1986–1990 recommended that a study of poverty in the country be conducted, and also proposed the establishment of the National Aid Fund (NAF) as a spin-off to the rehabilitation and aid section

---

2. Prior to the devaluation, the rate of exchange was JD 0.5564 to the pound sterling. In 1999, the exchange rate was JD 1.149 to the pound (Jordan, 1996; Jordan, 2000c).

of MOSD (Jordan, 1986a). Law number 36 establishing NAF was passed in 1986. As a safety net, the aim of NAF was to provide social security and welfare to Jordanians, through direct cash assistance or productive opportunities (Jordan, 1997).

To minimize the negative effects of the structural adjustment programme, towards the end of 1989 the World Bank supported the Jordanian government in establishing the Development and Employment Fund (DEF). Operating under its law number 33 of 1992, the purpose of DEF is to contribute to the alleviation of poverty and unemployment by enabling poor and low-income individuals, families and groups to become productive. DEF loans are targeted at poor or low-income families with high dependency ratios, as well as unemployed graduates of universities, colleges and vocational training centres. Priority is given to rural and underdeveloped areas with high levels of poverty and unemployment (Jordan, 1994b).

The revival of political liberalization

Recent years have seen a heightening of 'democratist' discourse in the Arab world. It has been noted that the conditions which have prompted this rise include 'the combined effect of internal social crises and international pressures for pluralism brought about by the final stages of the Cold War and in the disintegration of the communist bloc' (al-Azmeh, 1994: 116). Decisions on political liberalization are a common response among governments the world over when economic tensions threaten the status quo. In other words, the legalization of political parties and freedom of expression, and the widening of associational life, are looked upon as a means of restoring calm and social equilibrium:

> ... the purpose of liberalization from above is clear: it is to stabilize the system in a situation of acute crisis, to broaden its base of support, to enhance its legitimacy at home and abroad and to prepare the ground for a wider dis- tribution of responsibility for structural reform involving stringent austerity measures (Krämer, 1994: 202).

In April 1989 riots and demonstrations broke out in various towns and villages throughout the country in protest against the subsidy cuts agreed with the IMF. This came only a few months after Jordan's decision to dis- engage from the West Bank. By 1988 it had become clear that no progress was being made in the Arab-Israeli peace process. In response to requests from the PLO and Arab states, on 31 July 1988 Jordan took the decision to sever all legal and administrative ties with the West Bank, thus presenting the Palestinian people with the option of taking responsibility for their own future. The situation created by these two developments produced calls for a return to democracy. Due to parliament's formal approval in 1950 of the unification of East and West Banks, with equal parliamentary representation, no parliamentary elections could be held in Jordan while the West Bank was under occupation. The decision to disengage from the West Bank thus made it possible to return to a parliamentary system of government (Abu-Jaber, 1991).

In July 1989 King Hussein formally announced his decision to hold parliamentary elections. In the run up to the elections, scheduled for November of the same year, there were calls for the lifting of martial law which had been in effect since 1967, the legalization of political parties, a relaxation of security measures and a campaign against corruption. Despite the excitement that was caused by the decision to hold elections, the turnout on election day was quite low, with only 37 per cent of eligible voters actually casting their ballots. This could have been due to the complicated process involved in registering and voting, or to scepticism over government intentions. Nevertheless, observers judged the election to have been clean (Brand, 1998: 101–2).

The period that immediately followed the elections witnessed dramatic liberalization measures by which press control was relaxed through a more moderate law passed in 1993, the anti-Communist law of 1953 was repealed and martial law was lifted (Krämer, 1994; Brand, 1992). Local press reactions to the decision to revive the democratic process which had begun in the 1950s were positive all round. The development was hailed as one that would open up a wider space for political involvement and labelled 'the return of the spirit' (al-Ra'i, 1989a). With the press opening up to the public to express their opinions on the upcoming elections, there was a flurry of articles on what the new parliament would mean to Jordanians and, moreover, what was anticipated by the process of democratization as a whole. Some felt that the new parliament should devote itself to pressing domestic issues such as unemployment and its relation to the educational system, in addition to focusing on health insurance and other social development issues (al-Ra'i, 1989b). Opinions were also divided over whether the new-found Jordanian democracy was to be a replica of Western democracies, or based on the Islamic system of shura (al-Ra'i, 1989c; 1989d; 1989e; 1989f; 1989g). A few felt that in order to allow the government to take all the proper procedural measures, elections should be postponed for a year (al-Ra'i, 1989h). In analysing the various groupings that could succeed in the elections, some articles attacked the traditional and ideological groups while promoting the nationalists. These commentators were in turn criticized by supporters of the first two groupings who contended that traditional and ideological groups could not be separated from nationalist trends (al-Ra'i, 1989i; 1989j; 1989k). The position of women in the elections was also discussed at length, within the context of the ongoing power struggles, and from a religious perspective (al-Ra'i, 1989l; 1989m; 1989n; 1989o; 1989p; 1989q).

The results of the 1989 parliamentary elections, which brought in leftist and nationalist figures as well as a large contingent of Islamists, gave rise to much political analysis. The success of the Islamists (including independents and Muslim Brotherhood members) has been singled out as one of the distinctive features of the political liberalization process in Jordan. Some observers contend that the presence of Islamists in parliament brought with it conservative trends, for instance in legislation affecting women (Brand, 1998: 119). Yet there are those who believe that 'the Islamist movement in Jordan has been consistently in the forefront of democratizing the Jordanian polity since liberalization began in 1989 ... because greater democratization has served its organizational and political interests' (Robinson, 1997: 374).

The good results of the Islamists, who won nearly 40 per cent of parliamentary seats, has been attributed to their organizational abilities since they had been operating for many years as a voluntary society while political parties were banned. The decision of the PLO not to interfere in the 1989 elections also strengthened the position of the Islamists, who were able to attract the vote of the Palestinian refugee camps with slogans calling for the liberation of Palestine. On the other hand, the leftist and nationalist candidates, who won only 15 per cent of the seats, did not coordinate and organize themselves as efficiently, and some of them opted to follow tribal rather than party lines in the elections (al-Arab al-Youm, 1999). As the Islamists formed a weighty parliamentary bloc, some of them were included in the first cabinet to be formed after parliamentary elections, although none of them belonged to the actual Muslim Brotherhood. However, in a cabinet reshuffle at the beginning of 1991, five members of the Brotherhood were appointed to ministerial positions. According to Brand, a number of policies implemented by some of these ministers were controversial and created an uproar, a factor that in part contributed to the resignation of the government (Brand, 1998).

In addition to passing legislation to strengthen democratic processes, the elected parliament also voted on annual state budgets which were more stringent than previous ones due to the serious economic situation. Despite strong criticisms, especially of earlier policies, debates usually ended with the budget being passed. Although the 1989 Parliament has been described as more politicized than its successors of 1993 and 1997, over the years parliamentary debates at the time of state budget submission have shown a marked tendency among MPs to request increased services for their constituencies and to denounce the government's restraint in such issues. While macro-economic policies have always been debated, it is clear that parliamentarians seize the opportunity of the budget debate to highlight the needs of their constituencies. Demands have ranged from roads and silos to health centres, community development centres and schools. However, reflecting the severe economic hardships faced by the population, the overriding demand has been to focus on poverty allevia- tion (*ad-Dustour*, 1990; 1994; *al-Ra'i*, 1998).

In contrast to the political liberalization of the 1950s, which threatened Hashemite rule,[3] liberalization in the 1990s saw its consolidation. The National Charter, a document intended to supplement the constitution, was drafted by a sixty-member royal commission representing the politi- cal and social spectrum in the country. The Charter embodied 'advanced guiding principles for all aspects of life in Jordan' (al-Masri, 1999: 3). These included guaranteeing acceptance of the Hashemite monarchy, a pluralist political system, a solid basis for state-civil society relations and gender equality. The Charter was ratified in a national conference in June 1991:

> Seven years ago, the modern Jordanian system of nascent democracy and electoral pluralism was born through a process of nationwide, inclusive consultation … The National Charter process was meaningful because it was democratic and inclusive, because it affirmed majority positions while being sensitive to minority sentiments, and because it acknowledged the supremacy of a patient, open, deliberative process over the temptation of swift, narrow, expedient executive decrees and temporary laws (*Jordan Times*, 1997a: 6).

The new liberalization process with which Jordan entered the 1990s was to act as a major buffer for state and society against the critical political and economic circumstances that prevailed for the rest of the decade. While it did not replicate Western democracies, this home-grown

---

3. While King Hussein was consolidating his power in the first few years of his reign, he had to absorb the destabilizing attempts by leftists and Arab nationalists to make Jordan adopt Egypt's and Syria's stance of 'anti-imperialism' (Dallas, 1999: 43–59, 64–72).

model of liberalization allowed for a wider base of debate and freedom of expression, more democratic processes of legislation and a stronger belief in national institutions, all of which were needed when the Gulf War broke out.

Enduring regional tensions

The political and economic repercussions of the Gulf War were severe and long lasting. The close economic and political ties between Jordan and Iraq, coupled with Jordan's economic crisis and process of political liberalization, were the major factors to shape Jordan's position in the Gulf War (Brand, 1994). King Hussein's position on the issue was clear: 'We are principally always against the acquisition of territory by force' (*Jordan Times*, 1990: 5). Yet the King's main worry was that foreign intervention might have drastic repercussions: 'Any foreign intervention, be it Israeli or otherwise, in the Arab World will have a very, very bad reaction and could set the whole area ablaze' (ibid.: 1). At the popular level also, there was an outpouring of emotion against foreign intervention. Feelings ran high and the invasion of Iraq by foreign troops stirred nationalist sentiments in a way that could not be discounted. The mosques were a popular forum where nationalist feelings were voiced. Protest marches against the invasion of an Arab country by foreign troops, fund-raising campaigns and public rallies expressing anti-Western feelings also escalated at this time. Some analysts of the situation noted that state and society seemed to be of one accord: 'The harmony between the official and popular positions against Western intervention has accelerated the democratization process and fostered national unity' (*Middle East International* cited in Dallas, 1999: 220).

Its position during the crisis meant that Jordan's already severe economic problems were rendered yet more acute by ostracism from Gulf Cooperation Council (GCC) countries and isolation from the US. The state of turmoil in the region and relations between Jordan and the GCC countries brought a halt to direct foreign investments which amounted to US\$ 185 million between 1987 and 1989 (ESCWA, 1990: 17). Major sectors that were severely hit were trade, transport, energy, tourism, agriculture and industry. An increase in unemployment and the problem of returning expatriates added major burdens to the economy.

In 1988 an estimated 1.2 million Jordanians and Palestinians were living in Gulf countries and Saudi Arabia, of which 280,000 were workers. In December 1990, 200,000 expatriates returned. The problem was exacerbated by the fact that most of the returnees arrived without the savings they had accumulated in Kuwaiti banks. Without financial support for their daily life, the country was required to provide food, education, health services and job opportunities. The return of these expatriates increased the population by 6.7 per cent within three months. An equivalent number were expected to return from other Gulf countries and Saudi Arabia. Consequently, while 20 per cent of the population was estimated to live below the poverty line in early 1989, these events increased their numbers by half, accounting for a rise of more than 30 per cent; with a further 5 per cent living in absolute poverty, with no income for shelter, food supply and medical care (UNDP, 1991: 12).[4] In a Roundtable Discussion on the Impact of the Gulf Crisis on Jordan, held in Amman, the Regional Director of UNICEF made a presentation based on results of a rapid assessment done by UNICEF on approximately 500 families spread across Jordan. The results, he said, were shocking in their human dimension. Mothers and children had been so severely affected by the staggering blows Jordan had received that for them the crisis would not be over when the war ended (Reid, 1991).

Economic deterioration in the aftermath of the Gulf War

In 1990 a mission was sent by the UN Secretary-General to assess the problems Jordan faced as a result of measures to comply with the embargo on Iraq set up under Security Council Resolution 661 (1990). The envoy's assessment stated that Jordan's location, history and the structure of its economy meant that it had been placed in an extremely difficult situation by the political crisis in the region and the implementation of Resolution 661. Jordan's difficulties were further complicated by the interruption of its usual trade and financial relations with Saudi Arabia. The report pointed out that the overall economic burden on Jordan, relative to its total economic activity, was far greater than on any other country except Kuwait, and came at a time when the country had only just begun to see some recovery from a painful correction of economic imbalances in 1989. The recovery had since been overwhelmed by developments in the region and the current economic outlook could only be described as grave (Ripert, 1990: 1–2).

By adhering to the Security Council's sanctions, Jordan lost 23 per cent

---

4. For further information on the official figures for poverty during this period see chapter 6, notes 1 and 2.

of its export market to Iraq, with an additional loss of 16 per cent of other export markets due to Gulf countries cutting links to Jordan. Loss of the country's total exports was estimated at no less than half. In addition, all road transport to Iraq came to a halt in adherence to Security Council resolutions (UNDP, 1991: 7–9). The international sanctions imposed on Iraq placed Jordan itself under a de facto embargo, with restrictions on the movement of goods and an increase in shipping rates to al-'Aqaba port during the period 1990–1994. Since then, inspection teams situated by Lloyds have eased previous restrictions. However, these arrangements, which lasted until October 2000, cost Jordan around three million dollars each year (*al-'Arab al-Youm*, 2000). It is estimated that Jordan's losses as a result of the sanctions amounted to one billion dollars annually (*al-Ra'i*, 2000).

As a country that has always relied heavily on external aid, Jordan paid a high price for its stand during the Gulf crisis. Although it did receive some aid during 1990–1991 to help with the sudden influx of displaced foreign workers who had to transit through Jordan from the Gulf and Iraq to their various countries, foreign loans and grants declined sharply the following year. This expression of condemnation by Jordan's donors meant that in 1992 Jordan received only US$ 259 million, down by some 15 per cent on what it had received in 1989 (UNDP, 1997b). 'From 1989 to 1991, the Kingdom had reeled under economic hardship, domestic unrest, and a regional crisis in which Jordan's attempt at a middle ground had lost it the economic support of the Gulf states and its Western allies' (Ryan, 1998: 57–8).

In the aftermath of the Gulf crisis, Jordan faced a daunting economic situation, with major disruptions to aid, and no trade with neighbouring countries; this, coupled with a halt in the remittances of its expatriates, and the task of addressing their needs as they returned from the Gulf. Under such circumstances, Jordan's economic adjustment programme for the period 1989–1993 was interrupted. An amended programme for the period 1992–1998 was later launched, aimed at 'achieving economic growth and monetary and fiscal stability, and at removing imbalances' (Jordan, 1993a: 1).

In pursuit of peace

The regional instability and strained economic conditions caused by the Gulf War strengthened international and regional resolve to renew initiatives to address the Middle East peace process and in 1991 the Madrid

Conference was convened. Arab countries neighbouring Israel attended, as well as the PLO who participated as part of the Jordanian delegation. Direct bilateral negotiations followed between Israel and Jordan, Syria, Lebanon and the PLO; however, results were limited. After nine months of secret talks held in Oslo between Israel and the PLO, the Oslo Accord was reached in August 1993. This led to the exchange of letters of mutual recognition between Israel and the PLO on 9 September 1993 and the signing of the Israeli-PLO Declaration of Principles on 13 September 1993 in Washington. Jordan's inter-regional relations were redefined by these events as well as its isolation following the Gulf War. The country proceeded with the process of recovery demanded by its economic problems by moving towards a peace settlement. The revival of parliamentary life in Jordan in 1989 provided the democratic framework for endorsing a Jordanian-Israeli peace settlement (Abu-Jaber, 1991). On 26 October 1994 the Peace Treaty between Jordan and Israel was signed, restoring all occupied Jordanian territory, guaranteeing Jordan's full sovereignty over its land and defining its borders clearly and conclusively (Jordan Media Group, 1994).

Some have argued that the promotion of the peace process has in certain ways compromised the course of political liberalization begun in the country prior to the Peace Treaty. While legislation such as the Political Parties Law signalled a serious commitment to furthering democracy (more than twenty political parties registered after the law came into effect, including the Islamic Action Front as the political party of the Muslim Brotherhood), it was felt that certain public freedoms were being curtailed to prepare the way for the treaty (Brand, 1998). In 1993, a new temporary Electoral Law was passed by the government while parliament was in recess. As a result, the one-person, one-vote system was introduced in place of the previous multiple-vote per person which allowed each voter to vote for the number of seats allocated to his or her constituency in parliament. A Jordanian senator regarded this development as a 'retreat from democracy at a time when our country has evolved as a model of democracy in the region that we pride ourselves on' (al-Ra'i, 1993: 10). Some analysts consider that the new system was meant to reduce the presence of Islamists, Arab nationalists and leftists in parliament, in order to ensure that the Peace Treaty was passed. In the parliament which was elected in 1993 according to the new voting system only half the number of Islamists won seats (Brand, 1998; Dallas, 1999).

Since 1994, dealing with economic recovery and the peace process have been the two main issues on Jordan's economic and political agenda.

While from an international policy perspective both issues are inextricably entwined, internally they are often separated by a paradoxical divide. In order to address the debt burden, the economic aim has been to meet the conditions of international donors by pushing forward with structural reforms and other processes of liberalization and democratization in the face of the potentially destabilizing consequences of rising poverty and unemployment. However, there is a body of opinion, expressed through democratic channels, which believes that the interrelation between political and economic solutions is a deeply controversial issue. For example, international efforts to boost the peace process by promoting normalization measures in an economic context are sometimes perceived as externally-imposed political conditionality. Consequently in handling issues related to Jordan's political and economic transition, interventions by state and society have had to steer an often difficult course between different positions within a fluctuating political climate.

The peace process raised expectations in Jordan of increased opportunities for improving economic conditions, but even in 1999 peace had failed to deliver prosperity: 'Nearly four years after Jordan's peace treaty with Israel, the period of prosperity and stability it was supposed to herald has still failed to materialise' (MEED Report, 1998: 29). Nor could the fears and inhibitions harboured over the years by the Arab-Israeli conflict have disappeared overnight, particularly as major problems which affected Jordanian society, including its large component of Palestinian origin, were not resolved. Furthermore, the potential for changing perceptions and building confidence by fulfilling expectations through tangible outcomes was considerably restricted by the demands of ongoing structural adjustment measures. Jordan's transitional phase requires it to play an effective role in the ongoing events of the region; as a partner in the peace process, in withstanding the competitive pressures of participating in the global economy, and in implementing its own economic and political reform agendas.

The political role and position of the country before Oslo demanded that priority be given to its defence and security needs. Therefore, much external aid went towards military spending and maintaining an adequately sized and well-established army. Indeed, due to its strategic significance Jordan has received greater attention than its size and limited resources might otherwise have merited. Recognizing this fact it has been able to direct its efforts accordingly, resulting in considerable accomplishments not only at a material level but also in the development of its human resources. While the previous and largely problematic chain of political events created a certain resilience and an ability to adapt to changing conditions, the changes of the 1990s required a different response – namely initiative from within. The prospect of peace did not remove the threats to stability in the region, nor could it be assumed that they would disappear in the future. Nevertheless, in this phase Jordan was presented with new challenges such as keeping up with the competitive pressures of the global economy and increasing self-sufficiency. Hence, there was a growing awareness within the country that in order to find its place in the region, new directions would have to be taken (IMF, 1996: 4).

The Pressures of Reform

Economic adjustment and the shift to Western aid

With the resumption of the structural adjustment programme in 1992, economic policies were directed to fostering a more efficient and transparent business environment, focusing on legislative reform through amending existing laws or introducing new ones. These include the investment promotion law, sales tax law, intellectual property rights and companies law. Structural adjustment also centred on downsizing the government's direct participation in the economy through the privatization of major public industries and companies (Jordan, 1998b: 39). Another aspect of economic reform was to improve the competitiveness and efficiency of Jordanian firms through global integration. Among the policies, measures achieved are the Jordan EU Association Agreement, Jordan's accession to the World Trade Organization, the creation of the Qualifying Industrial Zone and bilateral investment treaties with several Arab and foreign countries.

Jordan's efforts to liberalize its economy and to integrate itself more fully into the world economy found support from international donors. The signing of the Peace Treaty was accompanied by significant changes in the pattern of foreign aid. The overall sum increased to US$ 853 million in 1995: more than triple what Jordan received in 1992 (UNDP, 1997b). There was also a shift from Arab support to Western aid: Jordan became the fourth largest recipient of US foreign assistance with aid rising from less than US$ 10 million to over a billion dollars in a three-year period (*Jordan Times*, 2000e). It has been noted that USAID specifically 'sought to guarantee Jordan's freedom of action by preventing it from becoming too dependent on any one source of assistance' (Amawi, 1996: 78). Hence, US assistance to the country is perceived as arising from its strategic interests, among which are the need to support Jordan's ability to maintain a moderate stance in the area. Besides the US, Jordan's main grant assistance donors during the 1990s were Japan, the European Union, Germany, the United Kingdom, France and Italy. Principal providers of concessional aid were the IMF, the World Bank and the European Investment Bank (UNDP, 1997b: 4). International donors also engaged in advocacy for foreign investment in Jordan, leading World Bank officials to describe it as 'an ideal country for foreign investors' (MEED, 1997: 10).

The 1995 World Bank report stated that Jordan was beginning to reap the rewards of reform. Jordan was considered to be an exceptional per-former, by both regional and international standards, on virtually every indicator of human development – life expectancy, school enrolment rates and infant mortality (World Bank, 1995b: 54–5). What cannot be reflected by these figures, however, is the erosion of social cohesion caused by structural adjustment. The negative consequences of the economic reform programme were again seen in August 1996, when riots broke out in the south of Jordan after the government's decision to lift the subsidy on bread (*Jordan Times*, 1996). While there is no doubt that structural adjustment is essential in addressing the problems of Jordan's economy, it must also be pointed out that before the favourable outcomes of such measures can trickle down, the hardships of already vulnerable groups are inevitably intensified.

Periods of intense transition, such as experienced in the 1990s, require not only a change in political perceptions, but also a change in previous patterns of behaviour in order to adjust to emerging economic realities. A point particularly relevant to the Jordanian situation, given its com-mitment to liberalization and its well educated population, is that while taking on numerous reforms and interest groups simultaneously may be economically optimal, politically it could be suicidal. It is therefore necessary to reconcile economic reform with the broader political context, while setting priorities in the interim (World Bank, 1995b: 81). Within the specific context of Jordan, adjustment measures should not only be viewed from an economic perspective, but should also take account of wider considerations, especially the pressures of structural reform in the system.

Development planning

In 1993, after a four-year halt in development planning during the economic crisis of 1988–1989, national planning was resumed. The Economic and Social Development Plan 1993–1997 complemented ongoing adjustment measures by dealing with policy issues rather than sectoral development, and directed the public sector to address social and economic policies and regulatory reforms. It sought to reinforce the structural adjustment and economic recovery programme by addressing social aspects. The targets of the plan were to alleviate poverty, reduce unemployment and strengthen the democratic process through public participation in decision-making to the greatest possible extent. Taking the democratization of political processes in Jordan into account, the plan recognized that new methods of action and decision-making, as well as appropriate implementation mechanisms were required (Jordan, 1993a: 2).

Despite some improvement in the country's macro-economic indicators, poverty and unemployment continued to rise in the 1990s. Jordan therefore requested the World Bank's assistance in conceptualizing a programme aimed at raising the productivity of the Jordanian economy by combating these two major problems. Thus the Social Productivity Programme was introduced in 1997. The first phase, from 1998–2000, consisted of measures directly targeting poverty, including income supplementation for the poor, improving the infrastructure of low-income communities, supporting institutional micro-enterprise development and enhancing the job skills of the unemployed poor, as well as providing a labour market information system. The second phase was expected to incorporate these areas into a broader strategy, with emphasis on using ongoing programmes in health and education to assist in poverty alleviation, and directed to bringing the poor into the mainstream of social and economic life (Jordan, 1998c: 2).

Comprehensive planning initiatives continued through the Economic and Social Development Plan for 1999–2003. The general aims of the plan included further liberalization of the national economy, strengthening the private sector, attracting local, Arab and foreign investment, increasing productivity, alleviating poverty and unemployment, and improving the quality of life through achieving greater harmony between economic and human development (Jordan, 1999a: 1). In line with its policy-oriented predecessor, the Economic and Social Development Plan centered primarily on policies aimed at improving the investment climate in the country, developing financial markets and encouraging privatization. At the same time it promoted the concept of sustainable human development through four basic principles: development and economic growth leading to employment opportunities and poverty alleviation, with total poverty eradication as the final objective; gender equity; practising good governance and enhancing participation in public administration; protecting the environment and the proper management of natural resources (ibid.: 44). This shift from project-oriented to policy planning, reflected by development plans in the 1990s as part of structural reforms, redirected the approaches of different players in the social sector, particularly in addressing the problems of poverty and unemployment.

Governance

As the New Policy Agenda advocates, a strong and effective public sector based on the rehabilitation of state functions in areas of regulation and accountability is the key to promoting development (Edwards, 1994; Archer 1994; Woods, 1999). In Jordan the process of structural adjustment and the drive towards privatization saw a greater emphasis by successive governments in the 1990s on civil service reform. In the climate of political liberalization, both parliament and the press were calling for an end to corruption among government officials, better service delivery and greater transparency and accountability. In 1992, all government departments were instructed by the prime minister to immediately activate the administrative reform units stipulated by the Civil Service Regulations of 1988. According to this directive, the units were to incorporate people with leadership skills and the capacity to perform the tasks required, starting with the process of simplifying administrative procedures, particularly in relation to service delivery. In addition, measures to achieve decentralization and delegation of authority and responsibility were to be identified (Jordan, 1992b). This drive was further strengthened through a Ministry of Administrative Reform, created in 1994, which embarked on drafting a comprehensive plan for administrative reform in the public sector (Jordan, 1995b). Letters of designation from the King to several prime ministers began to place greater emphasis on public sector reform. This culminated in 1996 with directives from the King to the new government of the time to undertake a comprehensive change in government institutions and their leadership (The Official Gazette, 1996).

The political implications of transitional change

As noted earlier, economic reform must be reconciled with the broader political context in order to address tensions which can erupt. From this perspective, the decision to adopt a policy of political liberalization helped to reinforce social cohesion following the riots which broke out in 1989 as a result of emergency adjustment measures. Thus, when the government decided to lift bread subsidies in 1996, by contrast to its approach in 1989 when emergency adjustment measures were imposed, various attempts were made to lay the ground for an eventual announcement. Moreover, with democratic channels in place, parliament and the media were actively involved in debating the subsidy issue. In a press conference, Prime Minister 'Abd al-Karim al-Kabariti explained the new measures, in which subsidies on bread would be lifted but citizens would be compensated through a cost-of-living allowance. According to one observer: 'The very fact that the government bothered to hold a press conference at all reflected the changes in Jordan's political liberalization process since the previous economic crisis' (Ryan, 1998: 59). Within the broader political context, however, the riots which broke out following the announcement were a sign of people's disillusionment with the economy, the peace process and political liberalization (ibid.: 65; Brand, 1998: 117). While in 1989, the state responded with democratization, the response to the 1996 bread riots was uncompromising and as such was interpreted as another sign of retraction from the process of political liberalization.

Reinforcing this feeling was the new Press and Publications Law, which was passed as a temporary law while parliament was in recess. This was viewed as an 'authoritarian drift in government policy that has come in the treaty's wake' (*The Economist*, 1997a). The government's justification for passing a restrictive law was that some of the weekly tabloids, which had grown dramatically in number and circulation with the liberalization process, were hurting Jordan's ties abroad. Although this law was later repealed by the High Court as unconstitutional, it had already caused the closure of more than ten newspapers for non-compliance with the amendment (Wiktorowicz, 1999: 616).

In protest against restrictive measures, and more importantly to protest the one-person one-vote electoral system, nine opposition parties, including the Islamic Action Front, decided to boycott the parliamentary elections of 1997. 'Most of the 524 candidates ... were independents or tribal leaders, running on local issues rather than the grander questions of peace with Israel or Jordan's IMF-driven economic policies' (*The Economist*, 1997b). As the first elections to take place after the Peace Treaty, those of 1997 did not arouse popular enthusiasm. Among the reasons put forward to explain this indifference, was the ineffectiveness of the previous parliament, its failure to have any impact on the government's internal and foreign policies, as well as a loss of confidence in its ability to improve the living conditions of the people (*al-Arab al-Youm,* 1999).

Significant challenges were posed by the often conflicting issues facing

Jordan's political transition in the 1990s. Bridging the divide which appeared at different moments between the process of liberalization and national interests was one such dilemma. In the past, numerous circumstances have put Jordan to the test, making it a tough survivor. Although still evolving, Jordan's democratization process will be crucial to withstanding a future that might be equally contentious.

Civil Society Negotiates its Role

Reflecting the climate of liberalization emerging in the 1990s, civil society in Jordan began redefining its own role and its relationships with different groups in order to become a more active advocate of citizen participation and social equity. While such a process is common to civil society in any country undergoing change, the Jordanian case is of interest because along with the process of negotiating its role, civil society has also had to fill certain gaps which governmental institutions, given the economic situation, could not cover. This meant that civil society organizations had to actively seek sources of funding, which sometimes created a new set of problems.

Whether due to the opening up of the political system, or a combination of this and other factors, the number of organizations which make up civil society has clearly grown since 1989. While the average annual increase in the number of NGOs registered at MOSD was 15.3 per cent before 1989, by 1999 it had risen to 31.7 per cent (al-Kafawin, 1999: 25). Besides this quantitative increase, there was an obvious qualitative change in the types of organizations which were established. Human rights groups were the first to take advantage of the political opening, with a few registering themselves officially as early as December 1989 (Jordan, 2000d). Research centres became popular, conducting studies and holding seminars on current issues, as well as opinion polls on the performance of governments, something virtually unheard of before the liberalization process began. The adoption of more democratic processes by the state meant that civil society could also function in roles that it had not been able to undertake before, as advocates, or in holding the state accountable for certain issues.

Political activism or national concerns?

The focus of the international conferences of the 1990s on issues such as human rights, the environment, population, social development and women, created a new awareness within Jordanian civil society of the impact that such agendas could make at the national level. Hence, international commitment to the themes of the conferences, combined with the climate of political liberalization in Jordan, prompted civil society organizations to begin using their newly discovered clout by urging the government to redress development failures, and to actively pursue policies to promote human rights and social equity.

On other occasions, spurred by the liberalization process, civil society organizations became more involved in political issues. Since the 1950s, professional organizations have acted as one of the few vehicles for political expression in the country and were not discouraged from continuing their own political activities by the advent of the new political parties. Indeed, their participation has seemed more vigorous, especially where the subject of resisting normalization with Israel was concerned: 'In fact the quest to expand civil society in Jordan has become bound up with the campaign against normalization' (Hamarneh, Hollis and Shikaki, 1997: 8).

Debate has been raised over the matter of venues for political activism. Successive governments have maintained that political parties are the legal vehicles for political expression, specifically calling on professional associations to restrict their role to 'professional issues' (Wiktorowicz, 1999: 609). The associations have countered that their involvement is not tied to political but to national issues, which according to the president of the Jordan Bar Association, 'is an essential part of their aims as stipulated in the laws that govern the associations. The interest of associations in the Palestinian issue is not a political act, but an interest in national issues. [The Associations'] insistence on promoting human rights and furthering democracy is an interest in national issues' (ad-Dustour, 2000a). The position of professional associations was strengthened by the fact that political parties were too recent to have established a strong following among constituents. Yet one columnist, criticizing political parties for their failure to rally people around them, blamed their programmes, leaderships and methods of work for the lack of public support. He concluded that the only actual democratic development that could be felt ten years after the country embarked on its liberalization process was the press freedom which was achieved through the work of the press corps itself (al-Ra'i, 1999a). On the other hand, political parties complained that they were not able to fulfil their role because successive governments had not allowed them to do so, either through the one-person one-vote electoral system, or through restrictions on their use of the media (ad-Dustour, 2000b).

A broader agenda for Jordanian NGOs

Despite various setbacks the process of liberalization begun in Jordan in 1989 brought unprecedented gains for civil society and its institutions (Brand, 1995). This new reality also had its effect on the situation of Jordan's NGOs, offering them a broad base to address social conditions in the country as part of the wider political agenda beyond the delivery of services (Majdalani, 1996). The 1989 parliamentary elections, and later the Gulf War, offered the earliest opportunities for NGOs to become actively involved in a more politicized agenda. The premises of some NGOs were used to hold public debates between parliamentary candidates running for the 1989 elections. Although this could be considered in open violation of the Law on Voluntary Societies and Organizations, which does not allow NGOs to engage in political activity, the NGOs went ahead. Collecting cash and in-kind donations for the children of Iraq, without seeking prior permission from MOSD, was another violation; yet given the popular feelings at the time, the NGOs again carried this off.

As economic and social conditions in most countries in the Arab region have necessitated monetary policies to address budget deficits, Arab governments have, to various degrees, reduced spending on social services. The gaps created have produced demands on voluntary organizations to address social needs in areas such as population, the environment, marginalized groups and human rights (Kandil, 1995). Even as new horizons for Jordanian NGO activities opened up, their traditional role in addressing social problems continued. Indeed, their role took on a more significant dimension as issues of poverty and unemployment became ever more serious. By the second half of the 1990s there were clear indications that poverty in the country had become more widespread and more deep-seated. For the poorest 20 to 30 per cent of the population, the increased wealth of recent years provided no relief, and income distribution became more skewed than at the end of the 1980s. Meanwhile, high population growth placed severe strains on the carrying capacity of the country, both in terms of natural resources and social infrastructure, with the cost to government of providing social services growing at an alarming rate due to a very high dependency ratio created by the high proportion of minors in the population (UNDP, 1997b: 2–3).

Foreign funding: a controversial issue

Although in the 1990s Jordanian NGOs found themselves responding to increased demands due to deteriorating economic conditions, political liberalization, as well as the increased interest among donors in funding NGOs, offered certain advantages. While in the 1980s most Jordanian NGOs had to go through government channels to approach foreign donors, with liberalization they were able to forego this practice. Some foreign states also established small assistance programmes within their embassies which allowed NGOs to receive grants directly without going through Jordanian governmental channels. Moreover, the Framework Convention signed by the government with the European Union paved the way for direct funding to local NGOs. This arrangement also meant that the government could not turn down any funding requests, or intervene in a project once it was approved by the EU, although this was in direct conflict with the stipulations of the Planning Law (JOHUD, 2000a). At the same time, greater access to external aid, and opportunities for partnership relations with foreign NGOs and donors, created more competition for funding.

The increased access of civil society organizations to external funding, and the sometimes sensitive issues for which funds have been allocated – such as public policy, human rights, press freedoms or gender equality – occasionally provoked acrimonious debate about the issue of foreign funding. The press became a regular channel for such debate, as both pro- and anti-foreign funding activists expressed their feelings on the subject. Although the government was not involved in this debate, some accused it of working behind the scenes: 'The irony is that the activists who work in the name of democracy play into the hands of the government, which is happy because the activists themselves prevent the independent and civil society from acting and growing' (*Jordan Times*, 1998a: 1). Another article echoed this view: 'The foreign funding accusation against civil society organizations and individuals in Egypt and Jordan is not credible, but rather a simplistic, unconvincing smoke screen for other unstated fears and resentments (the Jordanian government is smart enough not to make the accusation itself, but rather to leave the task to the nominally independent [Jordanian Press Association] JPA)' (*Jordan Times*, 2000a: 5).

Observers have noted that the question of external funding for Jordanian NGOs, 'is raising a storm of protest in the country, with Islamists and leftists alike crying foul at what they see as new Western attempts to control the country' (*Jordan Times*, 2000b: 3). The campaign against foreign funding gained momentum after the signing of the Peace Treaty with Israel in 1994 (*Jordan Times*, 1998b). In 1998, it became more vocal, forcing a human rights organization to 'indefinitely postpone' a seminar which was funded by a Western NGO. A research centre was also obliged to 'postpone' a conference on the role of the country's professional associations in democracy building when the associations themselves pulled out at the last minute 'saying they had to verify information they had received about the organizers – namely whether or not the organizers had "normalized with Israel and been complicit in the Zionist conspiracy"' (*Jordan Times*, 1998a: 1).

Also seen was the professional associations' forceful stand when the Jordan Press Association's disciplinary committee started investigating a JPA member for accepting foreign funding allocated to a press freedoms centre which he was heading (*Jordan Times*, 2000c). In another incident, the Jordan Bar Association took one of its members to task for accepting foreign funding on behalf of a human rights organization, petitioning the government to investigate the issue and shut down centres that received such funds (*Jordan Times*, 2000d). A little later, the parliamentary Public Freedoms and Citizens' Rights Committee also became involved in the funding conflict when it requested the government to 'investigate the "legitimacy" of local non-governmental organizations (NGOs) and research institutions which receive foreign funding,' and stated that the funds were used 'to tarnish the country's reputation' (ibid.: 3).

By the end of the decade the debate was far from resolved. Pro-foreign funding activists accused their opponents of 'intellectual terrorism,' and warned that the country was 'on the brink of the "New McCarthyism"' (*Jordan Times*, 1998a: 1). They also maintained that in the absence of local funding, and as long as they were not coerced by donors to follow any specific 'hidden agenda,' foreign funding was the only means enabling civil society organizations to pursue their activities. On the other hand, there were those who perceived foreign funding to be tantamount to 'grand treason,' in direct violation of the constitution and existing legislation. This position contended that foreign funding was an invasion of Jordan's sovereignty and a form of questionable neo-colonialism; accusing recipients of external funds of being loyal to their sponsors, rather than to their country (*al-Mithaq*, 1998; *al-Sabeel*, 1998; *ad-Dustour*, 2000c; *Jordan Times*, 2000b).

The serious nature of the charges leading to this confrontational climate prompted MOSD to ask the prime minister to issue a circular to all ministries and other government organizations, as well as foreign embassies, requesting them not to accept any funding proposals unless they were cleared by MOSD. The justification for this request was to ensure 'public good and proper administrative, legal and financial measures, as well as to avoid any mistakes or violations that might ensue from individual and random communication' (*ad-Dustour*, 1999a: 3).

While the underlying threads of the previous discussion are defining features of Jordan's transitional phase in the 1990s, similar tensions apply to other transitional settings. In the Jordanian context, the conflicts which have been described lie basically in the space between economic, political, and national interests: in some circumstances this space ceases to exist, while in others the issues at stake appear to be totally unconnected. Consequently, it is in this fluctuating area that different ideologies and interests compete for the upper hand. Jordan's strategic directions have essentially been redefined by the implications of its economic conditions; hence ongoing adjustment measures, including the implications of 'the Good Government Agenda' have narrowed the country's margin of manoeuvrability. Furthermore, the context of Jordan's economic transition coincided with an uncertain peace process, creating a dimension the pressures of which cannot be underestimated. It is inevitable, therefore, that the process of democratization should have been imbued with the concerns of the prevailing climate (White, 1995).

The debate played out through the Jordanian media reflects the way liberalization in the country has evolved through different vehicles. To a considerable, and often justifiable extent, the position of various hardliners brought to the fore by this medium came from their perceived reaction to political conditionality (Robinson, 1994). At the same time, the serious social problems addressed by Jordanian NGOs in their attempts to fill gaps the government cannot cover, coincided with heightened donor interests in the activities of civil society within the liberalization process. Yet it is primarily the scarcity of local resources which has compelled Jordanian NGOs to look for external funding to cover their projects, even though it is well established that donor priorities, and often the priorities of local NGOs themselves, determine development interventions (Bebbington and Riddell, 1995). Rather than generalizing about the motives of foreign or local actors, and possible co-optation (Hulme and Edwards, 1997), critics must differentiate between the valid needs covered by numerous humanitarian projects which Jordanian NGOs implement through donor support, as opposed to other agendas. Given the difficult issues that are being negotiated within the Jordanian setting it is likely that the interface between different actors will continue to reflect disparities. Whether conflicts erupt under the guise of foreign funding, venues for political activism, or other issues, in such times of transformation it can be anticipated that vested interests will inevitably play a part.

Conclusion

In summarizing the Jordanian development process, one basic gener-
alization can be made: from the 1950s, where the analysis began, to the
end of the 1990s, the course of development was characterized by a continuous response to changes in the external environment. Hence during
the 1950s the consolidation of the Jordanian state was challenged by a
critical political transition. Later, major regional events including the 1967
War, the oil-crisis of the mid-1980s and the Gulf War, left few options for
the Jordanian state but to resort to crisis-management. Internally also, it
was only after the end of the instability witnessed at the beginning of the
1970s that a unique phase of economic prosperity and regional harmony
could be enjoyed. Compounding the country's vulnerability to regional
fluctuations and its limited resource base has been the rapid population
increase, largely perpetuated by the demographic consequences of regional
upheavals. The country's heavy reliance on foreign aid necessitated by
these factors has given rise to the political realignments noted at different junctures. Such shifts have, however, left it vulnerable to reactions of
varying intensity, both internally, and at regional and international levels.
At the same time, the positions it has adopted in certain situations have
meant that it has had to withstand the effects of political conditionality.

In view of such considerations, the task of advancing development in
Jordan has often been problematic. Policies have suffered from a lack of
continuity and setbacks to long-term planning. Even during the decade of
prosperity from the mid-1970s to the mid-1980s, socio-economic development consisted more of capitalizing on a windfall than strategizing for
the possibility of altered conditions, although it is understandable that
the focus should have been on seizing the opportunities presented by this
singular period. Whether under favourable circumstances or conditions of
austerity, the interrelation between political and economic factors has basically defined Jordan's development options. These linkages were redefined
by the transition of the 1990s. New considerations arose as Jordanian state
and society struggled with the setbacks to the peace process in the region
and the significant social tensions created by structural adjustment and the
impact of various reforms. Characteristic of this transitional period were
efforts to promote self-reliance. However, still accustomed to the role of
the patron state, people's expectations were slow to change – particularly
as a large proportion of the population continued to suffer the effects of
structural adjustment, including poverty and unemployment. While in the
1990s Jordan's political and economic transition modified its relations,

both regionally and internationally, the role of state and society was also being transformed. Hence, another indication of the transitional climate lies in the pressures which varying perceptions of national and political interests have created. Essentially, Jordan's development story shows that each decade has posed a different set of political and economic problems which Jordanian state and society have had to negotiate while endeavouring to move ahead.

Evidently, the reality of the Jordanian experience has created different coping mechanisms among the actors involved in furthering the development process. Moreover, a specific resilience for adapting in the face of continuous uncertainty has emerged, even though the tensions created by this climate have sometimes strained state-society relations. Nevertheless, taking into account the severe limitations which have hindered development efforts, as well as frequent shortcomings, it can also be said that in numerous areas notable progress has also been made. Foremost amongst the country's achievements has been the development of its human resources which has been a priority of national policies from the outset. As seen within the social sector, organizational and legislative measures go back to the 1950s with NGOs completing their representational structure by the 1960s. Moreover, the shift from welfare to development, which began during the 1970s, was initiated not only by the state, but by an increasingly vibrant movement of Jordanian NGOs. Indeed, throughout the different phases, the social sector continued to evolve. To some extent, the advancement of local NGOs can be interpreted as the state's endorsement of this particular component of civil society and moreover its long-standing role in addressing social problems. As with other national efforts, the role of Jordanian NGOs has been mediated by the special circumstances of the country's limited resources and political vulnerability. While reconciling the limitations of the local context with the agendas of international donors, alternative methods of development have been created.

Part Two

3

Questions of Method:
Definitions of a Researcher's Space

Part two of this book traces the history of one particular development NGO in Jordan – the Queen Alia Fund – over the period 1977–1999. The stages of the growth of this organization mirror the stages of development of Jordan analysed in Part One, and serve to illustrate the ways in which dependence on international donor funding required all the actors engaged in furthering the development process (that is, the state and NGOs) to constantly respond to changes in the external environment, over which they often had little control. During the period under study, NGOs emerged and established their position as significant actors within the Jordanian development scene. NGOs were also subject to the political and economic constraints which applied to the Government of Jordan during this period, and just as the state had to constantly mediate changing donor interests, the NGO actors had to negotiate a role for themselves which complemented and supported the state. NGOs also had to respond to the changing demands of foreign donors on which they were also increasingly dependent financially. For development NGOs, however, the need to adapt to external pressures and to balance these often conflicting sets of interests, was compounded by their obligation to respond to the needs of their primary constituents, the poor and marginalized who were suffering the impact of the political and economic processes affecting the country and the region.

The Queen Alia Fund, Jordan's longest established development NGO working nationally, provides an appropriate case study through which these issues can be made more explicit. It allows a greater focus to be placed on examining in depth the ways that these processes of negotiation at global and local levels are reflected in organizational choices and behaviour, from day-to-day operations to strategic decisions. The choice of focus was also influenced by the fact that I had been closely involved with the Fund throughout this entire period, in my role of chairperson. I could therefore draw on my own experience of the processes of change and the ways that shifts in theory and practice are interwoven and inseparable. This close involvement, however, also brought its own challenges, and limited the possible approaches that could be taken to the study. Clearly, I was an 'insider' with my own understanding of the complex reality of these processes, and yet my closeness might also be a barrier to allowing multiple perceptions of these processes to emerge from the various actors involved. Accordingly, I drew on the actor-oriented approach advocated by Norman Long.

In *Battlefields of Knowledge* (1992) Long sets out to address a central challenge in the field of development: namely that of 'reconciling funda- mental research and theory with the practical demands of policy making and intervention' (Long, 1992: 3). Instead of seeing 'knowledge for under- standing' and 'knowledge for action' as a dichotomy, he constructs his framework for research on the assumption that theoretical and pragmatic issues and activities are 'so closely interwoven that one cannot have one without the other. Just as policy models and measures are themselves underpinned by certain theoretical interpretations and methodological strategies, theorization and research are also laden with evaluative judg- ments and decisions of a practical nature' (ibid.: 3–4).

From this starting point Long builds upon theoretical work aimed at reconciling the perspectives of structure and actor. Recent elaborations of this work have stimulated treatments of social change and intervention which emphasize the interplay and mutual determination of 'internal' and 'external' factors and relationships and enable the researcher to provide accounts of the life-worlds, strategies and rationalities of actors in differ- ent social arenas (ibid.: 5). Because all social change 'involves a struggle between different social interests and the intersection of life-worlds,' Long sees the actor-oriented approach, which is essentially grounded 'in the eve- ryday life experiences and understanding of men and women, be they poor peasants, entrepreneurs, government bureaucrats or researchers,' as central to an understanding of development processes. Put in a more abstract way, the approach entails 'recognizing the "multiple realities" and diverse social practices of various actors, and requires working out methodologically how to get to grips with these different and often incompatible social worlds.' It also demands sensitivity to the process by which the researcher enters the life-worlds of the researched (and vice-versa) and thus achieves 'a more reflexive kind of ethnography' (ibid.: 5–6).

Applied to development research the actor-oriented approach 'requires a full analysis of the ways in which different social actors manage and interpret new elements in their life-worlds ... and a deconstruction of conventional notions of planned intervention' (ibid.: 9). Intervention should be viewed, Long argues, not as the implementation of a plan for action, but as an ongoing transformational process which involves the interests and struggles of different actors. An understanding of the process 'by which knowledge is negotiated and jointly created through various types of social encounter,' and a recognition of the power dynamics involved are, therefore, integral to this approach (ibid.) Particularly important here is the concept of 'social interface' which offers a framework for analysing the encounters between various parties in the development process who represent different interests, are backed by different resources and are often distinguished in terms of power. Long defines social interface as 'a critical point of intersection or linkage between different social systems, fields or levels of social order where structural discontinuities, based upon differences of normative value and social interests are likely to be found' (Long, 1989: 1–2). An analysis of 'interface situations,' which involves notions of 'knowledge, 'power' and 'agency,' stresses the 'reproduction and transformation of social discontinuities inherent in interface encounters including ... those between the researcher and the researched' (Long, 1992: 6).

The different elements of the actor-oriented approach are particularly suited to an examination of the diverse, often complex and paradoxical factors underlying Jordan's course of development. The perspective facilitates an understanding of the approaches adopted by different actors within the specificity of the Jordanian development setting, in addition to the circumstances through which such approaches were created. It also provides a means of looking at Jordanian state relations with external and local actors, as well as ties between the Fund and its donors, or between the field and the Fund. Furthermore, the varying interests and discontinuities which often affected relations between these different actors also became apparent.

The qualitative research methodology on which this approach mainly relies, which is both interpretative and processual between researcher, organization and beneficiaries, contrasts with the dominant quantitative approach of much development research on the Arab World in general and Jordan in particular. While useful and valid, quantitative methodologies, which seek to measure and give a numerical value to the social outcomes of development, can provide only a limited understanding of the process (Oakley, 1990: 29). Furthermore, as Salmen points out, analyses of social and economic phenomena which rely primarily on statistics are particularly inappropriate in developing countries where the data base is poor and the need for cultural, contextual understanding is great (Salmen, 1987).

A blend of both qualitative and quantitative techniques offers a more advantageous approach to an understanding of development projects. Although qualitative and quantitative research are sometimes viewed as opposites, and qualitative approaches are often dismissed as less reliable with few or no validity checks, some of the best research uses both modes: 'Without science we lose our credibility; without humanity we lose our ability to understand others' (Ager quoted in Omidian, 2000: 42).

The qualitative methodology used here is what Lawrence Salmen has called 'participant-observer evaluation,' a methodology he describes as 'an eclectic blend of techniques designed to interpret the real world of project beneficiaries, their perceived needs, hopes, and frustrations ...' (Salmen, 1987: 6). The emphasis of 'participant-observer evaluation' is on creating a relationship of trust between researcher and subject. Establishing such trust encourages people to articulate their interpretations of a project, which are then conveyed descriptively, and where possible, numerically as well. Participant-observer evaluation relies on the researcher's ability to listen and recognize the utility of issues arising in a particular context, rather than on pre-formulated questionnaires or sophisticated statistical analysis.

Participant-observer evaluation as used by Salmen is therefore an inclusive general term which 'involves some amount of genuinely social intervention in the field with the subjects of the study, some direct observation of relevant events, some formal and a great deal of informal interviewing, some collection of documents ... and open-endedness in the direction the study takes' (ibid.: 108). The quantity of information, and the precision with which it is recorded and presented, are far less important than the quality and reliability of the findings. For Salmen the interpretation of survey data is crucial, especially when the phenomena observed are complex and subject to widely-varying interpretation. As in the case of community participation, it is far better to give a reliable, if general, picture of what takes place than to present precise numerical measures out of context.

Qualitative research, as Omidian points out, is based on the value of the insider's view and attempts to understand people's world from their own perspective. This method has three advantages: viewing behaviour in its natural setting, gaining in-depth understanding from an indigenous point of view, and providing the researcher with the flexibility to change research designs to fit new data. Salmen, like Omidian, emphasizes the advantage of viewing behaviour in its natural setting. Conversational interviewing and participant observation, the two basic methods used in this context, are, he notes, intended to increase the reliability and relevance of evaluation. The basic problem with questionnaires lies in the artificiality of the interview setting. People are simply not apt to disclose important information about themselves to someone they do not know, regardless of the stated purpose of obtaining information and 'poor people in developing countries (project beneficiaries), are ... distrustful of anyone in authority or anyone who appears to be working for those in authority' (Salmen, 1987: 122–3).

The importance of gaining in-depth understanding from the indigenous perspective is, for both Salmen and Omidian, the premise for qualitative research; for how can people of one world effectively plan and manage activities for people of the other without understanding them on their own terms (ibid.)? Qualitative research is based on the need to ask different questions from that of quantitative research. Not 'how many?' but 'what kind of?' and 'what is the meaning of?' While both kinds of questions need to be asked, questions of meaning clarify a community's own notion of what this process signifies. Qualitative studies that attempt to understand the insider's view validate the researcher's understanding of cultural patterns and issues.

In order to ensure the validity and reliability of the research project to the greatest possible extent, I decided to adopt a rigorous combination of qualitative and quantitative methods. The analytical approach I developed to the study of the Fund centred on understanding the relationships between policy, implementation and outcomes, rather than treating these factors as shifts from one separate stage to another. The emphasis was on understanding the processes which create linkages between different actors and levels related to the Fund's operations. Because policies and outcomes undergo constant transformation due to different interpretations, and as they interface with other factors such as the external environment, this interpretative approach was required to analyse the factors which underpinned various processes of change in the organization and its environment.

In undertaking this research, my own place within the field of the study has been a challenging factor, both in relation to the context of Jordan, but most especially with regard to the Fund of which I was the chairperson. The first issue raised by such close involvement in the subject of study is that of the 'insider/outsider' which in turn gives rise to questions concerning the broad philosophical debate between subjectivity and objectivity. To some, the notion which underlies the insider/outsider dichotomy is simplistic because it presumes that, as an insider, an indigenous researcher reproduces the culture of his or her informants; for in any research situation both sides are in essence representatives of certain ideas and values. However, while all researchers should for this reason examine their own ideas or values critically, the main question is not objectivity per se, but rather, how the researcher's relative social position bears upon the methodology he or she uses (Shami, 1988). In the case of this particular study this consideration has played a major part in devising the methodological approach which I have adopted.

Some of the issues raised by the context in which the study was carried out are highlighted in *Arab Women in the Field* (Altorki and El-Solh, 1988), a collection of essays in which six women social scientists of Arab descent examine their fieldwork experiences in the Arab region and explore the implications of 'studying your own society.' Suad Joseph remarks in her contribution to this book that as someone with roots in the society she studied, her relationships with people and her identities were multifaceted – a factor that both facilitated her work and made it more complex (Joseph, 1988: 27).

A theme of particular relevance highlighted in *Arab Women in the Field* is the way in which the researcher's status and accompanying role among the people she is studying can, to a considerable extent, 'structure access to the field and knowledge of the social reality at hand' (Altorki and El-Solh, 1988: 11). Another important consideration is the ethical implication of fieldwork, and in particular the way in which researchers present themselves to the research community. Arab researchers are not only, like their non-native associates, held accountable by the demands of scholarship, but may also be required to take into account expectations of their moral obligation to the subject of their study (ibid.: 20).

Both these issues have had an important bearing on the design of my work. With them in mind I have sought to address the question of my own inherent biases, whether in relation to the national dimension or to the Fund. In order to conduct a valid research study, it was also necessary for me to define a methodological strategy for examining the organization with which I have been involved in managing since it was established.

My status and role in Jordan afforded me significant access to data from a wide range of sources, both within governmental and non-governmental sectors and the cooperation I received was very generous. However, it became clear to me during an initial attempt to gather data first hand from a government ministry that my enterprise was likely to create considerable inconvenience and disruption for those concerned. While the session at this ministry was enlightening, it was also time-consuming for my hosts as well as myself. For what was intended to be a search for data, became a protracted tour, covering areas far beyond my immediate needs, which under different circumstances I would have welcomed.

Attempts to gather information first hand from the Fund itself gave rise to different problems. My position in the organization gave me unique access to data and materials about its workings which, as in many institutions, employees would have been more reluctant to disclose to a researcher from outside. This was a decisive factor in my decision to carry out an in-depth study of QAF rather than a comparative study with similar NGOs. For besides the unequal access that this would imply, a comparative study could only have been properly implemented by an objective researcher from outside the organizations involved. From another point of view I recognized that, as chairperson of the Fund, my capacity as a researcher was likely to conflict with the requirements of my management role which involved interactions of a different kind with the staff of the organization. Moreover, in searching for data first hand, I would become a constant presence in various departments and might interrupt their work. Another issue I had to consider was my ability to acquire valid and reliable information if I were to conduct interviews myself, due to the possible inhibitions of informants. Compounding this was the possibility that within the Fund staff might feel that I was assessing their performance, and therefore would not be spontaneous. In the case of the Fund's beneficiaries, it was likely that I would be told only about what they thought I wanted to hear, which was the positive side of its work. Fortunately, the many field visits which I have carried out over the years have helped to shape my perception of the Fund's role, and in this sense I was able to draw on what might be described as my own participant observation.

A method adopted and described by Marilyn Porter (1994) known as 'second-hand ethnography,' has been of considerable help in allowing me to overcome some of the problems of 'studying one's own society.' This approach allows for the main researcher to be divorced from the major part of data collection. In 1988, Porter secured funding from the Social Science and Humanities Research Council (SSHRC) for a large-scale research project to explore women's economic lives in Newfoundland, Canada. The main part of the study was to be a comparison of three different communities, with a focus in each case on an ethnography carried out by a research assistant. The research model followed by SSHRC meant that Porter was not expected to leave her full-time university teaching position to implement the study herself, but could hire research assistants, interviewers, transcribers, coders and secretaries. 'In this model the principal investigator ... is responsible for the theoretical formulation of the project, for its administration and for writing the reports, but not for actually carrying out the research' (Porter, 1994: 72–3).

Consequently, in her final analysis and report writing Porter based her analysis on the data collected by her researchers. This included interviews and oral histories, as well as the researchers' diaries and personal jottings. Porter states that 'when I write about the study, I am asking the reader to trust not my ethnographic understanding of the communities, but my interpretation of my research assistants' ethnographic understanding of the communities' (ibid.: 76). Although Porter concludes that this approach is not without difficulties, she believes that the examination of her colleagues' field experience and field notes can be a source of knowledge itself. She contends that with this approach, 'The focus would inevitably be as much on the researchers and the process of research as on the original "subject," but that is not, in itself, a weakness' (ibid.: 85).

Although I drew on Porter's methodology to address the various limitations arising from my own situation, only parts of the study relied on second-hand ethnography; for its purpose varied, and hence its approach. In Porter's case the study was 'exploratory' (ibid.: 70). In essence, studies done and data previously collected had been so scant that she could not know exactly what sort of material she wanted or how it would be gathered. Moreover, geographical distance as well as the demands of her work meant that Porter had to depend on her ethnographers and was separated from the study as it evolved. The premise of my own work differed. Based on the overall framework which I had defined, I relied on research assistants for data gathering to support a study plan which I had already set out. In addition, having developed the conceptual underpinning of each chapter, I was directly involved in guiding the process of data collection in order to maintain the focus of my arguments. I then drew on the data which my research assistants had gathered through interviews, documentation and fieldwork to make my analysis.

Four researchers were engaged in collecting documents, conducting interviews and fieldwork on my behalf. While Porter's methodological approach was primarily related to fieldwork, in this case I also relied on the researchers to collect information of other kinds. In this way I was able to acquire the extensive data needed to inform the broad framework of the study. As this meant that I had to rely heavily on the skills of my research assistants, it was important to choose the people I felt were best suited to the methods I had selected. The diversity of the subjects I wanted to cover in the overall study, as well as the linkages I sought to highlight, required a pragmatic experience of the different areas under examination. For, as with Porter, some analysis of my research assistants' ethnographic understanding would be involved.

At the same time, I was aware of my place within the context of the study beyond the development field, specifically in relation to the historical and political content of the work at hand. In this sense I felt a similar moral dilemma to other Arab researchers who 'may not easily be able to evade the social and political responsibilities directly or indirectly emanating from their research findings' (Nakhleh cited in Altorki and El-Solh, 1988: 20). Of fundamental relevance to addressing this dilemma is a major insight to be gained from feminist research. Feminist methodology, unlike other kinds of social research, reflects 'a concern to record the subjective experiences of doing research' (Gelsthorpe cited in Maynard and Purvis, 1994: 16). In critiquing the dichotomy between objectivity versus subjectivity, which alternative approaches to social research bring out, feminist scholars argue 'that the researcher is also a subject in her research and that her personal history is part of the process through which "understanding" and "conclusions" are reached' (Stanley and Wise cited in Maynard, 1994: 16). Here, the fact that my research assistants shared an understanding of this premise, and furthermore that three of them worked on feminist issues was helpful given the interpretative nature of the methodology I was using.

As with most research projects in developing countries, the process of data collection was not without difficulties, often due to a lack of adequate documentation. Frequently, documents which were drawn upon for the study required further factual validation to verify sequences of events behind the formulation of national development policies. In certain cases, materials were incomplete due to a cultural tendency to rely on oral history, or because of selective documentation. Consequently, in gathering data for the national and regional contexts of the study, the background of the two resource persons I engaged from the government sector, was a valuable asset.

Dr Amal Sabbagh, Secretary-General of the Jordanian National Commission for Women (JNCW), had nineteen years experience in the Ministry of Social Development. Salem Ghawi, former Assistant-Secretary General at the Ministry of Planning, was with the ministry for thirty-seven years during which time he was seconded to QAF as Executive Director from 1990–1992. The knowledge that Sabbagh and Ghawi possessed of the workings of the government development sector provided clarification in a number of areas. Indeed, an enlightening feature of the research process, which helped me to interpret underlying factors that affected development policies, were the intense and often heated debates which took place between them. Although colleagues and friends, Sabbagh and Ghawi frequently had different views on Jordanian development issues. In a way that documents could not always achieve, these discussions brought out varying perspectives on what the implementation of national policies actually entailed.

More specifically involved in gathering data on the work of QAF and the Jordanian social sector, including NGOs, were Dr Taghreed Abu-Hamdan and Nicholaa Malet de Carteret. Abu-Hamdan began working for the Fund in 1989 and was head of the Research and Studies Unit. She prepared background materials and information and conducted interviews in Arabic with the Fund's staff at headquarters and at its Community Development Centres (CDCs). She also implemented the 1996 field study on the Impact of QAF's Programmes and Activities. De Carteret, a British and Canadian national with a background in journalism, began visiting Jordan in 1992 and has carried out management and PR consultancy and training for the Fund. She conducted interviews in English with QAF staff, Jordanian development specialists and policy-makers, as well as representatives of donor agencies. Interviews carried out by both research assistants reflected the qualitative research methodology of the study, and were based on semi-structured and unstructured techniques.

People's time constraints, and the variety of topics covered, meant that interviews sometimes took more than one session to complete. Triangulation, a process of cross-checking, often revealed discrepancies and contradictions, and in such circumstances the interviewer was obliged to arrange an additional session with the same person, or with a second or even a third party, to get further validity. Particularly with regard to the Fund's initial phase of establishment and the early workings of the CDCs, some reliance on oral history was necessary. Hence, the probability that in retrospect perceptions had altered, needed to be taken into account. Consideration also had to be given to the different biases of the respondents. At times, however, verifying events and understandings through documentation proved difficult, again due to a lack of proper records within the Fund.

As the interviewers were familiar to QAF staff, both at headquarters and within the CDCs, they were generally able to make respondents feel at ease in the interview situation. Although there were advantages and

disadvantages to the different cultural backgrounds and biases of the interviewers themselves, on the whole their perspectives contributed favourably
to the nature of the interviews which they conducted. The fact that de
Carteret did her interviews in English, which for the most part was not her
respondents' first language, sometimes made it harder for them to express
themselves fully; moreover some of the cultural nuances of what they said
may have been missed. However, most of the time not being an indigenous
researcher seemed to work in her favour, for a reading of the transcripts
shows that de Carteret was able to get her respondents to open up to a
notable extent; in this sense, perhaps respondents felt more spontaneous
in talking to a 'foreigner.' On several occasions, however, respondents asked
to have the tape turned off out of concern that they were touching on
sensitive issues which might be misconstrued; their request was respected.
Sometimes when interviewing QAF staff, de Carteret sensed that the interview was being used as a channel to convey a particular point of view to
the 'chairperson of QAF.'

This did not apply to Abu-Hamdan, who was already known and
accepted in the field for doing research for the Fund through the CDCs.
Nevertheless, in order to ensure as valid an account as possible of different
issues, respondents did not know at the time of the interview that it was
being conducted for the purpose of the research project. Permission to
use the material for the study was subsequently requested and granted.
Apart from not having to deal with language constraints, as an indigenous
researcher Abu-Hamdan's cultural understanding of the people she was
interviewing was vital, particularly with regard to people in local communities, including women at the grassroots level.

In many ways, the Fund was 'turned inside out,' whether through
interviews or by examining primary sources. While this process often
disrupted work schedules, it also heightened a determination within the
organization to create proper archives. It has been noted that qualitative
research methodology implies that respondents are seen as 'participants'
in the research, and actively shape the directions which interviews take
(Cassell and Symon, 1994). Many people participated in these endeavours,
including the Executive Director of QAF, heads of departments and staff,
as well as the Director of the Queen Zein al Sharaf Institute for Development. Indeed, the amount of effort made to provide information and data,
whether through interviews or written materials, was significant. At some
point, after yet another interview with de Carteret, one head of department exclaimed 'I don't know if I can help you any more!'

The dynamic of the research process created its own momentum and I noted how the understandings of the research assistants themselves were at times altered by the experience. During the many discussions which took place, Dr Sabbagh, for instance, gained new insight into the dilemmas that confronted the Fund which occasionally differed from the perspective she had previously formed at the ministry. On the other hand, by wearing her 'ministry hat,' she was able to provide useful criticism of the Fund. In particular when certain events were recalled through oral history and the Fund's achievements were exaggerated, her intervention helped to ensure that validity and reliability were not compromised. Furthermore, the contrasting experiences of the researchers, and the mix of culture and gender in the group, created a layering of interpretations and helped to a fuller understanding of the issues. Some views contend that the feminist debate, while focusing on the process of conducting research, pays less attention to the impact and significance that participating in a research project can have on both the person involved as well as those being studied (Maynard and Purvis, 1994: 4). To a great extent, doing my research at a time when I was also helping to guide the Fund through a period of transition and internal reform, sensitized me at a deeper level to the concerns which were being addressed. In other ways, seeking clarification for the study on different aspects of the Fund from people directly involved in managing its operations, often prompted different forms of re-evaluation and reconsideration of QAF's role and relationships, particularly with the field.

In order to lay the ground for the comprehensive examination of the Queen Alia Fund, and to reflect the voice of people involved on the ground with the Fund, two field studies were conducted in 1996 and 1997. In both cases, the fieldwork was carried out in QAF's Community Development Centres, which at the time of the studies were forty-eight in number. The centres provide the infrastructural framework for the majority of the development programmes and projects operated by QAF in local communities. The first study on 'The Impact of QAF's Programmes and Activities' (1996a) was conducted with the aim of assessing the effect of programmes offered by the CDCs. The study examined QAF's approaches in fostering change within the communities served by the centres; it drew on evaluations made by Centre beneficiaries, and committee members running the centres (see chapter 5). Local community leaders and various national institutions were included as well. The impact of CDC programmes in mobilizing community participation through social and economic activities was also investigated. In addition, the study examined women's initial experiences as members of municipal councils, as well as the role of the CDCs in promoting their participation in decision-making processes.

The research team was headed by Abu-Hamdan and included members of the women's committees from the centres under study. Three CDCs, located in the north, the middle and the south of the country were selected as samples. This geographic selection was intended to allow comparisons to be drawn between the regional specificities of the three communities. A random sample of 185 beneficiaries and committee members was taken from each Centre, representing 20 per cent of total participants at the Centre. Local leaders and women municipal council members from each community, as well as CDC directors, were all included. Among the government institutions with which QAF cooperated, and which were also part of the study, were the Ministries of Planning, Health, Education and Social Development. Other organizations included were the General Union of Voluntary Societies (GUVS) and the Development and Employment Fund (DEF).

Questionnaires were drawn up to gather data for the study. Three separate questionnaires were prepared for three different categories of respondents, namely: Centre beneficiaries, local leaders, and staff of national institutions. Each questionnaire included a combination of closed and open-ended questions. The latter allowed for a better understanding of the issues which the study sought to cover (Patton, 1990). The other part of the study adopted qualitative methods of data collection, based on semi-structured interviews. These aimed mainly at acquiring an in-depth understanding of the way people thought and in this instance the interviewer introduced the topic and guided the questions (Rubin and Rubin, 1995).

Different procedures were used to access the data. With national institutions, questionnaires were sent, and upon completion were collected. In the case of Centre beneficiaries and local leaders, questionnaires were filled during individual interviews. This approach not only guaranteed that questionnaires were answered, but also gave respondents the opportunity to fully express their views and experiences of the CDCs, ultimately creating a better understanding of their perceptions. Taped interviews were transcribed and categorized under different topics. By combining qualitative and quantitative research methods, and by including a variety of respondents from the public sector as well as civil society, the aim was to strengthen the scope of the study and to acquire a valid evaluation of the impact of the CDCs' programmes.

The second field study on 'Management Versus Decentralization' (QAF, 1998b), consisted of a pilot interviewing schedule which was conducted over a four-month period, between May and August 1997. All forty-eight

CDCs were covered by the Pilot Study.[1] The aim was to highlight themes and concerns relevant to the comprehensive study of QAF. The interview schedule for the Pilot Study was carried out by a team of four researchers. The team, which included two women and two men, was headed by Riyad Mustafa, a researcher then working for CERMOC (Centre d'Études et de Recherches sur le Moyen-Orient Contemporain). A set of open-ended questions was prepared, which formed guidelines for semi-structured interviews conducted by the researchers. The interviews were mostly recorded on tape (except when respondents preferred not to record certain details). Initially, questions were grouped into three main sections: the first section addressed questions related to the nature of 'development' and the way it was defined and contextualized by respondents. Questions in the second section, were directed to the policy implications of both governmental and non-governmental development interventions. The last section included questions intended to allow respondents to make suggestions, which they thought could assist in formulating a hypothetically more 'positive' kind of development approach.

The researchers made preliminary visits to the CDCs in order to introduce the study and record data through structured interviews concerning programmes, Centre facilities, numbers of workers and beneficiaries etc. These visits provided the researchers with the opportunity to focus on the specific character of each Centre, and to prepare material related to its situation. They also allowed for respondents to be given notice, so that on the following day when the researchers returned to conduct interviews, their subjects would be available. This was a necessary measure owing to the distances between centres, especially in more remote areas, and the fact that people had different roles which did not necessarily entail being present at the CDCs on a daily basis.

Subsequent interviews conducted in this study included QAF staff, beneficiaries, local NGOs, pre-school and vocational training teachers carrying out the different programmes, as well as the *ra'idat rifiyyat* (rural woman leaders) who were responsible for the daily running of CDCs' activities; government workers involved in development programmes at the centres were also interviewed. Structured and semi-structured interviews were

---

1. Although this fieldwork was intended to be a pilot study for a broader survey of certain communities, the data collected through the pilot phase was sufficiently comprehensive not to merit further investigation. However, for purposes of identification, throughout the book this undertaking will continue to be referred to as a Pilot Study.

not the only form of data collection; the researchers also photographed the centres and other subjects that they thought could help them define contexts. In addition, the team wrote their impressions in diaries and other types of notebook. Generally, these techniques are not commonly used in development-oriented research in Jordan, which tends to rely mainly on quantitative methods.

The fact that the interviews in the Pilot Study were conducted by researchers from outside the Fund contributed to the reliability of the data. Due to the nature of the questions, many of which were related to the Fund's management approach, the respondents felt more at ease with interviewers who were not part of the organization. The data gathered included 103 hours of transcribed tapes covering 106 interviews. These were coded according to topics. The data was then categorized under seven main topics related to management and decentralization, and thirty-two subtopics.

In addition to the field studies, thirty-five interviews were conducted with different actors, both within governmental and non-governmental sectors. These voices grounded the arguments raised by the study by providing further insight into the circumstances surrounding various issues.

The adoption of a qualitative research methodology to analyse factors which have given the Jordanian development experience its specificity allowed the research project to tune into ethnographic reality largely influenced by local circumstances and requiring a recognition of the diversity of local contexts (Pottier, 1993). Moreover, in drawing on the actor-oriented approach, which combines various perspectives with process, the scope of the study was enhanced by a rigorous combination of written materials and interviews.

I was troubled by the limitations which in different ways prevented me from conducting certain aspects of the research first-hand; but I was fortunate to have capable and motivated research assistants. Like Porter I was able to see the strengths and weaknesses of the research assistants and the various ways in which they were affected by the research process. In the case of Abu-Hamdan, who had worked most of her professional life with the Fund and had certain ideals about the organization, the research project was an eye-opener in the sense that she became more aware of the Fund's shortcomings. As a result of the problems of data collection, moreover, she was increasingly motivated to create an efficient information base of the Fund's field activities. Ghawi, who with a long-standing career in the civil service, was closely associated with the national development plans through his work in the Ministry of Planning, began to recognize that while the plans called for the involvement of the private sector, including NGOs, in fact the participation of this sector in project identification and design was extremely limited. In the final analysis, it was the ministry that set the tone of development policies, and thus perpetuated a centralized approach. Through the research process, Sabbagh came to see the potential which really existed within the organization: hence, if the Fund could genuinely succeed in carrying out its reforms and listen closely to the field, with the spread of the CDC network it would be in a unique position in the country to impact the development of local communities. As a Westerner who, despite the fact that she had been coming to Jordan and working with the Fund for a number of years, de Carteret was more directly exposed to the complexities of the Jordanian development process. Thus, through the research project she gained a better understanding of some of the dilemmas faced by a developing country.

While I am sure that some of the biases of my research assistants influenced the findings of the study, because more than one assistant was involved I was able to draw on a mix of perspectives from which to form my own conclusions. Moreover, interpreting these different perspectives added another dimension to the research. From my perspective, the close interaction which I had with the research assistants over a long period of time, deepened my awareness of issues related to the Fund and beyond, that previously I had probably taken for granted. Moreover, through the different understandings that emerged from our debates, I was able to make new and important linkages between the broad areas examined by the study. It can therefore be said that the advantage of the study's qualitative methodology and its second-hand ethnography was to challenge assumptions, widen perspectives and sensitize everyone more acutely to the specific characteristics of the Jordanian development process.

4

Beginnings:
The Queen Alia Fund: 1977–1984

Royal Decree by His Majesty King Hussein officially establishing the Queen Alia Jordan Social Welfare Fund:

To our dear sister HRH Princess Basma, may God keep her.

I convey to you my warmest brotherly greetings together with my pride and appreciation.

Your continuous efforts in working for the country and in the service of our people have earned all my appreciation and support. Your faithful endeavours and the steady and positive steps which you have taken to foster social and humanitarian work in our beloved country, which include the fulfillment of our wish to create the Queen Alia Social Welfare Fund are commendable efforts in furthering the causes begun by the late Queen Alia, for which she sacrificed her life. Her dedication to these causes stemmed from a belief that social responsibility to the country was a duty in its most humanitarian sense.

Therefore, in achieving the aims of this honourable vision you have my patronage and full support. I am confident that this evolving social organization will with the grace of God and through your dedicated efforts, fulfil the aspirations of us all in effectively contributing to building our social structure and advancing voluntary work in our beloved country based on strong foundations, while preserving the noble spirit of our culture.

I ask Almighty God to protect you and all who work with you and to help you in your efforts to achieve and take forward this worthy cause.

Your loving brother who is ever proud of you.

Amman 30 Dhul-qa'da 1397H
Amman 10 November 1977
Reference: 3/3/1/24

On 10 November 1977, the Queen Alia Fund was established by Royal Decree. It thus entered the Jordanian social field with the highest level of support and a broad mandate. The creation of the new organization was spurred by personal tragedy, the untimely death of Queen Alia, the wife of King Hussein: 'When it was first established, we were all very emotionally involved in the tragic accident. The country needed a high level NGO that could take a lead in more than one way' (al-Mufti interview). The Queen Alia Fund (QAF) carried deep symbolic significance as a memorial to the causes upheld by the late queen. However, once founded, the Fund had to create a space amongst the already existing actors in the arena of social work in which it could define its role and justify its establishment. It was, in other words, necessary for the Fund to develop an operational approach through which to carry out its mandate.

Issues of Establishment

A theme of the 1973–1975 Development Plan had been the need to create social policy. In order to achieve this objective the Plan recommended that a Higher Council for Social Work be set up, consisting of representatives from government, private and other organizations working in the social field (Jordan, 1973). It also pointed to a lack of planning in rural areas, an absence of essential social services and insufficient data with which to address these problems. The 1976–1980 Five Year Plan raised many of the same issues. Various problems relating to social work were highlighted including a failure of the social sector to stem internal migration from rural to urban areas, resulting in overcrowded urban communities and underdeveloped rural areas; the lack of a clear-cut, comprehensive national social policy; poor information about the scale and nature of the social problems that faced the country and their dimensions, and a shortage of pre-school and nursery facilities, especially for working women (Jordan, 1976a).

The focus of both plans on the shortcomings of social work was an indication that the government, despite its efforts, was not dealing with these issues effectively. 'Development terms did not exist at that time and social work used to be charitable. Public perception of the ministry's role was in delivering in-kind assistance' (al-Iss'iss interview). The proposal to establish a Higher Council from related sectors to act on a national level and to set a policy for social development was not acted upon. Furthermore, the attempts of numerous committees set up by the government to redefine social work had limited results (Jordan, 1981a).

Despite the absence of a clear social policy around the time of QAF's establishment, and the largely unsuccessful attempts by the government to organize the social field, the impact of the non-governmental sector and other institutions was increasing. The General Union of Voluntary Societies (GUVS) had begun to carry more weight financially with the award of the management of the National Lottery and was consequently less reliant on government support. Furthermore, other bodies such as the Sociology Department at the University of Jordan were promoting new approaches to social work.

As a new organization, QAF was thus entering a vibrant setting where long-established actors, both governmental and non-governmental, had previously consolidated their roles. For all the differences between them, the interface between governmental and non-governmental actors was well established, enabling the two sides to coexist. On one level, then, the newly created Fund was an intrusive factor whose advent implied a change in the equation. The singular support with which QAF was founded, and the status this afforded the new organization, inevitably created certain sensitivities amongst other actors. 'Some doubt and cynicism existed among the existing NGOs as to whether the new organization could add anything substantial to what they were already attempting. Few were of the opinion that the new body would actually improve existing efforts; some felt it would weaken or duplicate them' (Abu el-Ata interview). Government organizations expressed similar apprehensions: 'For instance, the Ministry of Labour and Social Affairs had some concern that QAF would take over its role, and GUVS thought the Fund would take the lottery money from them' (al-Iss'iss interview).

Another controversial issue which provoked a range of reactions was my own role as Chairperson of QAF's Board of Trustees: 'Between us, I think there was a resentment in government towards QAF, in the sense that "you are doing our work." They couldn't do much because a member of the royal family was involved … various ministers harboured some kind of personal resentment, the idea that they couldn't check on QAF' (Nassir interview). Some believe the royal connection to have had a bearing from the outset on certain aspects of QAF's work. It has also fostered the perception that the Fund was to some extent an extension of the state: 'I think first of all that getting royalty involved in the work was a way of building a bridge to the grassroots. And when the King backed Princess Basma that meant another contribution to society. Also the availability of resources, royalty's connections, could be of so much importance to the work. At the same time, I had a feeling that the money that was going to be available to the Fund would be more than the money that would be available to us [GUVS]. They had more access to resources inside and outside which could help our cause' (al-Khatib interview).

There were, however, other interpretations among those who reflected on the significance of the new organization. Among them was the view that the addition of such an organization to the social sector could be regarded as a sign of support to social work as a whole: 'I think it was perceived that there was a recognition of social development – that was the perception – and to establish a Fund or similar institution meant that there was a recognition of the importance of social work … In fact I felt such an institution might be of help rather than threaten our work. In general, it was a welcome recognition of social work' (Nassir interview).

During the early phase of its existence the Fund faced, and tried to address, a variety of issues. To begin with, the distinctive manner in which it had been launched into the social field generated considerable pressure on the new organization to show early results. However, this feeling of urgency, which became a primary concern, was largely at the expense of the slow task of building relations with other key actors and gaining acceptance through a gradual process of evolution. In seeking ways to strengthen the organization fast, the Fund relied heavily on its Board of Trustees which included several cabinet ministers and heads of public and private sector institutions, together with leading figures from Jordanian society (al-Ra'i, 1978). This influential body of men and women had the contacts to generate support for the Fund, as well as the professional experience to develop an initial strategy to take it forward. In some ways the composition of the Board bore a resemblance to the Higher Council that had been recommended by the Three Year Development Plan (1973–1975) but had never materialized. In order to facilitate its efforts the Fund frequently drew on the extensive social capital embodied in its Board. For instance, at first QAF was registered as a non-governmental organization with the Ministry of Labour and Social Affairs (Jordan, 1977b). This meant that it was obliged to operate in the same way as other NGOs according to the regulations of the ministry. However, soon after it began its work, members of the Board began to lobby the government to secure a separate legal status for the Fund and in January 1979, Law No. 6 was passed giving the Queen Alia Fund complete autonomy.[1] Consequently, like the Red Crescent Society, QAF acquired a

---

1. Law No. 6 was provisionally passed in 1979, but was passed in its final form as Law No. 37 in 1985. Under this Law the Fund was recognized as a national non-governmental institution under the name 'Queen Alia Jordan Social Welfare

unique position as a national non-governmental organization operating independently under its own law.

The Fund's autonomous status gave it freedom from bureaucratic interference, as well as the flexibility to set its own agenda and approach. However, contrary to some impressions, the task of generating financial support involved considerable effort. 'It was an independent institution. It did not have to submit to the government. It was headed by a member of the royal family. It had funds. The other NGOs didn't have much. I remember we used to go ask businesses for a bag of cement. Imagine! So because QAF was headed by a member of the royal family it had the financial means' (Nassir interview).

Kamel Abu-Jaber recalls that QAF's situation was in reality far more challenging. 'Of course, the major difficulty was financial, and this was a backbreaker. In fact when I took over we hardly had money to pay the salaries, not to mention we didn't even have a car to run errands ... We were starting literally from scratch. There was a building, there were a few people on the staff, and there were some meeting rooms but hardly anything else. So we literally started building from that very narrow base' (Abu-Jaber interview). In fact, the office premises allocated to QAF upon its foundation formed the bulk of support from the government. In addition, it was granted a sum of thirty thousand JDs to finance research aimed at identifying the needs of the social sector at the national level and developing viable projects. However, once QAF acquired an autonomous status, the government felt that it should no longer receive financial support. QAF could use government land on which to build projects, but the government considered that part of the Fund's role was to assist the public sector by raising additional funds for the social sector (QAF, 1979a).

Members of the Board tried to generate income in different ways: 'We got quite a bit of help from local sources, but again in kind ... I started at that time to build a library for the Fund. The Cement Factory ... donated the cement. People donated doors and things like that. A small modest amount, but they were significant for us, so we started the library' (Abu-Jaber interview). In order to encourage donations from the business and commercial sectors, the Board succeeded in obtaining partial tax exemption status in 1978.[2] Through other efforts by the Board, QAF obtained a

---

Fund,' and was granted the right to enjoy administrative and financial independence (The Official Gazette, 1985).

2. This decision was passed by the Council of Ministers in its meeting in March 1978 and based the decision on Income Tax Law No. 10/25, 1964 (Jordan, 1978b).

Fatwa from the chief Mufti of the Kingdom permitting Muslim citizens to pay their *zakat* through the Fund.[3] This decision enabled devout people with religious motivation to help the needy in accordance with Islamic tradition.

Although QAF came into being during the boom period in Jordan, its early fundraising efforts from local sources were not sufficient to meet the needs it aimed to address.[4] This was to some extent because it had not yet established sufficient ties with potential sponsors who were either involved in supporting their own special causes or were already inundated with requests for financial support from other NGOs. In addition, the Board and original staff of five were faced with many other problems and were not professionally experienced in fund-raising methods. Finally, despite the focus on economic development there was limited awareness of the developmental dimension of social work. It soon became apparent to members of the Board that part of the Fund's role should be to foster such an awareness within Jordanian society through its activities, and to iden-tify development priorities and address them through its approaches.

To achieve these aims it was necessary to consolidate QAF's role by defining a clear set of objectives, as well as to promote more effective fund-raising efforts:

> At that time the most important thing was to get the Fund established because it had just begun ... Neither the staff nor the financial aspects of the Fund were sufficiently established, and I was in charge trying to help Princess Basma in setting up the Fund, you know, consolidating its roots. That was one aspect. Secondly, what kind of areas should the Fund focus on? What kind of activities should it engage in? The broad outlines and ideas of its hopes, aspirations, its goals, and exactly how these could be accomplished ... The last and the most important issue was finance, where could we get financial support? (Abu-Jaber interview).

Creating a Role

In order to define its role and determine the way it would direct its efforts, the Fund needed to gain a clearer understanding of the nature of social

---

3. *Zakat* represents one of the five pillars of Islam, whereby Muslims are obliged to give a percentage of their income to charity.

4. Over the first seven years the average annual support raised by local contributions (individual donations and donations from 125 different companies and institutions) was JD 131, 014 (approximately £251, 087 at that time).

work in the country. For this reason, much of QAF's activity during this initial phase focused on familiarizing itself with the situation in the social field. Members of the Board examined a range of issues, and in particular problems relating to the social sector highlighted in the 1976–1980 Five Year Plan. In addition, the Board tried to assess existing services with the aim of avoiding possible duplication of public and private sector efforts. An evaluation was also carried out with consultancy support provided through the Rockefeller Foundation (QAF, 1979b). Meetings with government officials and representatives from various groups involved in social work in the country provided further insight. Another approach adopted to assess ongoing efforts and needs was through field visits which provided us with a sense of how needs and expectations were viewed at the grassroots. Through such interactions, the difficulties faced by NGOs in rural areas were also uncovered. For instance, it emerged that an almost universal constraint on these organizations was lack of funding which frequently prevented small NGOs from seeing projects through to completion. Moreover, when funds were available they were often not well used because volunteers and social workers lacked training for the programmes they were trying to implement (author's recollection).

According to national surveys, social services in the late 1970s centred mainly on urban areas whereas services which catered to rural areas, where 40.5 per cent of the population lived, were generally insufficient (Jordan, 1982a). The reality of this situation was underlined each time a field visit was made. Hence QAF's decision to focus most of its efforts on rural areas was largely influenced by conditions observed on the ground. It was also felt that NGOs working in Amman had greater access to local funding, technical experts and influential contacts than those in other parts of the country. In addition, part of its role as a national NGO implied that QAF should develop a national outreach.

After a year spent largely on evaluating the social sector a course of action had begun to emerge. A set of objectives was formulated by the Board, which defined QAF's role and laid out the areas of concern which it would address in relation to both governmental and non-governmental sectors.

1. To act as a catalyst in the field of social work among private voluntary organizations, governmental agencies and international organizations in order to improve the quality and quantity of basic social services available in Jordan.
2. To seek funds on the national, regional and international levels.

3. To use these funds to support programmes and projects that would strengthen its own organizational and technical capability in social work:

   i)   strengthen the organizational and technical capabilities of private voluntary organizations through programmes of training, exchange of personnel, etc.

   ii)   participate with government agencies in formulating a clear and programmable social policy. Such a social policy must determine the types of social services needed and set minimum quality standards for each.

   iii)   improve the linkages between private organizations and government agencies delivering services.

   iv)   cooperation with private, government and international organizations in fulfilling social policies.

   v)   pioneer programmes that would emphasize preventive rather than curative social work.

   vi)   support directly and indirectly social, health, educational and cultural programmes that put into operation new concepts or models to be standardized and later transferred to government agencies (QAF, 1978a: 8–9).

With the passage of time, and as QAF's efforts began to take shape, some of these objectives were found to be overly ambitious and in certain ways unrealistic. For as the Fund gained operational experience, it became more aware of its limitations as well as its strengths. Eventually, as relations evolved with other actors, QAF's first approaches were redefined. Different forms of cooperation were established through interaction with related bodies such as the Department of Social Affairs, GUVS as well as local NGOs and communities. The development of such relationships was not only one of the stated objectives of the Fund, but also essential to consolidating its efforts and fostering credibility.

Some of QAF's first efforts at the grassroots level during the late 1970s centred on meeting basic needs. Although this was characteristic of prevailing development trends, for the Fund it was also a way of building ties with local communities for whom it provided tangible benefits. Also, the prosperity enjoyed by certain parts of society during this period was not visible in many of the rural communities where QAF was creating a presence: 'Our point of departure at that time was that our government was too burdened with a lot of other activities and obligations … And our government needed help to take care of these underprivileged groups'

(Abu-Jaber interview). One aspect of the Fund's basic needs approach within local communities consisted of restoring school buildings or donating funds for the construction of schools in remote areas (QAF, 1978a: 31; QAF, 1979c: 23). Additional activities included building water and sanitation facilities in villages where unhealthy sanitary conditions prevailed. On other occasions, in response to requests from local bodies for various services, the Fund interceded directly with relevant government offices to fulfil their requirements (Hassanein interview). This approach was not, however, entirely welcome: 'Even though QAF's intention was to speed up the process of providing communities and people with immediate services, its interference with the government's role created sensitivity … QAF was perceived as overseeing the government's efforts. As a result of this experience, QAF modified its approach and transferred peoples' demands to the related ministries' (Abu el-Ata interview).

During the course of its fieldwork, the Fund came across situations of severe hardship and poverty, particularly in remote areas where government services were inadequate and there were no NGOs. In numerous situations of this kind, the Fund responded according to cultural traditions of social solidarity. For example, a field visit to a village in the southern governorate of Ma'an in 1978 revealed cases of malnutrition amongst the children and health problems including tuberculosis. Living conditions in the village had also deteriorated to the point that some of its people had sought shelter in caves (QAF, 1978b). Here, the Fund played the role of an ombudsman by bringing the situation to the attention of King Hussein. The result was immediate action in the form of a housing project with adequate sanitation and electricity. Playing a similar role in other situations, the Fund facilitated the admission of sick people to hospitals and sometimes covered their medical expenses. Other cases eligible for financial support were brought to the attention of the Department of Social Affairs, which could assist under a provision which catered to such categories.

Such interventions were somewhat patrimonial and depended largely on the cultural framework of interactions with the Fund's chairperson. However, by responding to different grievances through whatever means were available, the Fund sought to increase awareness and motivate various elements of society to address existing disparities. The other aim was to bring to the fore the human dimension of development needs within a local context.

It may be considered that these approaches, as well as the achievement of some of QAF's objectives, were in certain respects facilitated by the position of its chairperson. However, this factor also fostered dependency and created high expectations, especially at the grassroots level and in relation to the Fund's intermediary role: 'I think people did not quite know what QAF was doing. People looked at QAF as a place where they could get help. I don't think QAF was able to challenge their imagination, and have them really look up to it, and say "look what it is doing." Unfortunately that was missing' (Nassir interview).

The need to build up credibility for QAF's role as an institution within the social sector recognized for its developmental efforts meant that such considerations were of significant concern to both the Fund and its chairperson. The nature of the Fund's leadership often provided grounds for debate among parties with varying interests over whether its interventions bore more relevance to the position of its chairperson than to its role as an NGO. Even as QAF's activities were seen to take effect, a certain scepticism remained owing to a view which maintained that the Fund enjoyed greater advantages than other NGOs and in particular, 'unlimited' access to funding.

Promoting Links with the NGO Sector

The Fund adopted a wide range of approaches in pursuit of its objective of working with the NGO sector. Some were geared to providing technical, financial and in-kind support to enhance NGO performance and projects; but QAF also took steps to create linkages and foster partnerships with local NGOs as a means of mobilizing social work and reaching target groups. Based on the needs revealed in field visits and meetings with NGOs, most of QAF's efforts centred on programmes for women and children (QAF, 1978a: 10–11; QAF, 1992a). To promote NGO children's programmes, financial aid was given to improve conditions in a number of orphanages, pre-school classes and children's clubs. In-kind support included books, toys and furniture, while technical assistance centred on teacher-training for pre-school classes (ibid.: 23).[5] In many villages NGOs operated from old buildings which had fallen into disrepair, creating unsuitable conditions, particularly for children. In such cases, the Fund allocated money to pay rent for better premises or to help the NGO in question to build its own facilities.

---

5. Between 1978 and 1984, 10 training courses and 13 workshops were held for a total of 300 pre-school teachers and 350 children's clubs were set up with local NGOs.

QAF's early efforts to promote women in development were similarly implemented through local NGOs. In the largely traditional communities where these activities were carried out, they created different opportunities and fostered new perceptions of women's occupations. Technical support was also provided by the Fund's staff who conducted courses to train rural women leaders (see chapter 4), as well as vocational training in traditional skills (ibid.: 23).[6] In-kind assistance consisted mainly of typewriters, sewing, knitting and weaving machines. In addition the Fund provided financial support for income-generating projects such as production and marketing units for clothing and handicrafts. Occasionally it set up a girls' library or donated musical instruments for a girls' band (QAF, 1984a: 34).

> Part of the activities of the Fund was, and remains, to provide the smaller NGOs with the means to operate ... because we are not talking about Amman, we are talking about remote areas. Sometimes a sewing machine makes a difference. It provides a voluntary society with the wherewithal to sew dresses and sell them, and make a little bit of money on the side to keep it running. So, to these small NGOs, and there are hundreds of them, for them the Fund was literally the backbone (Abu-Jaber interview).

All in all, during the period from 1977–1984 QAF made at least 600 allocations for NGO funding (QAF, 1992a: 23).

Building Cooperation with Other Actors

A major difficulty for the Fund as it tried to define its priorities was the lack of information about social work. Although problems related to this area were highlighted by national plans, further data was essential if the issues in question were to be examined in greater detail and recommendations made. Moreover, such input needed to come from the social sector itself. Inadequate research meant that the work of the social sector consisted largely of reacting to immediate demands rather than pursuing clear priorities. Without sufficient preparation, resources and efforts were sometimes wasted and NGO projects were often not sustainable. One of the Fund's own capacity-building objectives was to adopt a scientific approach. Equally important, was the need to conduct studies in cooperation with related bodies in order to strengthen links

---

6. Between 1978 and 1984 QAF conducted 60 training courses for vocational training instructors.

with them, as well as to identify social policies which would foster developmental approaches. Thus, through joint investigations of the social field, new processes of institutional cooperation with other governmental and non-governmental bodies were initiated by QAF.

The efforts of the Voluntary Social Work Coordination Committee, which was formed at QAF's invitation and which included representatives from the Department of Social Affairs, QAF and GUVS, provide an illustration of such processes. An evaluation of voluntary social work in Jordan was initiated by the committee (QAF, 1979d). The study, which was carried out by social workers from the Department of Social Affairs and graduate students from the Jordan University Sociology Department, evaluated the work of 238 active registered NGOs. The survey for the most part covered the activities and services provided by NGOs in rural areas (ibid.). Its main purpose was to gather basic information about the major characteristics of NGOs, their geographic distribution, structure, finance and number of beneficiaries.

By identifying NGO concentration and programmes according to geographic location, existing gaps in the field were revealed. This information helped to pinpoint areas of weakness in the NGO sector and to formulate recommendations to address these problems; the survey was also a useful planning tool and provided QAF with guidelines for addressing NGO needs. It showed that the majority of NGOs were located in Amman and Irbid, the two largest cities, while only 8.4 per cent were operating in underdeveloped rural areas in the southern governorates of the country (ibid.). These findings influenced subsequent decisions by QAF's Board of Trustees to implement projects in these areas. The conclusion of the study was that 'the voluntary social work sector is fragmented, provides a limited range of services and operates under financial and technical difficulties' (ibid.: 12). Identifying ways to increase the effectiveness of the NGO sector was consequently an important consideration for the Fund.

Prompted by the findings of the joint evaluation, in 1980 the Fund invited GUVS to work with it in preparing joint projects together with the newly-created Ministry of Social Development (MOSD).[7] This approach provided a means of addressing NGO needs with input from all three organizations. In order to promote sorely-needed linkages the Fund brought heads of NGOs together with district directors of the ministry in annual meetings to discuss NGO needs for training, financial and material

---

7. At the end of 1979 the Department of Social Affairs was upgraded to the Ministry of Social Development.

support. As part of this arrangement, the Fund concentrated on providing around sixty NGOs with financial assistance and technical support annually. It also continued to offer advice, staff training and educational materials to other NGOs as a way of maintaining ties and general support to this sector (QAF, 1980; 1981a; 1982a; 1983; 1984a; 1985a; 1986a).

All in all, whether through processes of coordination or evaluation, or as a result of participatory planning and programme implementation, the Fund was able to create significant linkages and build bridges of cooperation with key institutions within its sphere of activity. During this time, the Fund played the role of a catalyst, as reflected in its objectives, with various degrees of success. The implementation of new approaches by the social sector in effect reinforced a growing trend which emphasized the developmental dimension of social work.

Institutionalizing the Shift to Development

At the governmental level, the establishment of MOSD may be regarded as a significant step because it institutionalized the shift to development. However, there are varying interpretations of the institutional change which took place. For instance, Sari Nassir believes that the formation of the ministry did not, in itself, play a major role in promoting the shift from welfare to development: 'It was the University and also Princess Basma because then came her work. It began to reinforce the work we were doing. Together we were able to change the image of social work and development in the country. So things were happening' (Nassir interview). However, according to In'am Mufti, Jordan's first woman minister, the establishment of MOSD was a key factor in institutionalizing a comprehensive approach to social work:

> I was talking all the time about the importance of shifting the work of the Department of Social Affairs from just welfare and giving assistance to the poor and caring for a few people, such as the handicapped, to a developmental approach. Of course there was that trend. It wasn't that it wasn't there. But because the department was within the Ministry of Labour, not enough attention was given to development … The trend was established very strongly after the establishment of the ministry and calling it the Ministry of Social Development … it was starting already, but on a very small scale; people were feeling the importance of these matters but it had never been institutionalized as such (al-Mufti interview).

In fact the new phase which the social sector entered during the late 1970s was ushered in by a combination of factors. Political will was clearly at the time another important element to assist the transitional process: 'A new government was established under Sharif Abdul-Hamid Sharaf;[8] a new lady came to the scene, the first lady to be a minister, In'am al-Mufti. I think one of the things she was after was to start to change people by changing the concept itself, and try to push it forward along the social development path' (al-Saqour interview). Others consider that, at the governmental level, the main advocate for change was the prime minister himself: 'Really it was the insight of Abdul-Hamid Sharaf. He wanted very much to have a shift' (al-Mufti interview). The social development component was part of a larger package of new policies which the prime minister was keen to promote at the national level in order to address emerging needs (Tukan, 1983): 'He really was after social change and he introduced a lot of concepts along this line ... that we should be rational in our consumption, we should be rational in our expenses' (al-Saqour interview). The aim was to stem, through such policies, the negative effects of the high increase in public and private sector spending during the boom period in Jordan. However, within the social field, the changes which both government and NGO sectors were trying to promote had favourable consequences for the nature of social work as a whole.

Creating a Joint Focus: National Survey of the Handicapped

Besides upgrading development efforts, a significant aspect of the joint studies initiated by QAF in cooperation with other institutions was to raise awareness and focus attention on key issues related to both government and non-governmental bodies in the social sector. One of the most important means of promoting this objective was the National Survey of the Handicapped in Jordan (QAF, 1979e). This initiative was launched after consultations between the Department of Social Affairs, GUVS and QAF highlighted the lack of data on the situation of the disabled (al-Khatib, 1993). The survey was carried out in 1979 by the Fund in conjunction with the Ministries of Education and Information, the Department of Social Affairs, the Royal Scientific Society and the Faculty of Sociology at Jordan University. It aimed to gather basic information about the socio-economic conditions of the disabled and existing services for them. It was also intended to serve as a database for more specialized research (QAF, 1979e: 7), and help social planners and policy makers to formulate

---

8. Sharif Abdul-Hamid Sharaf became prime minister in December 1979 until his death on 3 July 1980.

plans and improve the quality and outreach of services. This survey was a landmark because it was the first of its kind to be undertaken not only in Jordan, but also in the region. It covered the entire country and involved the registration of 18,829 disabled individuals.[9] Despite this large figure, some of the disabled were probably not covered. In some cases this may have been due to their own inhibitions about revealing disabilities, or the inhibitions of their families. In others it may have been because people were not aware of the effort and did not come forward, or simply because the Fund did not reach them.

Besides aiming to change societal attitudes, the study also helped to change perceptions amongst the disabled themselves of the role they could play within the community, given appropriate services and rehabilitation programmes. Families with disabled children also began to feel that they were not isolated and that disability was a national concern. As a home-grown initiative this process helped to sensitize different local elements and prepare them for the worldwide attention created by the International Year of the Disabled in 1981. Reinforced by the focus of international donors, disability was given greater priority by the Five Year Plan 1981–1985. As stated in the Plan, the Ministry of Social Development aimed to establish fourteen centres for the disabled in different governorates, as well as to set up and equip four rehabilitation centres and vocational training centres in Amman, Irbid and al-'Aqaba, one of which was purely for women (Jordan, 1981a: 288–9). Before 1981, the ministry had only eight centres for the disabled (Jordan, 1980a).

Most of the Fund's early projects were driven by the findings of this study. By the mid 1980s, QAF had built four major custom-designed centres for the disabled in different parts of the country. The first centre for special education in the southern governorate of al-Karak was built in 1983 for the rehabilitation of youth with mental disabilities. Around the same time, in order to increase services in the three largest cities, the Fund built two centres for the physically disabled in Amman and Irbid, as well as a centre near al-Zarqa for children with impaired hearing. Considerable work was entailed in preparing plans for these centres, and architectural expertise was sought from abroad.

The centres for the disabled represent the Fund's earliest attempts at decentralization. Once completed, the administration of these centres was handed over to local NGOs, although the Fund maintained different levels of technical and financial support through regular visits and follow-

---

9. The survey did not include the occupied West Bank.

up. The focus on disability meant that QAF was widely perceived to be concentrating on this particular area of social work. At the same time, it was becoming clear within the Fund that extensive attention to this domain would make it increasingly difficult to address other long-term objectives (Abu el-Ata interview). Consequently, by the mid-1980s, as QAF's programmes within local communities expanded, the scope of its work with the disabled was gradually reduced so that it could focus on its community-based activities. New approaches were adopted by QAF for working with the disabled which were compatible with its ongoing programmes and yet still covered the special needs of this group. Projects which targeted the disabled continued to grow substantially through the activities of GUVS. Over the years, annual financial assistance was given to NGOs working on special needs according to GUVS' own criteria. The rise in the number of specialized NGOs was a gradual one, due to the high cost of service provision (al-Khatib, 1993). But by the mid-1990s, there were forty-six specialized NGOs in the social sector which addressed different kinds of disabilities (GUVS, 1996).

Identifying Priorities through Research

The emphasis on research during the formative years of the Fund was underpinned by a variety of factors: the lack of basic information about the social field, the need to promote joint interactions with other actors, or the need to raise awareness of different issues. Essentially, however, QAF was aiming to create a credible role for itself by addressing its objectives and defining its priorities systematically. The Fund's effort to provide a methodological model of social work contrasted with many of its own early interventions which were often spontaneous and geared primarily to building relations with local communities and NGOs. However, developing such a model as the basis for its operations was a key to consolidating the Fund's national status. While studies such as the National Survey of the Handicapped called attention to important areas of neglect and inspired QAF's early projects, smaller surveys such as those which examined women's issues, helped form the basis for its development priorities. Subsequently, women became one of the main target groups of programmes carried out by the Fund.

The Fund's first study of women was conducted in 1979 in cooperation with the Population Council and the Ford Foundation. A pilot study, it looked at the economic status of 300 women living in Amman and their activities within and outside the home (Salti, 1979). Also in 1979, QAF together with experts from the German Agency for Technical Cooperation (GTZ), undertook a preliminary study on rural women in the governorate of al-Karak (QAF, 1979f). This resulted in German financial assistance of half a million marks allocated to the Fund for further surveys and to support capacity-building programmes for women as well as training in traditional craft skills. In 1980, a second survey was carried out together with MOSD, NPC and GTZ (QAF, 1981b). The socio-economic conditions of rural women in al-Karak governorate were evaluated with the aim of designing model programmes for rural women in the area, which could be replicated in other regions of the country.

In addition to helping the Fund identify its primary target groups, the surveys also provided QAF with vital information about the areas in which to implement its development programmes. For instance, in 1979 the Fund together with the Department of Social Affairs carried a comprehensive study of villages in the Badia areas of the governorates of Ma'an, al-Tafila and al-Mafraq (QAF, 1979g). The findings of the survey, which covered 251 Bedu settlements, revealed inadequate basic services in health and education, particularly for women. Harsh living conditions coupled with a lack of job opportunities were major factors contributing to rural-urban migration. As a result of the study, twenty-eight villages were identified by the Fund as sites for the establishment of centres for social services by the Fund, including health and education programmes and development activities for women and children.

Although surveys provided QAF with an overview of the needs of vulnerable groups such as women, children and the disabled in rural and marginalized areas, studies initiated with local bodies or interna-tional agencies were generally conducted for the purpose of planning or policy-making rather than specific project implementation. As often happened when development workers went to the field, expectations of assistance and projects were unnecessarily raised. People at the grass-roots automatically assumed that studies were a preliminary to project implementation, and when no action followed they became disillusioned. As a result, the Fund tried to conduct studies only when resources were available to carry out at least some of the recommendations that emerged from them. Although it was not always possible to honour this princi-ple, the policy helped to foster the Fund's credibility at the grassroots level because people felt that research activities in which the Fund was involved were likely to be followed by some concrete benefits (author's recollection).

Essentially, QAF's subsequent community development programmes derived mainly from the needs identified by local communities through studies. However, without the cooperation of different concerned bodies within the social sector, whether governmental agencies or other institutions, it is doubtful that the Fund would have been able to achieve the kind of research that was undertaken in this early phase. Although governmental agencies were often hampered by their own bureaucracy, they had substantial resources of manpower and logistical support upon which the Fund was able to draw. Consequently, it was by combining efforts with other institutions that the best results were achieved. Through these different processes of interaction, the Fund was not only able to consolidate its efforts, but also to form a better understanding of the spheres of interest and areas of concern, as well as the priorities of other actors working to promote development in Jordan.

The Fund's first phase was characterized by diverse activity at all levels. This was to some degree a period of exploration and consequently elements of trial and error were considerable. Propelled by the sense that it needed to make an impact on the social field and from the outset consolidate its role at the national level, the Fund often opted for rapid action at the expense of setting carefully considered priorities. Although in many ways QAF's very diverse efforts helped it to identify its priorities, the range of its early activities was difficult to sustain. Moreover, while the Fund's role grew rapidly, the range and variety of its activities put off the task of focusing on one area and building its capacity accordingly. It must also be said that had the nature of its charter, as well as its leadership differed, quite possibly expectations of QAF as an organization may have been lower and greater scope would have been allowed for a more deliberate process of evolution. As it was, the operational experience required to carry out the Fund's envisaged role was an essential factor its chairperson could only acquire with time.

The Challenge of Funding

As its work began to unfold, an issue of obvious concern to QAF was funding. How could the necessary funds to set up projects and meet growing demands from the field be raised? As already noted, domestic resources were limited and competition among NGOs for local funding was already intense. It was therefore felt that external donors should be targeted rather than the local funds which were a primary means of support for most of the country's NGOs (QAF, 1981a). At this time, the Fund was able to draw on connections made by its chairperson, especially within the Arab region. Reference has already been made to the advantage the Fund was reputed to enjoy in this respect. However, it can also be argued that QAF used its advantages and connections to bring external contributions into the country and in this way created substantial new resources within the social sector without encroaching on existing funds.

As we have seen, during this period the political climate between Jordan and Arab oil-producing countries was particularly favourable. As chairperson I visited a number of countries in the region, accompanied by the Fund's executive director in order to present the Fund and raise support for our projects. These included Iraq, Oman, the United Arab Emirates, Qatar, Bahrain and Kuwait; contacts were also made with Saudi Arabia. As a result, QAF received generous donations from many heads of states and governments of many of these countries:

> ... We set up appointments with all the leaders of the Gulf. The Princess and I, we went with a delegation and we met with the leaders of these countries, except King Khalid. He sent us a cheque and thanked us actually, which I think was very kind of him. I remember his words through his ambassador in Amman. They thanked us for giving him the opportunity to do some good to humanity ... The Emir of Qatar, again the same thing, he donated and he didn't want his name to appear either. It is really in the Arab tradition to do good without anybody knowing. There is no public donation, people don't like that; quietly, or Mastoura in Arabic (Abu-Jaber interview).

The financial support received by the Fund was similar in its terms to most Arab donor aid to Jordan, namely in the preference given to infrastructural development. Consequently, the largest donations were earmarked for QAF's major construction projects during that time, which were centres for the disabled. This focus was, moreover, reinforced by the fact that, from the early 1980s, disability was gaining much attention in the Arab countries we visited, primarily through the establishment of large specialized institutions (ESCWA, 1992). Once funds had been allocated, the Fund was able to implement its projects with a high degree of flexibility without the restrictions of donor conditionality. The centres for the disabled built with Arab support were thus completed more easily and with greater speed than many other projects. Since, once built and fully equipped, they were turned over to NGOs, the bulk of financial contributions first generated by QAF from Arab donors contributed to a marked increase in the quality and quantity of local NGO services for the disabled.

On the other hand, as QAF's focus on comprehensive development increased, and its main priority became the creation of community development centres, it became more difficult to generate funding on the same scale. This was mainly because the support which the Fund had already obtained made it reluctant to request further donations from the same sources for some time. While the scope of funding procured for individual institutions could have made a considerable impact on expanding QAF's community services, it should be pointed out that the generous nature of Arab aid was more inclined to building institutional landmarks than to a spread of smaller community-based projects. At that time, Arab donors were also building similar institutions and creating national infrastructures themselves. Nevertheless, the unconditionality of Arab contributions helped the Fund to address a critical issue, which was organizational sustainability.

With no regular income from the government or other sources, QAF did not have steady resources with which to cover the running costs of the organization. As its areas of activity became more clearly defined, links were established with diplomatic missions in Amman as well as relevant international and regional donors such as UNDP, UNICEF, WHO and ESCWA. However, these development agencies provided funding for specific projects and technical support; their donations did not cover administrative overheads for programme implementation. Consequently, QAF's Board of Trustees decided that a Trust Fund should be set up in order to cover the 'core' costs of running the organization and ensure its continuity, as well as to provide a financial framework to sustain its programmes (QAF, 1979h).

The creation of a Trust Fund was one of the Board's main concerns; but it was not possible to accomplish this at the beginning. The primary aim of early fund-raising efforts was to build a role for QAF among existing bodies through a wide range of activities. Although this early approach did not foster the kind of strategic planning that would strengthen the Fund's financial resources, gradually, as the Fund's role was consolidated, the development of a long-term financial policy became feasible. It was mainly by setting aside Arab contributions which had not been earmarked for specific projects that the Board was able to achieve this objective. Through the Trust Fund, QAF has been able to cover some of its basic administrative expenses as well as certain overheads for its projects in the field. Nevertheless, the steady expansion of new projects coupled with the effort of maintaining a reasonable standard of delivery for ongoing programmes, have continued to pose a serious challenge.

The Way Forward

By adopting different approaches the Fund was able to consolidate its presence amongst other actors in the social field. While certain objectives were achieved in this way, others could not be addressed during this early stage. For instance, although in various situations the Fund did act as a catalyst, it was still too young an organization to play a pioneering role. However, QAF's wide-ranging activities did enable it to consolidate its role in implementing social work at the national level. A few years after it was founded, QAF's efforts were recognized by the National Planning Council:

> An outstanding achievement of this period (1976–1980) was the establishment of the Queen Alia Fund for Social Work by special law, to serve as a major corollary to the efforts expanded by the charities and the General Union of Voluntary Societies. The Fund's activity supports voluntary social work through establishing social development centres as well as centres for the handicapped. It extends technical and financial support to voluntary societies, undertakes studies and sponsors seminars, workshops and training courses (Jordan, 1986a: 177).

On the governmental level, upgrading the Department of Social Affairs to the Ministry of Social Development also signalled increased public sector awareness of the significance of the social component of development efforts: 'The measures reflected a new emphasis on the social dimension of development, manifested in the new Ministry's contribution to overall development. In co-ordination with other ministries, public institutions and private-sector groups, the Ministry of Social Development embarked on a program aimed at rising to the challenge posed by rapid socio-economic development, upgrading the efficiency of social services and satisfying basic needs' (ibid.).

Such statements were a clear indication that during this period, the social sector as a whole was seen as a key element in advancing overall development efforts within the country. At the same time, however, the Fund's experience in the field showed that development processes could not be effectively advanced by providing services and funding alone. For example, when working with NGOs, QAF frequently discovered that funding which it had allocated for a specific programme was largely spent on administration, resulting in limited impact on the quality of programme delivery. Furthermore, while financial support did not always bring about new practices, it often created further dependency. Ultimately, rather than increasing the number of passive beneficiaries, the challenge was to foster approaches which mobilized target groups to interact as active participants in the development process:

> It wasn't an easy task at all. The expectations of NGOs were very high and all of them thought that they would just receive money, although that was not the concept. Because it was called the 'Fund,' they thought that the money would go to them, although backing and support was to go to training, to raising their abilities, to enable them and help them to raise funds ... but people had different hopes from the Fund. They wanted financial help and whenever they came to the Fund, they came to request money. But later they recognized that wasn't what the organization was about (al-Mufti interview).

Taking these different factors into consideration, a strong belief developed within the Fund that, for its efforts to be effective, it should create its own approach: 'QAF's early efforts provided enough evidence that no matter what work was done through local NGOs, change could not occur without a model for social development. Transforming traditional attitudes would be difficult and therefore a model was essential in order to gradually bring about a change at the community level' (Abu el-Ata interview).[10] By 1982, QAF was in a position to embark on this process. The network of community development centres which the Fund proceeded to establish across the country, eventually came to represent QAF's own development model and became a primary vehicle for promoting its specific approaches within the social field.

---

10. In 1972, the Ministry of Labour and Social Affairs introduced a pilot project to encourage people's participation in the development process by establishing a community development centre in Sama al-Sarhan/al-Mafraq (Jordan, 1972). Later in 1977, another centre was set up by the Ministry in Thaiban/Madaba in addition to the centre built by the University of Jordan in Hay Nazal/Amman. QAF eventually adopted a similar concept, but with the broader vision of creating a network of CDCs throughout the country to serve as a pragmatic model for NGOs in order to enhance their community-based services.

5

Mobilizing for Development: The Fund from 1984 into the Late 1990s

This chapter explores the ways in which QAF mobilized development efforts at the community level. Endeavours by the state and other actors to promote participatory development are examined and the impact of these different approaches is compared. The network of community development centres, the CDCs, is introduced and the origins of the network, QAF's primary vehicle for advancing its working agenda, are described. The dilemmas of building partnerships in the field, as well as problems of recruitment and capacity-building, are analysed. An account is given of the CDCs' programmes for women and children, QAF's main target groups. The impact of these programmes on external actors beyond the CDCs is also explored. An underlying theme is to highlight the process of negotiation between the Fund, the CDCs and the communities, which advancing local initiatives constantly entailed. The discussion also seeks to show the differing perspectives and interests on the ground which have played a part in shaping the evolution of the CDCs and their developmental role. As this chapter unfolds, it reveals the importance of the CDCs' permanent presence within the communities, in providing access to local actors and furthering understanding of their realities and needs as a premise for QAF's development approach.

Participatory Development in Jordan

From the beginning of the 1980s, state discourse in Jordan centred on participation as a means of achieving development objectives. One of the goals of the Five Year Plan 1981–1985, was 'to increase popular participation and widen the base of decision-making in the development process' (Jordan, 1981a: 25). By advocating that people should share in the state's responsibility for advancing development as active participants rather than passive recipients, the Plan also aimed to bring about a change in existing perceptions of the government's role as the sole service provider. The theory behind 'participatory development' was that local resources could be mobilized and substantially increased by means of self-help and community development schemes that operated through broad-based local participation. Moreover, schemes of this kind could, in their turn, provide a foundation for more self-reliant development (Lisk, 1981: 9).

The 1981–1985 Plan reflected the state's decentralizing goals and its decision to give greater attention to rural areas by encouraging popular participation in the design of development plans for local communities. The government adopted various measures to promote these aims. For instance, in 1982 the Municipalities' Law No. 29 of 1955 was amended to facilitate popular participation in the municipal elections. Following, in 1983 municipal councils in different parts of the country began to hold public meetings in order to discuss development needs at the local level (*Baladi*, 1983). The aim of these debates was to address qualitative and quantitative disparities in social services as well as the unequal distribution of economic gain between various income groups and regions (Jordan, 1981a: 25).

Another important aspect of the Plan was that it highlighted some of the problems faced by rural women. These included 'illiteracy, a lack of awareness of proper methods of child-rearing and the benefits of home economics, a low level of productive skills and a shortage of effective women's organizations capable of developing women's ability to solve their problems' (ibid.: 235). Earlier, in 1977, a Women's Department had been set up within the Ministry of Labour. Its purpose was to facilitate women's entry into the labour force in the face of a serious shortage in the domestic labour market during this period (Jordan, 1979a). In 1980, the Department was moved to the newly established Ministry of Social Development and in 1981 the ministry began to form women's NGOs in rural and urban areas. The aim was to develop women's skills in various ways so that they could play an effective role in social and economic development (Jordan, 1981b: 32):

> At the same time we did many pilot projects with new concepts and new ideas on how to develop the abilities of women, particularly in remote rural areas with women who were illiterate. They needed real assistance. We did a pilot project to focus on how that could be done, what industries we could develop that women could be engaged in, and also be self-employed. We extended training and the possibilities for them to develop (al-Mufti interview).

Between 1981 and 1983 a total of twenty women's NGOs were established in rural areas (Jordan, 1981b; 1982b; 1983). In effect these rural

NGOs provided a vehicle for training and did not, in practice, promote participation. In general, women's NGOs at that time have been criticized for encouraging a charity-based approach instead of helping poor women to become independent: 'A group of well-off women get together and decide to help the poor. The outcome is charitable organizations' (Dajani, 1984: 195).

Among the other approaches adopted in the effort to achieve greater participation in the development process was the creation of community development centres. In 1972, the Department of Social Affairs, at the time part of the Ministry of Labour, had established its first community development centre in the governorate of al-Mafraq (Jordan, 1972). The aim of the project was to promote the concept of integrated development, based on 'people's participation in all facets of economic and social development for the purpose of enhancing family income and progressively raising the family's social level' (Jordan, 1973: 266). Later, as a way of mobilizing people, the Local Communities Development Department at MOSD began to form local councils in areas adjacent to its CDCs. Although reports published by MOSD contain no information on the role of these councils, or their activities within the centres, reference is made to their participation in various local community projects. These included agricultural and infrastructural projects as well as vocational training and nutrition programmes. Here, participation consisted mostly of financial contributions which covered around 50 per cent of the total cost of the projects. Only occasionally did people share in the task of planning (Jordan, 1982b: 23–4; 1983; 1984).

By 1984, MOSD had built four centres, three of them in rural areas (Jordan, 1984: 93–4). Meanwhile, various other organizations had also adopted the concept of CDCs. The Family Welfare Charitable Organization had five centres for women in refugee camps (Dajani, 1984: 163–4) and the University of Jordan had two centres in Amman. Activities and services at the CDCs run by MOSD and other organizations were largely alike. As In'am al-Mufti maintains, a common problem for all CDCs at that time, whether they were run by the government or by NGOs, was the duplication of programmes:

> If you do one thing and see that it is successful, then you will duplicate it everywhere, in the same format, same services, same approach. And this does not work, because any community centre has to fit into the needs of its own community. But this is not done. For example, with training for women in typing or sewing, you go to a little village and you find a community centre with typewriters people cannot use, and they are out of order and there are

no jobs. It's not wrong to teach them how to type, but it is (wrong) to expect (them) to get jobs out of it (al-Mufti interview).

Duplication, which in some cases resulted in the implementation of inappropriate programmes, was not the only constraint to affect the nature of CDC activities. A number of studies have pointed to the wide gap between the rhetoric of participatory development and its practice the world over and among the impediments to participation they have identified is centralized administration, largely a result of bureaucratic and conventional methods of operation (Schneider and Libercier, 1995).

In Jordan, according to al-Saqour, the aim of government CDCs was to achieve social change, develop human resources and advance the economic welfare of local communities. He recalls, however, that in trying to achieve these objectives, participatory methods were not fully applied as decisions relating to the centres were generally referred back to the 'higher, central administration' (al-Saqour interview). Dajani voices similar views, although she maintains that partial participation was a feature of the University of Jordan's Hay Nazal Centre where students discussed with local residents what programmes they needed. Nevertheless, she admits 'that the initiation of the idea arose in the classroom itself, not within the community itself, nor by the local residents themselves. Local people were brought into the picture later on, at the operational stage, when the initiators consulted with them on new activities and problems which arose' (Dajani, 1984: 176). In essence, especially during the first half of the 1980s, the role of CDCs in fostering participatory development was generally not clear, even to those concerned, and still revolved around centralized methods of service-provision. Across the board decision-making processes for the centres were mostly top-down and programmes were designed 'for' rather than 'with' people (ibid.: 10).

Promoting participatory development in Jordan was, in general, not a simple process. At the beginning of 1984, King Hussein had called for people's greater participation in the affairs of the country. Consequently parliament, which had been dissolved as a result of the occupation of the West Bank in 1967, was reconvened with its old membership. The aim was to enhance participation not only in decision-making processes, but also in the development, education and agricultural sectors (al-Ra'i, 1984). Yet the country was still under martial law and, as is often the case when participation is attempted in these circumstances, the situation was not conducive to the full revival of democracy. At the local level too, efforts to promote community development activities often met with reservations because people believed they might be construed as political activism.[1] Combined with such considerations, was a widespread lack of knowledge and practice of what the concept of participation really meant.

Within the Jordanian context, as Dajani (1984) maintains, although state policies advocating greater participation during this period were sincerely intended, the complexity of the country's cultural, economic and political situation combined to create a variety of impediments. While opposition to popular participation is not an issue, Jordan's specific experiences have created an awareness that potentially destabilizing forces may sometimes flourish under such pretextws. In this situation, it is often easier for planners and civil servants to keep to established administrative methods than to adopt novel strategies which might shake the status quo. Socio-political factors may also have played a major role in impeding participation. Al-Saqour, for example, observes that the policy did involve some transfer of power from traditional local leaderships to other groups. However, the absence of free democratic practices, bureaucracy, a lack of concern with issues of integration and the hidden mutual interests of official decision-makers and local leaders hindered popular participation (al-Saqour, 1986).

Yet the fact remains that national policies have placed significant emphasis on participation, even though the aspiration has not always been fully achieved in practical terms. While clearly the participatory process has faced a variety of impediments, during the early 1980s the seeds of an indigenous grassroots participation were sown in certain sectors and communities, and were beginning to grow in a manner that fitted and merged with the larger context of Jordanian culture and politics. Some contend that, given the existing socio-political situation, a comprehensive multifaceted approach would have been difficult, and that popular participation through development projects had to be increased gradually. In such circumstances 'a limited single-purpose organization has a better

---

1. While the need for greater popular participation is now more fully recognized, the concept itself carries different meanings in different situations. Increasingly, by linking it to democratization, the notion of participation has acquired political connotations (Schneider and Libercier, 1995: 10). For some, the emergence of civil society in the international development arena is the political complement to economic adjustment. However, others view the premise on which such an agenda is built as too historically narrow and geographically Western. It is also criticized as a harmonious model which is too partial and far removed from reality, for 'civil society is an area of dynamism, conservatism, competition, collaboration and conflict' (Fowler, 1996: 29).

chance of success' (Dajani, 1984: 203). The structure of QAF and its increasing focus on community development was in this sense well-suited to dealing with the range of issues faced by any attempt at participatory development in Jordan.

The Fund's Community Development Centres: A Home-Grown Model

The vision of a national network of community development centres emerged from QAF's early experience in the field and from studies which revealed the varied needs and limitations of its projects, especially in rural and nomadic areas (QAF, 1979c). The Board also thought that a wide presence within local communities would reinforce the Fund's role as an NGO working at the national level. The advantages of such an approach were underlined by a later evaluation: 'In the first place [QAF] was serving not just one city but was spread all over the country. Two, it started having centres all over the country. Three, it began to attract people to work with it. Four, perhaps it introduced in these centres skills that are needed' (Nassir interview).

A network of CDCs would also, it was felt, enable QAF to participate directly in national development concerns. For instance, one of the major issues QAF sought to address through the CDCs was that of rural-urban migration which previous efforts by the social sector had generally failed to stem (Jordan, 1981a: 285). The aim of the Fund was to engage people in socio-economic activities that would eventually contribute to increased job opportunities and encourage them to remain in their communities. By fostering such approaches in the field, as part of its catalyst role the Fund's objective was to mobilize local NGOs in advancing the development of their own communities: '... Big institutions like that should be catalysts, should be the think tanks and should gear the work in the country to new ideas, with approaches that work' (al-Mufti interview).

The CDCs thus had the potential to create an effective vehicle through which to pursue QAF's objectives of improving the quality and quantity of basic social services, strengthening the organizational and technical capacity of NGOs and offering new concepts or models to the social sector. For this reason, a significant aspect of the role envisaged for the CDCs, was to run comprehensive educational and training programmes at the grass-roots level that catered to the new development orientations the social sector was trying to advance. By establishing an infrastructural presence of its own within local communities, the Fund would acquire the tools to promote evolving concepts such as participation, sustainability and self-reliance. These approaches required fostering change, an objective which could only be advanced through a gradual but sustained process which built on different stages as they were reached. By creating its own working environment through the CDCs, the Fund could acquire a more reliable means of supporting such a process than would have been the case had it chosen to operate through local NGOs, which as already noted, implied being diverted by many other issues. The aim of the Fund was to adopt a pragmatic approach to the CDCs which took account of new realities on the ground as well as new concepts. Ultimately, the purpose was to create a working model on which both local communities and NGOs could draw in order to devise tangible methods of promoting development.

From 1984 QAF's network of CDCs expanded throughout the country, reaching a total of fifty centres in 2000. The map shows the geographical spread of QAF's network of CDCs (p. 144). Table 5.1 shows the chronological growth of the network.

The launch of the network in Madaba

The Fund established its first group of CDCs in the governorate of Madaba in 1984 (QAF, 1984a). The choice of this location was in part dictated by the need to build the first centres in proximity to QAF's headquarters. Madaba is some 30 kilometres from Amman – a manageable distance which enabled QAF staff to make the daily journey in order to oversee the centres' construction. Since this was a pilot project, our staff had to be on the spot to address initial issues such as administration, recruitment and training, and later to monitor and evaluate programmes as they took shape. The accessibility of the Madaba centres helped maintain a steady level of interaction between QAF staff and the local community, which in turn provided the essential working experience needed to expand the network.

Another reason for choosing Madaba to launch the CDC network was funding. In order to finance these first centres, QAF approached the Delegation of the European Economic Community (EEC) as it was then known.[2] The EEC funding mechanism for NGOs at this time stipulated that financial support should be channelled through a European NGO which had a counterpart in Jordan. The German Caritas Association

---

2. Now known as the Delegation of the European Commission – European Union.

Table 5.1
Chronological Growth of QAF Community Development Centres

Year	Type of Centre	Location	Urban/ Rural	Governorate	Run by
1984	Main[1]	Madaba	Urban	Madaba	MC[2]
	Satellite	Hisban	Rural	Madaba	MC
	Satellite	Ma'in	Rural	Madaba	MC
	Satellite	Mulayh	Rural	Madaba	MC
1985	Main	al-Mafraq	Urban	al-Mafraq	Main
	Satellite	al-Za'tari	Rural	al-Mafraq	NGO
1986	Main	al-Nuzha	Urban	Amman	NGO
	Satellite	Ghawr al-Mazra'a	Rural	al-Karak/ Jordan Valley	NGO
	Main	Ma'an	Urban	Ma'an	Main
	Satellite	al-Tayyiba	Rural	Ma'an	NGO
	Satellite	al-Basta	Rural	Ma'an	NGO
	Satellite	al-Sadaqa	Rural	Ma'an	NGO
	Satellite	al-Muraygha	Rural	Ma'an	NGO
	Main	al-Shawbak	Rural	Ma'an	NGO
	Satellite	al-Baq'a	Rural	Ma'an	NGO
	Satellite	Bir al-Dabbaghat	Rural	Ma'an	NGO
	Satellite	al-Juhayir	Rural	Ma'an	NGO
1988	Main	al-Tafila	Urban	al-Tafila	Main
	Satellite	Ruwaym	Rural	al-Tafila	NGO
	Satellite	Busayra	Rural	al-Tafila	NGO
1989	Main	al-Karak	Urban	al-Karak	NGO
1990	Main	Idoun	Urban	Irbid	Main
	Main	al-'Aqaba	Urban	al-'Aqaba	Main
1991	Satellite	Rihab	Rural	al-Mafraq	NGO
	Satellite	al-Khalidiyya	Rural	al-Mafraq	NGO
	Satellite	al-Qatrana	Rural	al-Karak	Main
	Main	Ghawr al-Safi	Rural	al-Karak/ Jordan Valley	NGO
	Satellite	al-Hisa	Rural	al-Tafila	Main
	Satellite	al-Husayniyya	Rural	Ma'an	Main
1992	Satellite	Rawdat Basma	Rural	al-Mafraq	NGO
	Satellite	al-Ba'ij	Rural	al-Mafraq	NGO
	Satellite	al-Dafyana	Rural	al-Mafraq	NGO
	Main	al-Kafrayn	Rural	al-Balqa'	Main

Table 5.1 *Continued*

Year	Type of Centre	Location	Urban/ Rural	Governorate	Run by
1993	Main	Sahab	Urban	Amman	Main
	Satellite	Ghawr al-Haditha	Rural	al-Karak/ Jordan Valley	NGO
	Satellite	'Ayma	Rural	al-Tafila	Main
	Satellite	al-Disa	Rural	al-'Aqaba	Main
	Satellite	al-Quwayra	Rural	Al-'Aqaba	Main
1994	Main	al-Wahadina	Rural	Ajlun	Main
	Main	Jarash	Urban	Jarash	Main
	Satellite	Mu'ta	Rural	al-Karak	NGO
	Satellite	al-Risha	Rural	al-'Aqaba	Main
1995	Satellite	Dabbat Hanut	Rural	al-'Aqaba	Main
	Satellite	al-Humayma	Rural	al -'Aqaba	Main
1996	Satellite	al-Sheikh Hussein	Rural	Irbid	Main
	Satellite	al-Qadisiyya	Rural	al-Tafila	NGO
1997	Satellite	Faqou'	Rural	al-Karak	Main
2000	Satellite	al-Mansura	Rural	Irbid	Main
	Satellite	Dair al-Sanieh	Rural	Irbid/Tayyiba	Main
	Satellite	Thaghret al-Jub	Rural	al-Mafraq	NGO

1. The size of main centres varies, from 450 sq.m. in al-Mafraq to over 800 sq.m. in Jebel al-Nuzha. Satellite centres average around 220 sq.m.
2. Municipal Council.

and Caritas Jordan, which are part of an international confederation of Catholic organizations, met this criterion.[3] Accordingly, these two NGOs were selected by the EEC as its funding channel. Since Madaba has a substantial Christian minority, it was particularly appropriate that this area should be the recipient of EEC funding through Caritas.

The operational infrastructure for the CDC network was to consist of a main centre in the principal town of each governorate with satellite

3. Caritas International is a confederation of Catholic organizations mandated by their respective Episcopal conferences. All member organizations seek to contribute to the socio-pastoral mission of the Church through spreading solidarity and social justice. The German Caritas Association is one of six main central welfare organizations in Germany acting in all areas of social work. Caritas Jordan is recognized as the social welfare arm of the Catholic Church in Jordan.

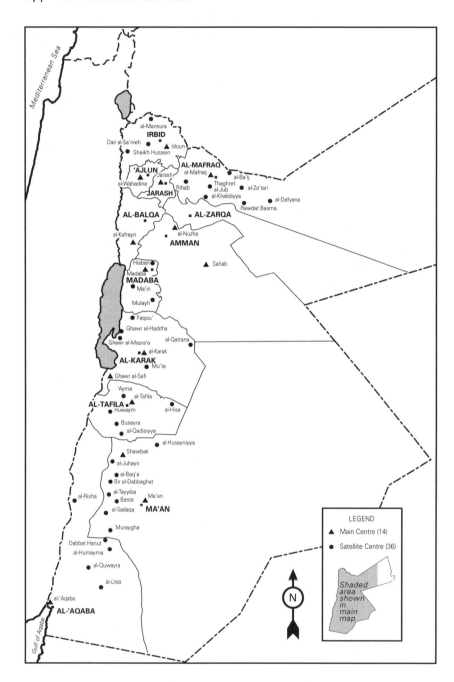

Map 5.1: The Fund's Network of Community Development Centres
(Courtesy of the Royal Jordanian Geographic Centre, 2000)

centres in the outlying villages (QAF, 1984b).[4] 'The idea was to establish projects as models, one key centre in each governorate in different areas of work. That was the initial concept of QAF' (al-Mufti interview). Once the satellite centres acquired sufficient skills and expertise, they in turn would work with local NGOs in their vicinity. By extending their outreach, the main centres and their satellites would create a ripple effect so that different communities could benefit from the programmes which were being implemented. 'The idea of the centres was that the Fund should involve other NGOs in projects and support them professionally through training and marketing and support them financially wherever possible' (al-Mufti interview).

In building the CDCs, the Fund moved beyond the sphere of cooperation with various national institutions to forging working relationships with local entities. This process was facilitated by drawing on social capital within the community in the form of different groups and individuals from both the public and the private sector. The traditional nature of Jordanian society meant that to gain support for the centres it was important to involve men during the conceptual stages of the process (Abu-Jaber, 1980). Such endorsement enabled QAF to reach its target groups, including women. The strategy of seeking men's approval for women's participation was a reflection of the patriarchal tendencies of society and was in contrast to development concepts which advocate that target groups should be directly involved from the planning stages of the development process. However, cultural considerations meant that the Fund could not have addressed the issue differently. Nadia Hijab has observed that, throughout the Middle East, it has generally been the case that women's advancement has first been championed by men and subsequently women have followed (Hijab, 1988). In the same way, it was essential to foster a positive attitude to the CDCs through men as this also affected women's perceptions and their willingness to participate in the centres' activities.

Another method of generating support for the CDCs was to build ties with local representatives who could contribute in their official or personal capacity to the running of the centres. These included tribal leaders, municipal council members, the business sector, NGOs, local authorities

---

4. The CDC network of main centres are responsible for following up and monitoring the work of the satellite centres. The director of a main centre also participates in managing satellite centres in the same governorate, as a member of the local administration committee. Accordingly, all official communications from the satellite centres go through the main centre.

and government departments and other prominent individuals. Such groups formed local committees which represented the centres' interests, and the interests of QAF's community-based partnerships. In areas where no suitable NGO partner could be found to administer a satellite centre, its operations were overseen by a main centre (see table 5.1). To formalize the commitment and spell out the means of cooperation between QAF and its local partners, agreements which outlined each side's role and responsibilities were drawn up and signed. Taking into account the specificity of different areas and the most appropriate arrangement for managing the centres, three kinds of formal administrative mechanisms were adopted by the Fund:

Local Committees of Volunteers: In the larger towns, the main centres were run by a local committee of volunteers headed by a high official such as the governor. While this method of operation gave QAF the greatest input, it was more bureaucratic than others and involved the least local initiatives. In decision-making and other work-related matters, QAF dealt mainly with the governor or his representative, as they were the most influential figures and could expedite matters faster than anybody else. Committee members did not carry the same weight and consequently their role was less significant. The authority of official channels combined with QAF's expertise proved to be an efficient system of work, particularly for the main centres which were required to deal with diverse issues and demands (QAF, 1986b). However, this top-down approach meant that the contributions other committee members could offer were not fully utilised.

Local NGOs: In the smaller villages, after studying the area and its needs, a local NGO was selected to administer the satellite centres. The NGO's executive committee became the satellite centre's management committee.[5] QAF staff worked with the committee to strengthen its capacity while the centre was being built. Regular field visits, training and systematic follow-up by QAF staff, particularly in the initial stage, set the standard for services required by the Fund. The NGO was responsible for covering the running costs of the centre through its own fund-raising activities. However, in many poor communities where local NGOs could not cover their expenses, QAF eased financial demands by partially subsidizing programmes (QAF,

---

5. Registered Jordanian NGOs consist of an executive committee of 7–13 people and a general assembly (Jordan, 1992a). Usually the general assembly is divided into subcommittees (social, membership, fundraising etc) according to the NGO's activities.

1991a).[6] While this method of administration involved substantial local participation, it also played a part in reinforcing local elites. As in any traditional society where hierarchical structures exist, the cooperation of the local leadership was a significant factor in facilitating the rest of the community's participation. At the same time, within the framework of such partnerships, conflicts occasionally arose. In some situations, the appointment of rural woman leaders by the Fund to run the satellite centres was resisted by NGO partners. For example, many of the activities suggested by the rural leader of the al-Tayyiba centre in Ma'an were at first rejected by the head of the local NGO, who then went on to propose the very same programmes to QAF. Hence differences between the two sides were not related to the programmes and activities themselves, but to who presented them (al-Hmeidat interview). Essentially, this was because in many rural areas NGO partners were run by leading figures from local tribes who were not ready to share the social prestige and position afforded by heading an NGO with the CDCs' rural woman leaders.

Local Councils: This type of council was formed only in Madaba. It included representatives from the Joint Services Councils,[7] the head of the Madaba Municipality, the district directors of Health, Agriculture and Public Works and a QAF representative. The local council undertook to administer and finance the running of the Madaba CDCs. This semi-formal arrangement was recognized as providing the greatest local autonomy. It was, however, a response to local circumstances rather than a model for other centres (QAF, 1986c).

Under all three administrative arrangements, once a centre was completed and fully equipped it was handed over to a local partner responsible for implementing programmes agreed upon by both parties. However, the agreements QAF concluded with such partners stipulated that the Fund reserved the right to monitor activities, both directly and through regular progress reports. The Fund also had to approve any changes in the agreed projects or programmes (QAF, 1986c; 1991a). For QAF, this was an indis-

---

6. In practice, QAF annually contributed JD 1, 500–3, 000 to support local NGOs in running the satellite centres and JD 8, 000–10, 000 for the running costs of main centres (the amount varied from centre to centre). Since 1997, QAF has been working with the CDCs to achieve financial autonomy (QAF, 1997a).

7. The Joint Services Councils were formed in 1977, joining together a number of village and municipal councils. The aim of the government was to form centres for basic services to cater to a number of villages in close proximity, in order to help expand council services in rural areas with minimum cost and better service delivery (Jordan, 1980b).

pensable provision needed to ensure that the centres were not diverted from their original objective to serve the interests of any given individual or group. QAF's approach was, therefore, largely centralized. Nevertheless it still gave its partners a share in the responsibility of developing their local communities.

Operational considerations

As the CDC network grew over the years, it was not always easy to strike the right balance between two key aspects of its working approach: the need, on the one hand, to maintain the function of the centres in accordance with the Fund's original vision, and on the other hand to nurture a true sense of ownership amongst QAF's local partners. As is often the case with large organizations, QAF's extensive outreach gave rise to conflicting situations. Moreover, each of QAF's management methods created its own dilemmas. Ironically, certain problems arose from the Fund's attempts to promote a participatory management approach.

The Pilot Study conducted for the Fund in 1997 on Management versus Decentralization offers some examples (QAF, 1998b). As revealed by the study, centres managed by a local committee or NGO experienced occasional conflicts between QAF, local partners and the CDCs, especially over salary scales. Sometimes the staff of satellite centres run by local NGOs would compare their situation with main centre staff and feel discrimination. As QAF employees, the staff of main centres received better pay, as well as the advantage of social security benefits; the staff of satellite centres, on the other hand, were hired by NGOs at lower salaries. When a decision was taken by QAF's central administration to increase the salaries of teachers employed by the CDCs, it became a bone of contention between local NGO partners and the staff of satellite centres. The teachers felt that the decision should become effective immediately, but the NGOs refused to raise their salaries. Consequently, the teachers blamed the Fund for not ensuring that the NGOs followed its directives. 'If a decision is taken by QAF, it should be implemented. QAF should supervise our centre and other centres. Why isn't there any follow-up?' (QAF, 1998b, Pre-school Teacher interview, al-Khalidiyya 2: 154). The position of local partners was that QAF should cover the salaries of all CDC staff so that they could focus on their perceived role as NGOs. 'If QAF covers the salaries, we will be able to concentrate on other things. We can help poor families. Why are we called a charity? The purpose is for us to offer charity to people who need it. If each year I were able to support two or three families, within a few years I would have covered my area' (ibid., Treasurer of NGO interview, al-Khalidiyya 2: 185). However, QAF's central administration also appeared to be sending conflicting signals; one NGO partner which decided to increase its teachers' salaries was reprimanded by QAF headquarters for taking an 'individualistic' decision (ibid.: 198).

Giving local NGOs administrative authority over the satellite centres in theory meant that QAF was ceding some of its powers to its partners. Its commitment to encouraging local governance of the centres necessitated this approach. Indeed, establishing the satellites in rural areas was in itself a means of handing over responsibility, and hence authority. But this process, often painful, was sometimes ignored at QAF headquarters, resulting, in practice, in disagreements over who had the final say. The appointment of rural leaders was sometimes viewed differently by QAF and the NGOs. For instance, while the Fund tested applicants to choose the best candidate for a position, local NGOs would often have their own agendas for such appointments in which tribalism and nepotism were significant factors (ibid., CDC Sewing Trainer interview, Rihab 3: 256; CDC Director interview, al-Tafila 8: 13). Often, local NGOs believed that they could run the satellite centres without the Fund, provided they had enough income. Some even considered that a centre was tied to QAF only because it owned the building. For their own part too, the directors of the main CDCs had reservations about local NGOs running the satellite centres, preferring to have them completely under their control. 'Then I would know the details one hundred per cent, while in the other centres my information is not as precise … I am one of the people who has written about the need to review the agreements between the Fund and NGOs and the internal regulations of those centres' (ibid., al-Tafila CDC Director interview 8: 13).

Such examples illustrate how QAF's interventions in the arena of the CDCs' activities were often defined by the power struggles between different interest groups in local communities – for communities, as Guijt and Shah have noted, 'are neither homogeneous in composition and concerns, nor necessarily harmonious in their relations' (1998: 8). The Fund's widespread presence at the community level has itself given rise to considerable diversity within the local context. However, this factor was at times overshadowed by the effort required to establish an expansive structure of this kind. Consequently, a homogenous perception of the CDC network was created which did not always fit the reality on the ground. As the CDCs' experience matured, the Fund became increasingly aware that its vision, often difficult to achieve, had to be underpinned by a pragmatic focus. As Abu-Jaber has said, efforts should be directed at getting local communities to sustain projects and to encourage participation so that people feel they play a part in the development of their own areas; in effect, 'to get people to feel that this is their effort' (Abu-Jaber interview).

This approach was fostered early on in Madaba through cooperative ties which were developed by the Fund with the local Joint Services Council. As a result, QAF's first four CDCs were built on Council land. 'The Council, which represented the local community, played an effective role with QAF in facilitating the establishment of the centres because there was a feeling that they would address the needs of the community. As well as its discussions with QAF, the Council consulted the local community to get people's views about having a centre' (al-Shawabkeh interview). Another means of building relations was through studies carried out with the participation of the local community to identify areas most in need of satellite centres. 'QAF implemented a number of studies in Madaba and the surrounding areas. A field study was conducted by the Social Development Department at QAF to examine the conditions of the local communities, especially women and children. They found that Hisban, Ma'in and Mulayh were most in need of CDCs; they were still villages at that time, before they grew. The local community participated in the study' (al-Shawabkeh interview).

The Fund's subsequent experiences with various centres proved that involving the local community in its studies had other significant purposes besides identifying target groups and programmes. In addition to the training it gave them, participation in surveys helped to raise people's awareness of their communities, and motivated some of them to work closely with a centre in addressing different needs. Through this approach, people's relationship to the CDCs moved from the first stage of passive participation, in which management would inform them unilaterally about what had happened, or was going to happen, to interactive participation. This more advanced stage of participation, which involved joint analysis leading to plans of action, promoted local decision-making and enabled people to become stake-holders.

The research teams consisted largely of women and those who were interested later became members of the women's committees in the centres: 'I appreciate the opportunity that you gave me to participate in the study. Even though I have lived in this village since I was born, I did not know it as I do now. Participating in the study gave me the opportunity to understand my community better. I am looking forward to joining the centre and taking part in the centre's efforts to improve the conditions in my community' (a comment made by one of the participants in the study which took place in Rawdat Basma/al-Mafraq governorate) (QAF, 1992b).

Changing grassroots perceptions: the role of the CDCs

When the Madaba centres began their work, people in the area had a preconceived idea of a community development centre. This derived from an existing centre in nearby Thaiban which was built in 1977 by the Department of Social Affairs. At first, the conventional understanding of government as a service provider created similar expectations of QAF's own centres. These were reinforced by assumptions about the Fund's relations with the state. Expectations of the CDCs were partially shaped by this factor, as well as interpretations of the government's development model in Thaiban:

> When people approached the centre they used to ask for subsidies … people perceived that the centre's role was to provide them with services for free. The idea was that the centre must provide services. That is because Princess Basma established the centre. People used to be surprised if we asked them for the programmes' fees and used to argue. They used to say 'even if the other organizations ask for fees, you should not. You should provide the programmes for free because this is a community service centre'. I told them that the centre charges symbolic fees that will not cover the cost of the programmes, but we want you to participate and share the responsibility with us in the development process (al-Shawabkeh interview).

It has taken a number of years for the CDCs to bring about a change in the understanding of their role: 'It was not easy in the beginning as people were expecting to receive subsidies similar to the ministry's centre. We used to stress that they should contribute financially to programmes when they attended them and gradually people started to understand. Later, they began to ask for loans' (al-Shawabkeh interview). In fact, it was eight years later, in 1992, that the Madaba centres first started to give soft loans for income-generating projects (QAF, 1992c). The replacement of subsidies with loans offers a positive illustration of people's growing acceptance of the centres' developmental role; but the time-span involved shows that the process of fostering self-reliance is gradual and continuous. It needs to be primarily activated by the centres themselves and requires recognition that the process must begin by building from where people are, not where others want them to be (Marsden, 1994).

Before QAF's first satellite centres were established in the Madaba villages no development programmes had been carried out by other NGOs. Consequently people's expectations of the centres revolved around their own basic needs. In Hisban, 'People thought that they would have a mother and child care centre not a community development centre. People were not familiar with the idea of community development. Even when we told them that the centre was going to carry out programmes for them, it did not mean anything to them. But they wanted to have something. They did not reject the centre' (Saudi interview). As the CDCs have moved into different stages of their development activities, building trust has been the keystone on which the promotion of different concepts has rested. Such trust has been particularly important given that new directions rarely have a visible impact in the short-term and some outcomes remain intangible, even after a period of time.

Recruitment and capacity-building

Finding qualified staff was one of the main problems to face the CDCs when they began their work. The centres needed two kinds of personnel: administrators and people who could conduct training and implement specific programmes. The term *ra'ida rifiyya* (rural woman leader)[8] was first used in Jordan by the CDC network to describe women selected to run the satellite centres. The responsibilities of a rural leader included administering the centre on a daily basis, in cooperation with the local management committee. Another important part of their job was to mobilize the community to participate in the centre's activities by forming local committees and integrating them into the centre's planning processes (QAF, 1984c). However, the most significant aspect of the rural leader's role was the access her gender gave her to other women in the community – the CDCs' main target group. In traditional communities where the satellite centres were located this was a key factor in enabling the CDCs to pursue their objectives. A more detailed discussion of this important aspect of the rural leader's role follows later.

Finding candidates for the new kinds of work required of the rural leaders was not a simple task, particularly in village communities where women had no previous experience of this sort. Prospective candidates generally fell into two categories: women who had only partially completed secondary levels of education, or university graduates whose degrees were

---

8. QAF was the first organization in Jordan to use this concept. The term itself has been used in Egypt since the late 1960s (al-Saqour interview).

usually unrelated to social work. Neither category automatically fulfilled the CDCs' requirements. In order to overcome this problem, QAF decided that specialization should not be the main concern, and that recruitment would be based on the supply of candidates.[9] The lack of previous experience in specific areas of the CDCs' work could be dealt with through specialized training (QAF, 1986d; 1987a; 1988a; 1989a).[10]

The training process for staff of the Madaba CDCs was conducted over a six-month period at the Fund and other specialized institutions (QAF, 1984d). 'The training turned out to be very useful for me and helped me a lot in my job, as I was specialized in nursing not social work. We learnt how to integrate with the community, about communication methods and about the nature of social work' (Saudi interview). In the second stage of training QAF moved to the field, reaching smaller villages through a cascade-down approach. 'Training was systematic. In one year, QAF staff would conduct six training sessions of a three-day duration in each village' (Hassanein interview).

In the governorate of Ma'an, rural leaders were trained over a year. Twenty-three women from villages with satellite centres (QAF, 1988b) were selected to undergo three days of training a week. In this area particularly, training was an arduous process in part due to the distances involved, and in part to the conservative nature of local society. Trainers from QAF had to travel for nearly three hours from Amman and then between villages which were often a fair distance apart. Logistical arrangements included not only accommodation and transport but also considerable planning by QAF staff in order not to neglect other duties at the Fund. In addition, when training sessions for the *ra'idat rifiyyat* were held at QAF's main centre in Ma'an, local circumstances had to be taken into account. To be able to come from their villages to attend sessions at the centre, women were accompanied by their fathers, brothers or husbands. Consequently, schedules had to make allowances for the trainees' family situation as well as institutional demands (Abu el-Ata interview).

Substantial effort also went into preparing the content of courses run for rural leaders: 'The training included confidence-building, needs assessment and data collection. Methods such as role-playing were used'

9. For instance, the rural leader in Hisban centre, Madaba, had a BA and working experience in nursing, whereas the rural leader in al-Tayyiba Centre, Ma'an, only had a secondary school certificate.

10. Jordanian professionals as well as regional and international consultants were hired by the Fund to provide the necessary technical support for training (Abu el-Ata interview).

(Hassanein interview). Such methods proved to be effective not only in improving the skills of rural leaders, but also in giving them the confidence needed to pursue their role within the local community. 'I attended the training programmes from 1986–1987 which focused on ways to raise community awareness and how to interact with the local community ... the training motivated me to contact women in the community, to listen to their needs and to find ways to help them' (al-Hmeidat interview).

Training programmes aimed at enhancing leadership skills and upgrading operational and financial administrative methods were also devised for the local NGOs which made up the CDCs' management committees (QAF, 1990a).[11] One means of assessing the impact of such efforts was through evaluations made by the rural leaders themselves. The motivation for QAF's trainers sometimes came from statements such as: 'The training became part of our personality and daily thinking. We feel our future will be different now' (Hassanein interview). In fact, as will be seen, the *ra'idat rifiyyat* eventually had a large impact on the general situation of rural women in local communities.

Building community relations through pre-school education programmes

Pre-school education was from the beginning a major priority for the CDC network. In 1979, statistics showed that 49 per cent of the population was below the age of fifteen (Jordan, 1979b) and that 11 per cent were children in the pre-school age group (Jordan, 1979c). The Jordanian Constitution safeguards children's rights to education by making primary education compulsory and free of charge at all state schools (Jordan, 1986b: 10). At the time, primary education started at the age of six and covered nine years of children's education.[12] This did not include pre-school education

---

11. QAF was not the first organization to conduct training for social workers. Institutions such as Princess Rahma Development Centre in Allan also ran similar courses. Approaches however differed. Training courses offered by MOSD were mainly carried out in Allan or in other MOSD centres for a limited duration. In contrast, QAF's training in different locations was extensive and repeated, giving trainees the chance to grasp and apply information on site.

12. The first National Conference on Educational Development took place in 1987. Accordingly compulsory education for children was increased to ten years. The primary and preparatory cycles were joined to form one cycle under the name of Basic Education. Gradually, more attention was given to pre-school education and in the nineties the Ministry of Education began to provide pre-school classes in state schools (*The Official Gazette*, 1994).

which was largely offered by the private sector in urban areas at high fees, as well as by a small number of NGOs. While the Ministry of Education set directives for kindergartens, including procedures for establishment, registration, licensing and supervision, it did not provide pre-school classes or teacher training (Jordan, 1980c). It was against this background, that pre-school education programmes were incorporated at a very early stage into the activities of the CDC network (QAF, 1984a).

The idea that QAF should start pre-school education programmes filtered up from the field. A 1979 study carried out by the Fund revealed a lack of services as well as malnutrition among children, particularly in rural areas (QAF, 1979d). Field visits by QAF staff in the early 1980s also highlighted problems within the existing pre-school education programmes provided by local NGOs: 'We found that most of the existing classes were not suitable. Children were crammed together, mostly sitting on the floor and the rooms were not healthy. In the first two years, through the field visits, we identified different needs and problems and then we started setting plans to address them. In those visits, the NGOs helped us to define their needs such as teaching manuals, furniture, equipment, teachers' training ... A good pre-school model needs all these things' (Abu el-Ata interview).

Besides responding to these very valid needs, there was another significant dimension to the Fund's provision of pre-school services since children's programmes proved to be one of the most effective channels for building community relations. For instance at the outset in Madaba, the main centre relied extensively on its pre-school programme as a means of encouraging people to come to the centre.[13] Parents, especially mothers, were regularly invited to meetings at the centre, during which they were asked to give suggestions about activities they would like to see carried out. 'In one meeting, parents raised the issue of women who could not finish their education and left school at the elementary level ... their suggestion was to open a sewing centre and a literacy class' (al-Shawabkeh interview). It was through such occasions that many of the early programmes were built around the prevailing needs of the community.[14]

---

13. Programmes were partially supported by Caritas and the EEC who covered 35 percent of the running cost of different activities in Madaba's four CDCs (QAF, 1986e).

14. In 1985, literacy classes were opened in the four Madaba CDCs in cooperation with the Ministry of Education. A total of 136 women benefited from the programme by learning to read and write. Besides increasing their self-esteem, such achievements had a considerable impact on women's day-to-day lives, as well

By establishing pre-school education programmes at the CDCs, QAF was entering a highly-specialized area of development. Without sufficient experience of its own, it was by drawing on the expertise of other institutions that the Fund was able to undertake this endeavour. In 1985, training programmes started in different governorates (QAF, 1985b). One of the first issues to emerge was that pre-school teachers in rural areas lacked a proper curriculum with the result that classroom activities were basically improvised. In 1989, a consultative committee was formed by the Fund which included experienced teachers from the private sector, as well as faculty members from the University of Jordan and other pre-school educators, whose task was to develop a curriculum and training programme (QAF, 1989b).

The shortage of qualified pre-school teachers in rural areas meant that QAF's training policy did not revolve solely around its own employees and those of the CDCs, but was targeted to reach as many NGO teachers as possible (QAF, 1989b; 1990b). However, stepping up training created a rapid turnover of participants and as a result sometimes brought about negative results:

> To me, if you are giving a short training course to people who are trained, that will not be bad because it will keep them up and will raise their standards. But when you give one week or two weeks to someone who never had a training course, and consider that you have given them training and think that they are now capable of doing the job – to me this is very serious because these people come to think that 'we know now, we're good kindergarten teachers or caretakers' (al-Mufti interview).

The Fund's training programmes nevertheless helped to address a real need by accelerating the establishment of pre-school classes at the grass-roots level, giving this aspect of the CDCs' outreach activities a significant impact. One of the strengths of the on-site training programme lay in 'training the trainers' to set up programmes based on locally available resources, which meant that their programmes were more likely to be sustained. Yet there was an obvious disparity between the kind of facilities, teaching materials and equipment available to a private kindergarten in Amman and that of a small village NGO.

It took the Fund several years to develop a methodology for training. In 1983, QAF started to gain some insight by joining with other national

---

as opening up opportunities for them to participate in socio-economic activities (QAF, 1985c).

organizations in preparing training courses. However, it was mostly through the training geared to pre-school education programmes at the CDCs that the Fund's experience grew. Eventually, with the help of local and international experts, QAF began to design training packages (QAF, 1989b). The outcome of these various efforts eventually earned QAF recognition from UNICEF as a national trainer in pre-school education (al-Himsi interview). As pre-school classes at the CDCs gradually became a model for local NGOs, demands to expand the programme increased. As a result, in 1990 an outreach project was carried out in cooperation with UNICEF aimed at setting up additional classes for local NGOs in different governorates. QAF was responsible for teacher training and providing equipment and furniture through UNICEF support (QAF, 1990c). Sixteen pre-school classes were established in four different governorates, reaching 485 children. By the end of 1994, a total of 266 new classes were being run by NGOs in eight governorates. Over five years, more than 7,000 children attended the programme (QAF, 1994a).

Although pre-school education had by then become a growing concern in both the public and the private sectors, the pioneering effort epitomized by QAF's training packages, was still of significance.[15] The director of the Madaba centre recalls that: 'The educational programmes carried out at the centre were gradually transferred to other kindergartens and other NGOs. For instance the pre-school guidebook:[16] now, in 1999, at a private school, I see QAF's guidebook with the teacher. I ask her where she got it and she says from a teacher in your centre ... we became a model for others' (al-Shawabkeh interview). The level of training reached by the CDCs contributed in other ways to private sector efforts: 'A private school opened a kindergarten which charges three times our fees. They contacted the teacher at the centre seconded to us from the Ministry of Education without telling me and agreed with her to take one year of unpaid leave from the ministry, and to go and work for them. She got the job. For me I lost a teacher. When I asked the school's principal about the matter, he said "well, we wanted your experience." Now they have a model kindergarten and although we lost our teacher, it's still a service to the community' (al-Shawabkeh interview).

15. New teaching methods introduced through the CDC pre-school classes differed from the existing traditional approach. Emphasis was on learning through play, using methods such as theme teaching whereby classes were divided into four playing corners, each one carrying a different theme.

16. *The Teacher's Guide-Book for the Pre-School Level*, published by QAF, the Ministry of Education and UNICEF in November 1991.

In other respects too the qualitative and quantitative advancement of pre-school services provided by different bodies, including the CDCs, had a favourable impact on subsequent stages of children's education:

> The centre has facilitated our work with children. They come to us ready for the system and well-organized. They also adapt very quickly and are ready to learn. Being already prepared makes it much easier for teachers than teaching children with no pre-school experience ... In lessons, they have confidence to express themselves and do well and teachers enjoy teaching them (QAF, 1996a, Hisban Primary School Head Teacher interview).

Pre-school education programmes at the CDCs were instrumental in achieving one of the Fund's basic objectives, namely to enhance the quality of service delivery within the social sector by providing working models. 'QAF has had a very good and effective role as far as training and capacity-building are concerned, training of manpower for the government as well as the NGOs. This is a clear and undeniable role' (al-Saqour interview). While pre-school education was one of the CDCs' more obvious success stories, an emphasis on capacity-building underpinned the Fund's approach to maintaining the quality of services in general. 'In most of QAF's work, particularly in the children's kindergartens in the community centres and the work for women, the training they provided helped a lot' (al-Mufti interview).

In her evaluative study of pre-school education services carried out by different organizations in Jordan, Srour (1997) concludes that QAF's pre-school education programmes were better than those provided by GUVS, the private sector, MOSD and the Ministry of Education. However, whereas the private sector made a profit from its services and GUVS was able to break even, pre-school programmes offered by QAF and MOSD did not cover their costs (Srour, 1997). As Srour shows in the case of QAF's pre-school programmes, one of the Fund's main challenges was the extent to which its various activities continued to be subsidized – a dilemma encountered in other projects carried out by the Fund.

In conclusion, the Fund's single most important initiative to further its objectives on the ground within the Jordanian development arena was the establishment of the CDC network. Through this effort, the Fund gained first-hand experience of the needs and constraints of its activities in the field. The diversity of QAF's interactions with local actors was a key factor in creating social capital and other vital linkages in order to advance the CDCs' operations. As QAF began to implement programmes through the CDCs, it also became familiarized with the different interests which played a part in shaping the outcome of their activities. Ultimately, such insight helped in forming grassroots interventions through approaches which were built pragmatically around local circumstances.

A new infrastructure

During the mid-1980s, state discourse emphasized the 'glaring' shortage of trained practitioners within the social sector. To address the problem, the 1986–1990 Five Year Development Plan called on the social development sector 'to upgrade the performance of existing social institutions and voluntary agencies, increase their capacity and expand their programs with a view to improving the level of service' (Jordan, 1986a: 179). As the 1980s drew to a close, a growing perception had formed within the Fund that it should, at this stage, take steps to consolidate its training programmes. QAF had acquired training experience and recognition through the CDCs and it was felt that building capacity at the national level through training, as stated in its original objectives, had become an essential part of its role as a national NGO. In 1989, therefore, work began in the Fund to establish the Queen Zein al Sharaf Compound for Training and Social Development.

The name chosen for the new institution merits comment. Of Hashemite descent, Queen Zein al Sharaf 'played a pivotal role in the political life of the country towards the latter part of the reign of the late King Abdullah and during the reign of the late King Talal' (al-Ra'i, 1999b: 8). The late Queen's overall contribution to the betterment of Jordanian society, especially in the social, cultural and educational fields, is well recognized.[17] Queen Zein al Sharaf is remembered for the leadership in advancing the cause of Jordanian women and for ensuring that women's rights should be guaranteed by the Constitution. In 1944 she launched the first women's movement, the Union of Jordanian Women. Subsequently, the women's branch of the Jordanian Red Crescent Society was formed with Queen Zein al Sharaf as its patron in 1948. Other women's organizations were established with her support in later years, as well as different charities

---

17. In *The Brink of Jordan*, Charles Johnston, who was British Ambassador to Jordan from 1956–1960, describes Queen Zein al Sharaf as 'a woman of charm, courage and considerable wit' (Johnston, 1972: 27). In his writings, Roland Dallas recalls that Queen Zein al Sharaf 'evoked her son Hussein's strongest adjectives when he described her: she was not only very beautiful but also very wise, tender and loving and full of advice and encouragement – "a major factor in my life"' (Dallas, 1999: 4).

(excerpts from *al-Ra'i*, 1999b). She was indeed a 'brilliant and subtle Queen Mother' (Johnston, 1972: 174).

In 1994, soon after its establishment, a memorial for Queen Zein al Sharaf was held at the new institution which bore her name. It was attended by her four children, together with family members and a large number of Jordanians from all walks of life, who had come to honour the memory of 'the Mother of the Jordanians' as she came to be known.

The Queen Zein al Sharaf Compound for Training and Social Development was established with the support of the Government of Abu Dhabi, channelled through the Abu Dhabi Arab Fund for Economic Development. This generous, unconditional grant, which covered construction and equipment, enabled QAF to build the 4,500 sq. metre complex over a four year period between 1990 and 1994.[18] It was located in al-Hashimi al-Shamali, a low-income, densely populated area of Amman, and designed to include two separate yet interrelated sections – a training centre and a social development centre. The aim of the training centre was to provide instruction in three related areas: community development and pre-school education, as well as capacity-building programmes and income-generating schemes for women. To ensure that training would be innovative and practical, rather than theoretical, these programmes were to draw on the experience of the CDCs, which served both as a laboratory for field training and a model for community development. Constant feedback between the centre and the field was envisaged, the objective being to instruct trainers for the social sector in various specialized fields who would in turn act as catalysts to revitalize local communities and promote local development (QAF, 1989c).

A basic part of the training was, therefore, to be achieved by drawing on the practical experience of the CDCs. However, in the Compound methods could be constantly monitored and evaluated, and new programmes could be tried and later transferred to the field. Furthermore, QAF's provision of training for NGOs could be reinforced to include other NGOs beyond the vicinity of the CDCs. A major drawback to training in the field was that the distances involved meant that QAF was unable to make regular use of experts from other institutions. The accessibility of the Compound in Amman meant that capacity-building activities could be enhanced by drawing on

18. It must be noted as a source of deep appreciation in Jordan generally, and within QAF in particular, that allocations by the government of Abu Dhabi for the Queen Zein al Sharaf Compound for Training and Social Development were kept up throughout the period of the Gulf War, at a time when the project could have been delayed or even halted due to regional conflict.

nearby expertise. It was also hoped that the interaction and exchange of experience between development practitioners would contribute to the formation of new ideas and approaches in the social sector.

The objectives set for the Compound, as with some of the Fund's other development efforts, were not easily achieved. There were a number of reasons for the difficulties. The volatile climate during the Gulf War and its aftermath, while the Compound was being established, was not conducive to focused activity in the early stages. As in the field, finding the human resources needed to carry out programmes was not easy. Moreover, in the initial phase particularly, a shortage of funds to operate the Compound and implement its programmes posed a serious problem. An active process had to get underway before the concept of the Queen Zein al Sharaf Compound for Training and Social Development could apply in practice.

Promoting Women's Participation: Local Reinterpretations of Global Perspectives

At the time QAF was established, the predominant discourse relating to women's advancement was embodied in the term Women in Development (WID). Inspired by Ester Boserup's study in 1970, which demonstrated that, far from improving the life of women in the Third World, development projects had created further marginalization, WID advocated an approach centred on the economic empowerment of women. Underpinned by liberal thinking, this approach called for greater equity between men and women but remained largely steeped in Western gender stereotypes. Essentially, women's development was viewed as a logistical question rather than an issue which required a fundamental reassessment of gender relations (Marchand and Parpart, 1995: 13).

During the 1970s, some development practitioners working on women's issues were influenced by emerging critiques of development and patriarchy. The arguments of dependency theorists for autonomous development, as well as assertions by radical feminists that women could only develop outside patriarchal power structures, gave rise to a new way of thinking about women's advancement. This approach, sometimes called Women and Development (WAD), promoted projects solely for women and discouraged close cooperation with male-dominated institutions. Numerous NGOs adopted these policies. Advocates of Women in Development responded to the new thinking by modifying mainstream development policies for women. Calls for equality between men and women gave way to a focus by planners on women's basic human needs, especially in health, education and training. WID proponents maintained that women's effectiveness and efficiency in their working environment, would be enhanced by such means and ultimately create positive outcomes both for economic development and women's lives.

By the 1980s, academics and activists both in the North and South had begun to advocate a new approach to women's development. Prompted by growing concerns over rising poverty among both women and men in the South, as well as certain feminist misgivings over global patriarchy, a socialist feminist outlook gradually began to take form in different parts of the world. The debate was heightened by feminists in the South, who sought their own solutions to development challenges. The specific problems of women in the South were further highlighted by the series of international conferences celebrating the UN Decade for Women (1976–1985).

From the resulting dialogue, which was largely an outcome of academic research, a further shift in approach emerged. Recognizing the limitations of focusing on women in isolation, this approach advocated instead the need to look at gender: 'not only at the category "women" – since that is only half the story – but at women in relation to men, and the way in which relations between these categories are socially constructed' (Moser, 1993: 3). A strong linkage also emerged between developmental approaches concerning women in the Third World and the social construction of gender relationships. If women's concerns are addressed separately, the real problem, which basically consists of women's subordinate status to men, is overlooked.

As in other areas of development policy, international discourse related to women has traversed different phases. The various approaches emphasized in each have created new ways of looking at women's issues at local levels. Throughout its interventions in the women's sector, as this section aims to illustrate, QAF's approach was made up of, and sometimes combined, different elements of these international trends. However, in many ways this was an organic rather than a deliberate process, frequently influenced by the characteristics and demands of the local context, as well as inconsistencies encountered on the ground and which were often far removed from prevailing trends.

Programmes for women

In 1978, just a year after QAF began its work, the first meeting of the Board of Directors of the Scientific Organization for Cultural Studies on

Arab Women was convened in Rabat. The resolutions of the Rabat meeting included the expansion of the organization to one that served the more general concerns of Arab women and operated from offices to be established throughout the Arab world. This event showed that the increasing attention being paid to women in the international development community was reflected at the regional and local level in the Middle East. It was time to call for 'the eradication and change of all the symptoms of ignorance and backwardness which hampered the development of women' (Princess Basma, 1978: 2), which were in turn regarded as an impediment to the development of the Arab World in general.

By the end of QAF's preliminary phase, activities directed to women had evolved from needs assessment through studies, and in-kind support through local NGOs, to programme design. A primary aim of the CDCs was to 'establish projects that specifically targeted women, while meeting their needs as mothers and wives and citizens, building their agricultural skills in rural areas and building their technical skills in urban areas' (QAF, 1981c: 1). By 1989, propelled by rising poverty in the country, the Fund's strategy specified that: 'Women play an active role in the family and society. This role can be enhanced through the development of women's skills, ability and productivity in various spheres' (QAF, 1989d: 8). The strategy went on to state that development efforts would have a restricted impact 'as long as women are not fulfilling their roles' (ibid.: 12).

Such documents conveyed a clear policy of incorporating women into the development process through the Fund's programmes. Statements of this kind were also very much in line with international donor discourse during the mid-1980s, which saw a clear shift towards incorporating the needs of women into development planning. This was best exemplified by the Nairobi Forward Looking Strategies of 1985, which called for placing women at the heart of the development agenda and gave particular importance to rural women. With the establishment of the first CDCs in rural areas during this period, the Fund was well placed to respond to these international trends. The CDC programmes reflected the priority given to projects that provided agricultural and technical training for women, as well as awareness raising in health, nutrition and reproductive health (QAF, 1987b).

Despite the stated aims of QAF's policy documents, women were, at this stage, still very much viewed as passive beneficiaries rather than active participants. However, certain views maintain that participation, whether among women or men, generally occurs in different ways and at different moments: 'A common pattern is a high level of participation early on, with extensive community consultation, which is followed by a period of less participation when decisions are made' (Guijt and Shah, 1998: 9). To what extent this observation applies to women's participation in the centres' early programmes is hard to determine in retrospect; nevertheless it can be said to describe the level of women's involvement during the CDCs' initial stage of operations.

From the mid-1980s, QAF began to involve women at a deeper level. Whether this was the result of international consensus, a reflection of a national process in which women were becoming more involved, or even an internal decision to activate the role of women in the Fund's work, or all these factors combined, is uncertain and a topic for further research.

A gendered perspective from the community level

In most countries in the Middle East, including Jordan, women are viewed as symbols of the 'integrity of the dominant culture in the country' (Chatty and Rabo, 1997: 7). Above other roles, women are distinguished as wives and mothers. This perception has generally meant that individual women have had to negotiate their gender relations with great care in order to overcome the cultural bonds which have so often impeded the fulfilment of other ambitions. In Arab societies, people's predominant ties are those of kinship. It is therefore customary for women to join together in a family setting. Outside this context, and particularly in conservative environments, the most accepted way for women to associate formally has been through involvement in charitable organizations.[19]

In 1987 considerations of this kind had to be taken into account when planning the first venture for women in al-Tayyiba centre in Ma'an. A religious lecture was chosen as the most acceptable activity for women to attend. As a rural leader from al-Tayyiba recounts: 'We planned the activity with the office of the Ministry of Social Development, who had a woman preacher who was known to al-Tayyiba community. Only two women attended the event. Girls were not allowed to leave their houses, how could they attend? That was difficult. The two women who did come were the mothers of male leaders of al-Tayyiba NGO. Even though it was only the two of them, we went ahead with the activity. We thought that by doing this, we would influence other women in the community' (al-Hmeidat interview). Cultural factors meant that involving women in the

---

19. Unless formal groups conform to cultural ideals upheld by the state, as well as society and kin, they are not well regarded (Chatty and Rabo, 1997).

CDCs was not always simple given the sensitivities of the local community where girls and women were concerned. As the rural leader explains: 'Actually the QAF centre was the first organization to open its doors to women. Before the centre was established, women used to be at home' (al-Hmeidat interview).

Conditions such as these resulted in rural leaders having to produce their own solutions and approaches to integrate the women of their community. Here we can see examples of the type of social skills that only the rural leaders as women themselves could draw upon:

> After that lecture, I started making home visits. I couldn't go directly to the women, knocking at their doors and asking them to come to the centre. So instead I used their children who were registered at the kindergarten as a reason for them to come to the centre ... The problem was with their husbands and fathers. Women used to suffer as a result of not being allowed out of their homes. So we talked about the possibility of organizing lectures. I worked together with the centre's administrative committee, as well as the men's local club, with whom I discussed the possibility of giving their wives, sisters and daughters permission to leave the house. And so we began to get them accustomed to ideas such as 'if your wife, or daughter came to the centre to attend a lecture on family matters, home economics, child raising ... then it will reflect well on you, your children and your family.' As a result, I achieved some acceptance among the men, which was encouraging ... although not all of them agreed. It wasn't easy, I used to hear criticism of me for attending meetings with them. But I continued to work as a rural leader (al-Hmeidat interview).

By building trust with the community, rural leaders were to play an increasingly important role in the work of the centres in coordination with the women's committees which were gradually set up. Because women were not always comfortable in the presence of strangers without their menfolk, the familiar figure of the rural leader made them feel at ease. Since the community's leadership was viewed as an important factor in encouraging community participation (Cohen and Uphoff, 1977), particularly in the case of women, candidates for the position of rural leader were often identified in consultation with local sheikhs and other community notables (Abu el-Ata interview).

One could say that QAF's approach had always been gender sensitive, well before the distinctions between a 'women in development' and a 'gender and development' approach were recognized in the international development arena. This was primarily because any interaction with women had to be negotiated with the largely male-dominated communities to which they belonged. QAF had to take into account gender relationships within the community and within families. Often, the successful integration of women into the centres was as much the result of communication with men, as with the women themselves.

According to Es-Said, although the level of women's education in Jordan was increasing in the 1970s, 'the basic motives were not to facilitate women's entry into the labour force and market, or to seek employment outside the home. [It was] more geared towards preparing a woman for her traditional role as a "better mother," a more "competent housekeeper" and to become a more "understanding wife"' (Es-Said, 1974: 4). By the mid to late 1980s, the situation was not very different. Even when our aims were different, the rhetoric surrounding attempts to enhance women's participation made use of such an understanding. Often, QAF itself had to present its programmes in this way in order to assuage the concerns of the men: 'We reinforced the woman's role in her family as a mother. That was an entrance for focusing on women's health, family planning, children's upbringing, social and economic topics and later on women's rights. It was not acceptable to go any other way' (al-Hessa interview).

The theme of gender equality, and the setbacks sometimes encountered, was highlighted by the processes of political liberalization which were advanced in the region during that period. As Laurie Brand contends, these processes are not bound by any law of nature or politics to produce only liberal actors. Given the overriding position of men, and the fact that transitions can activate the emergence of parties which sometimes uphold policies that may be reactionary and defensive, it is quite feasible that 'women's issues ... may be among the first that parties to the new political balance seek to use/exploit in political bargaining' (Brand, 1998: 3–4). Referring to Jordan, Brand notes how in 1990–1991, the Islamist-dominated parliament, while debating the state budget, argued for the adoption of a range of Shari'a-based economic policies. However, after eventually moderating their position, twenty-two Islamist MPs voted for the budget:

> Then again, quietly ... the Legal Committee of the house approved a law changing the formula according to which *miri* (state land) could be inherited. Up to this point, men and women had been eligible to inherit equal shares of such land. The new law made such lands subject to Shari'a, thereby reducing a Muslim woman's share to one-half that of her brother's. The law was proposed and passed by the house so quickly that there was no public reaction until after the fact, when it went to the senate, where it also passed, virtually unchallenged. The Islamists had been joined by a cohort of non-Islamist deputies, including Christians, who reportedly saw nothing detrimental to their interests in a proposal that compromised women's rights (Brand, 1998: 105–6).

Just as efforts to further gender equality on the national level are often impeded by the very mechanisms that are designed to promote it, so too can the attempt to involve local communities in decision-making and planning reinforce discriminatory practices and attitudes towards women.

QAF's awareness of the significance of gender roles and relations did not mean an attempt to challenge existing attitudes directly. It was, rather, a matter of trying to work within their context: 'The Fund has been good to us, (but) in the beginning we had our problems. They wanted certain things, but we are a village community ... We have our own customs and traditions. A girl shies away from talking to men, yet they wanted us to make home visits! This was solved by appointing a woman rural leader' (QAF, 1998b, Head of NGO interview, Ghawr al-Safi 7: 69). The attempt to involve women in programmes and activities had to be well thought out. Even so, it was likely to encounter opposition: 'The programmes presented by the Fund do not suit the community. When the Fund talks about women, it does not reflect reality because the village here has its own circumstances' (ibid., Head of NGO interview, al-Juhayir 9: 68). Such comments by the men who headed the NGOs working in partnership with QAF, who had a greater understanding than other men in the community of QAF's work with the women, clearly illustrate how sensitive the Fund had to be in addressing gender relations.

Resistance to women's participation was not limited to rural areas. As Sari Nassir recalls, when he began his work in the Hay Nazal community in urban Amman: 'I had many enemies as a result of our attempts to involve the women in the work of the centre, for coming to a traditional neighbourhood, and doing something that they couldn't understand ... To begin with, they resented us and tried to stop our work in any way possible' (Nassir interview). A study carried out among women in the squatter areas of Amman revealed similar attitudes. One woman explained why local inhabitants objected to having a football team in the neighbourhood community centre: 'The people don't want mixing [of men and women] – forming the football team means the mixing of boys and girls because the centre will be used for literacy classes and sewing classes as well – the centre should not be treated as a university' (Shami, 1997: 90). Shami maintains that people were not comfortable with the centre because it represented a space which was not under their control. The authorities controlled the public space of a university and they saw decisions about the centre's activities being taken in much the same way (ibid.).

Gender relations, as these examples show, were a deciding factor in promoting women's participation in both rural and urban areas. In order to activate the role of women, gender issues needed careful attention whether the Fund was working with male NGO partners or the community at large. Nevertheless, since the public space offered by the centre was predominantly under the authority of QAF, we were able to promote women's programmes in ways that the community itself might not have achieved. Essentially, the Fund's presence helped to moderate gender conflict which the varying attitudes and interests within a community could easily create.

Practical needs versus strategic interests

The efforts QAF made to increase the participation of women offer a compelling example of the way in which the empowerment of women is dependent on a range of factors which include, but are by no means limited to, practical interests and basic needs such as health. The literature on gender and development defines practical gender needs or interests as the needs 'women identify in their socially accepted roles in society.' They are 'a response to immediate perceived necessity, identified with a specific context [and] are practical in nature and often concerned with inadequacies in living conditions such as water provision, healthcare and employment' (Moser, 1993: 40). Practical gender needs do not, as Molyneux has pointed out, 'generally entail a strategic goal such as women's emancipation or gender equality ... nor do they challenge the prevailing forms of subordination even though they arise directly out of them' (Molyneux cited in Moser, 1993: 40). Strategic gender needs, on the other hand, 'are the needs women identify because of their subordinate position to men in their society. Strategic gender needs vary according to particular contexts. They relate to gender divisions of labour, power and control and may include such issues as legal rights, domestic violence, equal wages and women's control over their bodies' (ibid.: 39).[20]

This distinction between practical and strategic needs is an important one in analysing the impact and effectiveness of the Fund from a gender perspective since it 'helps to unpack the very real tension between policies which seek to distribute the resources in ways that preserve and reinforce these inequalities and those which use women's everyday practical needs as a starting point for challenging these inequalities' (Kabeer, 1994: 91).

---

20. One of the principal objectives of JNCW is to increase the focus on strategic gender needs of women in the country.

QAF's experience of working with women offers a valuable insight into the dynamics of women's emancipation, both from the position of women themselves, and the organizations that have sought to support them. 'Practical interests' or 'needs' were the focus of the basic services and skills that QAF offered women in its earlier conception of women's programmes. Given existing conditions at the grassroots level, it was essential for the Fund to address such needs. Yet it had to recognize that providing women with skills would not, in itself, empower them, or ensure that they became active agents in the development process and may even, short of a systematic transformation of social institutions, serve to perpetuate inequalities (ibid.: 87).

The early phase of QAF's work with women was not consciously intended to address strategic gender needs. Indeed, within the organization itself there was initially no awareness of the possibility of developing such an approach. Hence, in the first stage of the Fund's interventions, serving women's practical needs was a logical, if not deliberate, sequence. However, as our work with women evolved, a strategic dimension gradually emerged.

A step forward: establishing women's committees in the CDCs

The way in which QAF sought to empower and emancipate women was very much a 'home-grown' effort to develop an organic strategy and support practices. The idea of women's committees embodied this approach: 'When we visited the NGOs which worked with our CDCs, we couldn't see any female members in the administration committees. It was not acceptable to have women members, yet all the programmes were for women. We asked the NGOs to integrate women into their administrative committees, but this was not deemed acceptable, and they refused. So we suggested instead that separate women's committees should be formed' (Abu el-Ata interview).

The women's committees through which the Fund sought to respond to this situation were a pioneering move in the 1980s. Men were, at that point, still central to decision-making, administration and the planning of activities and programmes. The creation of separate committees as an alternative to integration would, it was believed, give women a practical option to become actively rather than passively involved in the centres' activities and would gradually shift the gender focus.

The centres had to devise ways in which to manage women's activities in order to ensure that they did not overlap with programmes for men.

Women's programmes and activities generally finished around noon and were soon in demand. This was attributed to the fact that many of the women had little else to do during the day once their house work was over, and also that their opportunities for socializing with other women were limited (al-Shahwan interview b).

The first committee was formed in Madaba. Generally, it was the prominent women of the community who were approached, including the wives of the local sheikhs and other local leaders. The inclusion of such figures in the committees may well have increased the likelihood of reproducing 'the structures of domination current in masculine arenas' (Joseph, 1997: 59). However, it was a necessary and often helpful strategy. Just as the support of male community leaders was important to the work of the CDCs, with the women's committees their female counterparts provided essential endorsement for the new concept of women's committees.

The women's committees were a bold and pioneering step which challenged both social perceptions of the role of women and women's perceptions of themselves. These committees were to be entrusted with the responsibility of defining needs and planning activities accordingly under the supervision of the *ra'idat rifiyyat* (rural woman leaders) in the satellite centres and programme coordinators in the main centres (QAF, 1989e). The purpose was to engage women in the development process of their communities, while increasing their voluntary work ethic and leadership potential. Through the committees, QAF offered women a platform from which to expand the sphere of their own activity, to enter into that of the community, to play a more proactive role in planning its development, and possibly to begin serving their own strategic interests. As the women's committees began to select their head and co-ordinators, 'They started to feel their value. You know that women in rural areas were repressed. When you give them authority, they start to ask for more. Nowadays, women have more of a role than before' (Abu el-Ata interview).

The inevitable problems varied from one area to another. However, the process of setting up women's committees gradually became easier. For example, in 1990, a newly formed committee in Irbid comprised seventy women. None of the centres could achieve such figures in the 1980s. The socio-cultural setting of Irbid, an urban centre, may have enabled women to participate more freely. Nevertheless, as the women's committees in general gained strength, they became one of the most vital mechanisms for the organizing of women's programmes within the CDCs.

The impact of the women's committees

The women's committees fostered new outlooks for numerous women, particularly in rural areas. However, their inadequate integration into the workings of the CDCs, meant that women were not fully empowered. While the committees were to play a major role in planning events and programmes which targeted women, and in fundraising for the centres, they were generally not involved in overall planning and they had to report to the centres' directors. Nor were the women's committees to play a role in the budgeting of the centres' activities and programmes, which often meant that they were allocated funds which proved to be insufficient (al-Shahwan interview b).

A 1989 evaluation also revealed that the activity of the women's committees was generally limited, and that even in the case of the more active committees there was a lack of planning and originality, as well as an absence of follow-up. The report noted that the women's programmes organized by the committees lacked financial backing, and that it was impossible for some women to pay the fees for certain training programmes. Transportation was another problem for women who lived in remote areas and therefore had no access to the centres. The report noted, moreover, that local and official authorities were often not supportive of the women's programmes. An important observation was that the contemporary definition of social development and a general understanding of their own roles were largely absent among those who worked in the centres (Ismail, 1989).

Other evaluations of the centres and their programmes also found the committees to be generally lacking in impact on the situation of women (*Baladi*, 1988; Kassabeh, 1994). Yet, when the women themselves were asked about their feelings, there were more positive responses. Seven years on, in 1996, a second evaluation carried out by the Fund indicated that 38 per cent of the women interviewed felt that the centres did serve the community. However, only 17 per cent felt that they participated in the decision-making processes of their own centre. Social interaction and making friends ranked higher as an outcome of their involvement in the committees (QAF, 1996a). For women who seldom left their homes, as al-Hmeidat notes earlier, the opportunities which the women's committees offered for making friends should not be underestimated.

Evaluation reports provide valuable insights into some of the drawbacks in the work of the women's committees, as well as the approach of the Fund and its CDCs. What naturally cannot be highlighted by a report are 'the internal dynamics and differences that are so crucial to positive outcomes' (Guijt and Shah, 1998: 1). The existing power structures within the CDCs, such as the administration, were no more likely to relinquish their authority to the women's committees than they would to NGO partners run by men. It is also difficult, in the light of different conditions in various localities, to make generalizations about women's potential to take on increasing roles in certain aspects of the centres' operations. Furthermore, 'women' may be 'just as much of an obstacle to collective action as differences between men and women' (Kandiyoti cited in Guijt and Shah, 1998: 50). Given the inevitability of this situation, an advantage to not fully integrating the women's committees into the overall work of the centres may have been that other operations were less likely to be affected by conflict. As for lack of planning and originality, these have always presented a major challenge for the Fund. Various reasons, including staff apathy or insufficient aptitude may play a part. Yet differing levels of skill amongst women's committee members can perhaps justify the decision to run basic programmes which lack originality but cater to existing capabilities and needs.

For the majority of CDCs, and therefore for the Fund, the overriding worry was financial constraints. To operate an extensive network of centres is a heavy burden. In addition to staff salaries, numerous programmes have to be subsidized by the Fund on a long-term basis due to the limited resources of local communities, particularly in hard economic times. Indeed, without this support, some programmes could not have been sustained.[21] This issue, as we will see, was to pose a serious dilemma for QAF's attempts to decentralize. However, in the day-to-day running of the centres the need to keep expenses down has always been a major consideration for administrators who remain answerable to the Fund. These circumstances are bound to have a bearing on the quality and types of programmes which the CDCs are able to implement.

Despite its dilemmas, QAF was able to reach women in the local communities in a way that no other institution, thus far, had been able to achieve. The Fund's success on this score was attributed to a number of factors, including its connection with the Royal Family. It is difficult to know how far this observation is correct. However, as in other countries where well-connected women have been associated with social causes, in

---

21. In 1999, the CDCs covered 69 per cent of their operational costs. The rest was covered by QAF (QAF, 1999a).

Jordan their participation has helped to facilitate and encourage other women's involvement.

A 1999 evaluation report conducted in the governorate of Ma'an states that one of the outcomes of the centres' work with women was that awareness of the needs and situation of women in Jordan was raised, resulting in greater activism which was in turn reflected in increasing membership in political women's fora (Muhtasseb and Habahba, 1999). The report notes that the women's involvement largely grew from a modest local context to one that had national impact. The international prize for rural leadership presented to Kawkab al-Ghnameen, the rural leader of al-Baq'a satellite centre, by the Women's World Summit Foundation in 1996 was noted as a significant achievement in this regard (ibid.: 12). Hind al-Hajaya of al-Hisa satellite centre became the second rural leader to receive the same international prize in 1998 (WWSF, 1999).

The importance of economic returns

The prospect of economic return undoubtedly contributed to the acceptance of the women's committees and their programmes in local communities. Women were questioned by their husbands and families as to whether or not they would be receiving anything in return for their participation in the centres. Indeed it was often difficult to maintain their attendance when it was felt that there would be no financial gain (al-Shahwan interview b). It has been noted that 'for women to sacrifice precious time, they need to be convinced that they will be better off for having been involved' (Guijt and Shah, 1998: 15). Within the local context, the men also needed to be convinced: 'When they see a woman going to the centre … The first day, the second day, the third day … they say "what is she doing going out of her house every day, not bothering about her duties … everyday she goes out, dresses up, goes for an outing"' (QAF, 1998b, member of Women's Committee interview, al-Risha 11: 111). As overall economic conditions deteriorated in Jordan income-generation became a significant issue for women: 'This is a development centre and all our beneficiaries are women … yet the mere fact that women leave their homes makes them open for criticism … people say "why do these women come and go without even getting a salary?" Had there been men in the centre, the women would not be allowed to come here' (ibid., Rural Leader interview, Mu'ta 7: 112). For the CDCs' activities to succeed, it was important to dispel these concerns.

The concept of rural markets did much to modify such views and gave added motivation for women to attend the CDCs. From the 1990s, the women's committees began to join the rural market programme introduced by QAF to promote women's participation in economic activities. The idea was simple: the women were to bring their home produce to the centres each month to sell at stalls to the local community. Often, the produce was the result of home-garden projects carried out by the CDCs which gave women in rural communities the technical training to increase their output of fruit, vegetable and dairy products. These programmes aimed to encourage families to use the land around their homes to meet their own food needs, as well as to sell surplus produce to generate income. To begin with, the notion of the rural market went against traditions and women would often give away their products free rather than ask for anything in return. 'Women were shy. They didn't want to be involved in selling their products. They used to send their products to the centre for us to sell on their behalf. We encouraged them to bring anything simple, like parsley, and would sell it ourselves. Gradually, they were encouraged' (Women's Committee group interview, Idoun).

In some rural communities the reaction was even stronger. When the rural leader in the southern village of al-Tayyiba introduced the idea, the women there would not accept it at all: 'When I told the women to bring anything to sell in the rural market, such as the local bread, the reaction was very strong. They said "You want us to take money in return for some bread? We don't want the money. We'll make the bread for the centre, and you sell it. No, we don't want the money"' (al-Hmeidat interview). With time, however, the success of the rural markets encouraged the women to sell their products. Gradually, the markets grew to include other items such as clothing and crafts, which women had learned to make through the centres. In al-Baq'a, despite initial difficulties in setting up the programme, sixty women joined the committee as a result of the market's success. By 1997, 165 members were participating in this activity (QAF, 1997b). Accordingly, the rural markets became an effective point of entry for the women of the community into the women's committees and into the other areas of activity they offered.

Although the CDC programmes included a range of activities designed to increase women's knowledge of their legal rights and the importance of their role in the development process, it is hard to ascertain whether or not the women themselves viewed their involvement as the start of a larger involvement with the life of the community and its development. However, participation in the centres indirectly gave many women the opportunity to gain confidence and skills hitherto denied to them; the rural markets offer a prime example. A staff member recalls one woman saying: 'In the past, we would have hidden if visitors came to the centre. I could never have imagined myself standing up and speaking in public to a group of strangers about our work' (al-Shahwan interview b).

The role and responsibilities of the women's committees increased with time. In 1996, they participated in the rural loan programme in cooperation with UNIFEM (see chapter 6), which involved conducting case studies on women who could benefit from the programme. Once they had submitted their recommendations, the committees were responsible for follow-up with women who established income-generating projects. By 1998, there were 5000 members of the women's committees in the Fund's CDCs (QAF, 1998c).

The impact of the Fund's approaches on women's participation

In an attempt to define participation in its varying degrees and forms, Pretty (1995) offers a classification beginning at the lower end with passive participation and culminating with self-mobilization at the other. In certain traditional contexts, self-mobilization, where 'people participate by taking initiatives independent of external institutions to change systems' may never be possible. Perhaps for now, 'functional participation,' which resides somewhere in the middle of the proposed spectrum, is closer to a Jordanian model. According to Pretty functional participation occurs when people form 'groups to meet predetermined objectives. Such involvement tends to be after major decisions have been made. These institutions tend to be dependent on external initiators and facilitators' (Pretty et al., 1995: 61).

While QAF did succeed in playing an important role in mobilizing women at the community level, it was, like other organizations in danger of substituting itself as an agent of change for those they seek to organize (Kabeer, 1994: 256). Mazumdar's appraisal of the Bankura experience shows that similar tensions existed in India:

> Neither the organizations nor the employment to be generated were to be ends in themselves. They were merely to be the means of mobilizing poor rural women to participate more effectively in the wider process of socio-political development, to wrest from society the rights, the dignity and the resources to which they were entitled for their own development, through collective action to increase their voice in development decisions that affected their lives (Mazumdar cited in Kabeer, 1994: 11).

In this light, the sustainability and durability of the women's involvement fostered by QAF's approaches may be questioned. Nevertheless, when asked what would happen if the CDCs shut down, one respondent maintained that 'the women would go ahead and form their own committees' (al-Shahwan interview b). For Kabeer it is only women themselves who can push forward their strategic demands, as the 'political will for taking on more politically controversial issues which address women's strategic gender interests is contingent on women themselves organizing to demand and promote change' (Kabeer, 1994: 91).

It is certainly true that most of QAF's attempts at promoting women's participation in development efforts stemmed from a concern for the practical interests of women, not just as determined by the women themselves, but as deemed appropriate and permissible by the local context. Yet, while serving practical gender interests alone may not result in a structural transformation in gender relations, significant social capital may be generated by the process which in turn may lead to women themselves eventually working towards strategic goals. It has indeed been pointed out that the step from the practical to the strategic must be internalized in order for change to really occur. Nevertheless, it may be argued that in the case of Jordan full participation, as characterized by the concept of 'self-mobilization,' cannot occur and moreover that strategic interests might only be defined and served by women themselves, as the result of a political will other than their own.

The extent to which QAF as an organization truly offered itself as a site of transformatory potential for women may be judged by the degree of responsibility it gave the women to create their own types of involvement, and the extent to which it systematically reformed itself and its own planning processes to allow this to happen (Kabeer, 1994). Beyond that, however, lay other factors, including the communities and society at large. When these factors are viewed in the context of the larger sociopolitical scene which has exerted tremendous pressures and restrictions, manifesting themselves in numerous and complex ways, the prospects for change seem small and the space for the dynamics of transformation limited. Perhaps the greatest challenge for the Fund lies in sustaining often intangible gains, such as those achieved by the efforts described. What must also be recognized is that 'if empowerment entails redressing power imbalances by increasing the "transformative" capacity of the relatively marginalized, then time is needed' (Thompson cited in Guijt and Shah, 1998: 12). In the Fund's work with women, this reality is brought to bear on a continuous basis.

Strategic directions evolve

…Where a space is created for women's own voices to be heard, either through participatory processes of needs identification or else by organizational practices that encourage participation in shaping and changing the 'decisionable agenda,' a different set of needs may come into view (Kabeer, 1994: 230).

How, within the context of the Fund's community-based interactions, did the 'new needs' which gradually emerged, contribute to a more strategically-oriented level of addressing women's interests? As we have argued, QAF's work with women was partly designed to play the role of a catalyst; but the momentum subsequently gathered, particularly in the general political atmosphere of the early 1990s, moved beyond the framework of the Fund. This section attempts to highlight certain linkages in the evolution of a process which helped to raise the level of consciousness within Jordanian society concerning women's strategic interests and to show how the attention brought to bear by the emergence of new mechanisms in turn impacted women through the Fund.

The period leading up to the Fourth World Conference on Women, held in Beijing in 1995 saw a greater focus among international donors on women's issues, as well as an increased interest in the promotion of national mechanisms through which they could be addressed. Hence, the establishment of the Jordanian National Commission for Women (JNCW) in 1992 came as a response by the state to the prevailing climate. It was decided that the secretariat of JNCW should be hosted by QAF – a decision prompted primarily by the special features which the Fund offered as a national NGO with widespread institutional linkages with women based on collective experience in the field. In addition, had it not been for my own long-standing association with the women's sector, largely through the Fund, it is unlikely that I would have been asked by the government to head the new Commission.

One of the first tasks of JNCW was to prepare the Jordanian National Strategy for Women in 1992. This effort was the first of its kind, not only in Jordan but also in the Arab region. The importance of the National Strategy was that it created a focus on the priorities of Jordanian women and that it defined them within the national context. As well as sensitizing society at large to this area of concern, the National Strategy provided a Jordanian 'Platform for Action' prior to the Beijing Conference.

A year-long process of consultations culminated in a national conference in June 1993 at which the National Strategy was officially launched. Here again, men's participation was particularly important in gaining overall approval for a pioneering national effort. Among the six main areas of priority identified by the strategy, was the need to address the role and rights of women in the political, legislative and socio-economic fields (JNCW, 1993). After gaining people's endorsement, the key areas highlighted by the strategy required activating by those elements of civil society and government who were involved. Hence, for the National Strategy to serve its purpose, women had to be mobilized in order to reach as many constituents as possible.

Based on this premise, it was the potential demonstrated by the women's committees within the Fund's CDCs which inspired a new initiative. In order to raise awareness amongst women at the local level about the different components of the strategy, JNCW promoted the formation of women's committees in different parts of the country. These committees were organized in much the same way as the Fund's women's committees, but their first aim was to promote the role of women as outlined in the National Strategy and bring them closer to the arena of public and political life. By 1995 the number of women participating in the 'new committees' had reached 15,751 (JNFW, 1995). In the same year, this initiative culminated in the establishment of the Jordanian National Forum for Women (JNFW).

The creation of the Forum raises significant questions about the degree to which grassroots mobilization in Jordan actually began at the grassroots level. The initiative was certainly pushed from above and in this respect the extent to which it may be called truly participatory is questionable. It was, however, characteristic of Jordan's home-grown model which blends a top-down approach to initiating change with efforts to achieve public acceptance and some degree of positive response – in other words a top-down approach followed by reinterpretation and augmentation at the grassroots level. The Forum had to ultimately resonate with the values and ideals of Jordanian society. It had to earn the approval of, and give a sense of ownership to, both the women and their communities. Here the more mature experience of QAF's women's committees did much to pave the way for the creation of the Forum, despite the differences in some of their objectives and approach.

Political empowerment versus basic needs

The fact that there were two types of women's committees operating in communities was sometimes a source of confusion. While the two were intended to serve different objectives, a certain degree of overlap, in membership particularly, meant that these differences were not always clear to the women themselves. My own role as head of the organizations working with each kind of committee may have added to the confusion. Since I felt that this linkage should not be allowed to compromise the identity and objectives of either mechanism in the field, deliberate efforts were made to maintain a distinction in the overall perception of the committees by emphasizing the more political nature of the Forum's work, as compared to the developmental dimension of QAF's women's committees. Interestingly enough, this distinction resulted in many women feeling disillusioned with the Forum, which they had hoped would also lead to income-generating opportunities (Abu al-Samen interview). This is an important insight into what appears to be the priority of many Jordanian women, and the fact that political activism and mobilization is often viewed as a luxury, far less important than meeting basic needs such as health and nutrition of the family.

Mai Abu al-Samen, a founding member of JNFW, recalls that despite the media attention the Forum received at its inception, and the large numbers of women it attracted, the predominant focus on political and civil rights in many ways deterred Jordanian women from joining (Abu al-Samen interview). As stated previously, the responsibilities of the committees which eventually became JNFW included the dissemination of Jordan's National Strategy for Women at the community level. Moreover, the strategy was intended to be a platform for enhancing women's participation in all spheres, including the economic. As a result, Abu al-Samen recalls, they were often compared with QAF's women's committees, which at least offered the opportunity for some economic activity, and 'didn't just offer talk' (Abu al-Samen interview).

On the other hand, QAF's centres were criticized by members of JNFW for their 'traditional programmes,' which they felt 'did not even try to educate women on their rights or raise their awareness on the political issues and other issues that are more important' (QAF, 1996a, Ghawr al-Safi Municipal Council Member interview). Nevertheless, many Jordanian women still felt that they benefited more from the 'traditional' programmes, which offered some financial incentives, than those which, in their eyes, merely talked about rights and failed to help feed their families. In this respect our efforts failed to illustrate and tangibly demonstrate how economic and political gains were complementary, and should go hand in hand.

While the work of the Fund provided an opportunity for economic activity, JNFW offered an opportunity for a greater political voice.

However, the division of the two continued to be a hindrance both to the full participation of women, and to the creation of a platform which could truly serve their strategic interests. Some grass-root views indicated that such a platform would be well received. Asked how she regarded the role of the Forum, the rural leader in Bir al-Dabbaghat stated 'you are asking about elements that might take our demands to the top? I would expect the National Forum for Women to do it' (QAF, 1998b, Rural Leader interview, Bir al-Dabbaghat 9: 58). In parallel, the rural leader in Mulayh maintained 'I can say that my victory in JNFW elections was due to my work in the CDC. People got to know me through the CDC' (ibid., Rural Leader interview, Mulayh 5: 82). Owing to the balance which I tried to maintain in my own role, given my association with women's issues in general, I was careful not to deliberately promote this kind of coalition. However, there were times when I felt that this decision had in itself been a liability to advancing the overall objectives of the organizations with which I was most directly involved. At the same time, one cannot overlook the fact that an enabling external environment, and a strong political will at the top, are still vital in certain contexts for the encouragement of such participation. Political and economic participation can be assisted, nevertheless, perhaps women themselves must mobilize for a more comprehensive participation to occur.

By the end of the 1990s, it was still too early to evaluate the impact of JNFW. As this women's movement evolved, it might offer Jordanian women a strategic window into increased participation, but this and its possible emergence as a grassroots movement would depend on numerous factors, many of which affect the prospects of change for Jordanian women in general. JNFW had already proved to be an effective mechanism for recognizing leadership potential among women and promoting and nurturing their growth. However, it remained centrally directed and driven. Its future ability to become a vehicle for participation and transformation for women at the grassroots would indicate the extent to which this type of participation could evolve in emerging circumstances.

The beginnings of local level political participation

In 1994, in a bid to support political participation, ninety-nine women were appointed to municipal councils by the government. A number of these were rural leaders and members of QAF's women's committees. Reactions to these appointments were not always positive and initially many of the appointees faced some resistance. Here again, it was felt that women's participation had to be supported by a central decision before it could be supported and enacted of its own accord. Yet although this unprecedented action was not the result of a democratic process, it gave women a window of opportunity to begin pursuing a more political role. The significance of the attempt to integrate women into the arena of local politics was, additionally, that it began to challenge gender perceptions of women's traditional roles. In some cases, women's involvement in the work of the CDCs, served as an effective base for raising their profile and furthering their political involvement. For example, Huda Saudi, the rural leader of Hisban centre, acquired some of the skills and knowledge that she needed in her new position as a municipal council member with the CDC (QAF, 1996a).

The appointment of women to local councils, served as an important stepping stone for Jordanian women to begin to envisage themselves as playing a greater role in the lives of their communities, and indeed for Jordanian society to begin to accept such an involvement. In subsequent municipal elections, some women actually ran. Among them were members of QAF's women's committees. In the 1995 municipal elections, fifteen women ran and ten were elected; in 1999, forty-two women ran while only eight succeeded (JNCW, 1999). Despite these modest results, this was a clear indication that women had been encouraged to attempt a more strategic involvement through political empowerment.

A member of QAF's women's committees, who won a seat in the municipal elections of 1995, states: 'The idea of nominating myself started at the community development centre, as the woman who was appointed for the first time in Hisban was the rural leader.' Before becoming a member of the women's committee, she had been involved in the vocational training programmes at the centre. She used her contacts at the centre as a base for going through the election process: 'Through the centre, I got the chance to know more women. I also got the chance to introduce myself and to know a large proportion of the women of Hisban' (QAF, 1996a, Hisban Municipal Council Member interview).

The same woman claims that, once elected, she faced resistance by members of the council. However, she maintains that this grew less with time. Her focus was mainly on health services in the community. It is interesting to note that she did not attribute the limitations on her role as a council member to her gender, but instead, to the role of the municipal council, which was to 'provide basic services to the community.' Criticism was levelled against her by the women of the community, and she felt that this was because they expected different things from her. While she felt that she might help in providing a library or a park, the women 'wanted me to help in the women's rights movement. For me, it is still unclear what the situation of the women's rights movement is. The centre trained women, educated them, raised their awareness through the educational and awareness programmes. But through the municipal council, as a provider of infrastructure services, I believe that I can help women with issues regarding their environment ...' (ibid.). Apparently, this councillor felt that the centre was more of a site for the social transformation for women than the council which had other obligations.

Interviews with some of the appointees at that time indicated, however, that certain notions regarding the role of women in local politics still persisted. When and if these women were finally accepted, they and their communities viewed their roles as pertaining mainly to issues of women and children's health, education and the environment, as well as services provided within the community. Often, however, this served to increase social acceptance of women's participation in the elections, precisely because the women were seen to be concerned with issues that were different to those of the men, and therefore did not impinge upon them (Abu al-Samen interview). Despite its shortcomings, it could be said that QAF's experience had shown how development efforts that targeted women could slowly begin to promote change at the local level, and might eventually lead to greater political participation by women at the national level. Nevertheless, while prevailing attitudes and conditions within the social environment remained an obstacle, government support would, as in other spheres, continue to be a necessary factor in promoting women's political participation.

Conclusion

Jordan's experience in initiating strategic changes for women at the grass-roots, and the difficulties the country has faced, is indicative of many things. It highlights some of the dilemmas societies face in general when fostering participation in the absence of a tradition of 'civil society' in its modern sense. It also shows how it is sometimes difficult for women's participation to grow without some kind of political will and support at a higher level. Moreover, Jordan's experience illustrates that notions of participation as they are generally defined and accepted in the West are not necessarily shared by women in a traditional Arab context. There is, therefore, an innate contradiction and paradox, which development efforts that seek to be participatory will often encounter when they attempt to bring about a change in the attitudes and socio-cultural practices of communities.

As such, the Jordanian experience of women's participation may always be 'home-grown' to the extent that it will always have to cater to the specificity of its own socio-cultural norms, hierarchies and the gender relations that flow from them. Here again, if participation of any kind is to be increased, Jordanian women themselves will have to play a greater role in defining their own strategic interests. Gradually, the importance of an integrated and holistic approach became clearer. For instance, JNFW realized that it could not promote women's rights and political participation in isolation, without trying to address their economic needs. QAF also came to realize that while it served as an effective mechanism for identifying women leaders at the local level, it would have to initiate multiple strategies for promoting and integrating women's participation there.

Municipal councils are an important venue for grassroots partici-pation and civil society involvement. However, the lack of resources and the nature of their work have limited their role in this respect. As council members, the scope offered to women stems from these factors, as much as issues related to their gender. Indeed, any attempt to analyse women's participation in Jordan must take into consideration the factors that affect Jordanian society as a whole.

In addition to societal attitudes that impede women's political partici-pation, it is important not to underestimate the significance of access to resources in assessing the advances of Jordanian women. Studies have revealed that both in parliamentary and municipal elections, discrimina-tory attitudes were not the only factor behind women's failure to reach decision-making positions. Women's inability to access sufficient resources for their campaigns was a major hindrance to their success (PBWRC, 1997).

At the end of the decade, the effects of structural adjustment still con-tinued to impose the harshest of living conditions on an increasingly large section of the Jordanian population, resulting in further marginalization for certain groups. These conditions created their own restrictions on the participation of women, and did not foster a climate in which access to decision-making can be increased. High unemployment meant that men were given priority in hiring practices in the work place, while the absence of political activity meant that there was little opportunity on the political front for change in the situation of women. In the absence of sufficient opportunities for women's self-mobilization, many of the changes that actually occurred could be ascribed to political will on the part of the state, or to the agency of the Fund and similar mechanisms.

Political will may challenge traditional societal attitudes and may promote certain changes that might not otherwise occur. Nevertheless, political will and any other strategies with a national dimension also reflect public attitudes, perceptions and priorities. Such is the case with women and gender issues in Jordan.

In this context, attempts to foster gender equality fell short of expectations, and would probably continue to do so while the political will remained insufficient and public support was still lacking. Complex political factors and a stagnant economic climate discouraged a process whereby traditional notions could be challenged and gender roles and relations reassessed. As such, women would still be excluded from the very platforms from which they could advocate such change and consequently they remained largely unable to serve their own strategic goals. In this context, the interests of Jordanian women are perhaps better served through vehicles such as JNCW as well as many NGOs. While the limitations on these organizations cannot be overlooked, in responding to the external environment their roles are subjected to continuous reinterpretation. Thus, through this evolving process, it is quite feasible that alternative approaches will gradually arise.

6

The Fund in Transition

During the 1990s structural adjustment signalled the beginning of an economic transition which placed a heavy burden on different sectors of Jordanian state and society. Significant pressures were involved for both state organizations and NGOs who were trying to offset the effects of economic reforms. The process of political liberalization, also a feature of the 1990s, represented another dimension of transition. At times, these processes combined to create additional tensions, particularly as the prospect of tangible benefits anticipated after the Peace Treaty with Israel failed to materialize. The problems that have confronted, and continue to confront the Fund during the 1990s mirrored the dilemmas of the country as a whole. This chapter discusses the way these problems have affected the Fund, the approaches it has adopted within the context of transition, and the directions it took at this time of change.

The Realities of Poverty and Unemployment

In 1988, as the country's economic crisis peaked, forcing a policy of structural adjustment the following year, socio-economic problems intensified for large segments of the Jordanian population. A Ministry of Social Development study of poverty, published in 1993, concluded that 21.3 per cent of families were living in absolute poverty while 6.6 per cent were living in abject poverty;[1] a notable increase compared to the findings of a study conducted in 1989 (Jordan, 1993c; al-Saqour et al., 1989).[2] The

1. People falling under the abject poverty line are those whose incomes are not enough to cover their food requirements, while those falling under the absolute poverty line are those whose incomes are not enough to cover food, shelter, clothing, education, health and transportation (al-Saqour et al., 1989).

2. The results of the 1989 study on poverty showed that 18.7 per cent of families were living in absolute poverty and 1.5 per cent of families were living in abject poverty.

185

government tried to minimize the effects of its stringent structural adjustment policies on the poor by providing social security and welfare through the National Aid Fund, as well as loans to low-income families and individuals through the Development and Employment Fund. However, the severity of the overall economic situation meant that government organizations could not reach many people in need, especially in rural areas. Consequently, NGOs such as QAF began to assume a more direct role in supporting state efforts, through gap-filling activities aimed at relieving some of the prevailing hardships.

The National Philanthropy Campaign

In 1991, in response to the Gulf Crisis, which saw thousands of evacuees and returnees flooding the country, straining an already weakened support system, the Fund launched its first National Philanthropy Campaign.[3] The initial aim of this drive was to provide immediate relief to families suffering from economic difficulties. The campaign, based on the Islamic values of solidarity and support, and emphasizing the importance of cooperation and participation, is organized each year during the Holy Month of Ramadan when people give *zakat* (donations) to the needy.[4] Many well-known Islamic and public figures participate as members of its Central Committee in Amman, responsible for overall planning and organization at the national level. Its subcommittees in the governorates, representing different public and private sector organizations as well as civil society, plan local activities. Hence the Campaign is a truly national effort.

Donations and direct participation in the Campaign's activities come from a variety of sources, including the Ministry of Awqaf (Religious Affairs), the Amman Municipality, the Ministry of Agriculture, GUVS, the Muslim Brotherhood, the Chamber of Commerce, the Chamber of Industry, the health sector, universities, the banking sector, the media, as well as youth movements such as the Boy Scouts and Girl Guides and different clubs (QAF, 1993a, 1993b, 1993c, 1995). Its broad outreach and inclusive approach, mean that many other bodies besides QAF, including GUVS and the Ministry of Social Development, referred needy people to the Campaign so that they can draw on its various means of support (QAF, 1994b, 1994c).

At first the Campaign was a largely charitable enterprise; but from 1993

---

3. *Himlat al-birr wa'l-ihsan.*
4. See chapter 4, note 3.

onwards the focus began to shift to supporting income-generation in order to improve people's socio-economic conditions (QAF, 1993d). Some private companies specified that their contributions should be directed to development projects rather than to charitable handouts (QAF, 1994d). While its activities peak during Ramadan, the Goodwill Campaign (as it was renamed in English in 1997) has gradually evolved into an all-year institutional effort (QAF, 1998d) that consists of two mutually reinforcing approaches. Welfare measures give help to poor families through in-kind assistance such as food packages, winter provisions and clothes; medical services including free operations and tests, as well as equipment for the disabled; educational support for poor children in the form of school supplies and uniforms, and, in the case of university students, scholarships. The development dimension offers equipment and financial resources to individuals and families to assist them in starting their own small businesses or other income-generating activities.

Over the years, the Goodwill Campaign extended its outreach to cover many different parts of the country. By the end of 1999, it had touched the lives of more than a quarter of a million people through in-kind assistance or income-generating project support. In addition, 378 NGOs were helped to carry out their own projects (JOHUD, 2000b). The Campaign had also made a significant contribution to promoting solidarity and reinforcing social capital throughout the country, as reflected in the media: 'The campaign is doing humane and noble work which citizens support, welcome, and give great attention because it is sustainable' (ad-Dustour, 1999b).

For the Fund, the Goodwill Campaign represented one approach to dealing with poverty through popular participation and immediate intervention. Other developmental approaches were more long-term, requiring greater investment in training and support. The following discussion looks at different methods adopted by the Fund to respond to the needs of local communities through job creation and income-generating projects.

Different approaches to income-generation and job creation

From early 1985, working through the CDCs, the Fund began to address the economic needs of people in local communities through small-scale agricultural activities and projects. For instance, in some vicinities the Fund established greenhouses with the aim of encouraging families to use more advanced agricultural methods through which to start their own income-generating projects (QAF, 1985a; 1986e; 1987c). By 1988 QAF had moved into other areas, helping women to use their existing skills and local resources to generate income for their families through craft-based enterprise with rug weaving, basketry, embroidery, sewing and other activities (QAF, 1988c). Eventually, a need was seen to establish production units within the CDCs which would enable women who had received vocational training in specific skills such as sewing and knitting to use these crafts productively. Other small projects were also launched at the CDCs for which QAF provided the training and sought out the necessary funding from donors. These included the production of dairy commodities, fruit and vegetable preservation, animal husbandry, industrial sewing, flower cultivation, as well as ceramics and tapestry-making. In 1989, around 548 families benefited from these projects (QAF, 1989f). The Fund's efforts to improve the economic condition of the poor relied on a comprehensive approach. Thus, income-generating projects were not isolated from other social development interventions such as capacity-building, awareness-raising and gender empowerment.

Although these income-generating projects promoted social as well as economic benefits, they also gave rise to new problems. The most obvious was that participants often regarded them as an opportunity for a permanent job which they then depended on the Fund to maintain. QAF, on the other hand, was faced with the additional burden of running a financially sustainable enterprise. In November 1990, supported by the Canadian government, the Fund opened a rug weaving project at Mleih satellite centre employing seventeen young women (QAF, 1988d). Although the women were trained before starting the project, the rugs they produced were well below market standards and were consequently difficult to sell. Despite its limited experience in this area, QAF had taken on the responsibility of selling the rugs. But with a glut of traditional rugs in the market, its already inadequate commercial skills were further put to the test. The Fund introduced measures to upgrade the quality and design of products, and to encourage greater community responsibility for the project (QAF, 1992d). However, the community was unwilling or unable to accommodate the Fund's suggestions and the project continued to face financial problems which the Fund had to absorb. In spite of the financial losses, the Fund chose to keep the project going because it gave the women a source of income and, in addition, because the fact that for women to work in the centre had become accepted was a gain which the Fund wanted to sustain.

In another situation in 1991, QAF was approached by a local NGO in al-Mafraq to help it establish a dairy production centre by providing financial and technical support. The NGO, the Khsha' al-Slateen Social

Development Society (KSSDS), was already running a small cheese production venture, marketing some of its product locally, and it wanted to
expand (JOHUD, 2000c). Since the Fund viewed support for small local
NGOs as part of its role, it prepared a feasibility study which was submitted to the Industrial Development Bank with a request for a loan (ibid.).
An agreement was signed in November 1992 between QAF and KSSDS
stipulating that the NGO would be responsible for production, sales and
marketing while QAF would supervise the instalment of the machinery,
train the staff, provide quality control, and stand as a guarantor of the
loan (QAF, 1992e). However, a subsequent evaluation made it clear that
KSSDS was unsuccessful in its attempt to market increased volumes of
cheese, 'with all of its working capital tied up in stock,' and the project
was becoming a losing venture (QAF, 1994e).[5] As the KSSDS was unable to
meet the payments on its loan, QAF was obliged to take over the project
and to try and make up the loss.

Experiences of this kind raise questions about the Fund's ability to
transfer to the community the skills necessary for people to manage
large-scale income generating projects. Such projects are often unsuccessful because they are incompatible with local needs or capacities. Additional
burdens are sometimes placed on communities by the introduction of
sophisticated technologies and a lack of operational know-how due to
inadequate training. Furthermore, limited marketing skills as well as limited local and national markets hamper income-generating efforts. These
selected examples show some of the initial problems faced by the Fund
in its attempts to implement income-generating projects in local settings.
Frequently, the communities viewed QAF as a 'parent' organization that
was not only obliged to help meet local needs, but also to absorb any
financial losses incurred by the projects. On the other hand, QAF often initiated projects without proper feasibility and market studies, and without
giving due consideration to the particularities of the local context.

Nevertheless, the deteriorating economic situation at the beginning of
the 1990s meant that income-generating projects steadily became a major
'growth industry' for the Fund (JOHUD, 2000c). Through the CDCs, the
Fund was keenly aware of the serious hardships faced by the majority of
its target groups. However, our projects were often not well planned or
properly designed and were not always financially sustainable. In many

---

5. Prior to the project's expansion, KSSDS produced 1,500–2,500 kgs of
cheese annually; in 1994 it produced 7,400 kgs, out of which only 1,100 kgs were
sold (JOHUD, 2000c).

ways the Fund was taking on more than its capacity could handle. Sub-sequently, as certain projects expanded and gained national significance the Fund would face the need to hire staff with better business skills and more sophisticated management experience.[6] The implications of such issues will be examined presently in relation to the changes in approaches which, like the rest of the country, the Fund was required to make within the context of the transitional process of the 1990s.

Alleviating unemployment and poverty through credit

From 1992 the Fund adopted credit programmes as a new way of promoting income-generation for the poor. A grant from the Industrial Development Bank[7] was used to establish a revolving loan fund (RLF) that would be self-sustaining and would preserve its loan base. The loan would be used to help unemployed or low-income individuals or families to start or expand micro-businesses (QAF, 1992f). QAF viewed the extension of credit as part of an integrated process through which it could 'enhance the self-confidence of individuals through training and upgrading their managerial, financial and technical skills' (QAF, 1997d: 1).

Its large outreach through the CDC network meant that the Fund was considered a suitable intermediary agency for loans in rural areas. Conse-quently, in 1994 the Development and Employment Fund (DEF) signed an agreement to allocate QAF an interest-free loan for the purposes of

---

6. An example is the Date Palm Plantation Project in Aqaba started in 1991 in cooperation with the Aqaba Regional Authority. The aim was to use local resources and improve the environment as well as to provide job opportunities (QAF, 1991c). By 1997, around 650 dunums of land were planted with high quality palm tree selections while members of the local community were trained in the production of handicrafts made from by-products of palms (QAF, 1997c). The National Ceramics Project was established in 1990 to train and provide job opportunities for young Jordanian artists, and to restore the Arab/Islamic cultural heritage through the high quality production of ceramics (ibid.). The project was expanded in 1993 to include the Qwara ceramics factory which produces more commercial items. In 1996, the National Ceramics Project was further developed to become Beit al-Bawadi, the Fund's design, training and production centre. The showroom at Beit al-Bawadi acts as the commercial outlet for all ceramics and crafts produced through the Fund's projects (JOHUD, 1999a).

7. An agreement was signed between QAF and the Industrial Development Bank (IDB) in 1991 (QAF, 1991d), in which the Bank gave QAF a JD 30,000 grant to be used as revolving loans to set up income-generating projects.

on-lending (Jordan, 1998d).[8] By 1996 QAF was running four main types of lending programmes with different loan criteria based on donor conditions and the Fund's own internal policies regarding credit schemes (QAF, 1997d). In this way, as recognized by a World Bank report, QAF became one of the main providers of microcredit in the country (Brandsma and Khayatt, 1996).

One issue that had to be addressed when introducing credit schemes into local communities was the subject of interest. In Islam, any amount paid on top of a loan is known as *riba* and is prohibited. However, in Islamic finance there are other means for recovering the financial transactional costs, including *murabaha* which involves the resale of goods to a borrower with profit and is viewed as trading (Syam, 1999; Dhumale and Sapcanin, n.d.). Like other Jordanian organizations, QAF used *murabaha* for some of its credit schemes and in others charged 'administrative fees' as a means of recovering some of its costs (QAF, 1991e).

Generally, alongside credit, the Fund offered the training necessary to ensure the success of any small income-generating project. For example, during the pilot phase of the Rural Women Groups and Credit Program funded by UNIFEM,[9] the project manager first trained the women in confidence-building, women's rights and how to conduct a feasibility study. Since some of the women were illiterate, innovative approaches were called for while carrying out the feasibility study for their sheep-raising project: 'We drew the sheep, we photocopied the money, and we drew the things they would need, water, the products etc. I sat with them and said, "okay, let's think about your project … how much money do you need to buy the sheep?"' (al-Shahwan interview a). The training was an important factor in raising the skills of this particular target group, and also of determining which women had the confidence to take a loan and manage their own small income-generating project.

---

8. This agreement came in response to EU conditions that DEF should involve NGOs in providing credit to people in rural areas. In 1996, DEF signed subsequent agreements with the General Union of Voluntary Societies (GUVS) and Noor al-Hussein Foundation (NHF) (Jordan, 1998d).

9. The project started in 1994 and was funded by UNIFEM as a three year project targeting women in local communities. Its main objective was 'to foster the economic and social empowerment of grassroots women working in agriculture by ensuring that women have a direct control over the product of their labour' (Bseiso, 1996: 11). A total of 126 women benefited from receiving credit (JOHUD, 1999b) and were trained in livestock and milk processing, and project management.

On the whole, the socio-economic impact of the project on the women and their families was 'positive,' with the women reporting a 'better standard of living, better time management of their activities ... they became more decisive, and the ties between the family members were improved' (Bseiso, 1996: 8). The project was nevertheless criticized by the same consultant for its low outreach and lack of financial sustainability due to the low level of interest rates (the 2.5 per cent flat administrative fee charged for the participants) (ibid.). However, the project manager had a different perspective: she felt that even with the low interest rate many women were still excluded from the project due to their inability to make the repayments and provide a suitable loan guarantee (al-Shahwan interview a). It was concerns such as these which QAF had to take into account in operating loan schemes in poor communities and among people who had few skills and little access to resources – in other words its main target groups.

Although the Fund's income-generating activities did not necessarily achieve sustainability, they did help to ease some of the economic problems suffered by local communities. As such, the provision of subsidized credit for low-income groups was in line with national efforts to combat poverty and unemployment. Subsequently, however, as new donor trends emerged, the effectiveness of such approaches came into question. This issue will be highlighted later through the microfinance case study.

Negotiating Donor Approaches

By the mid to late 1990s, a shift in donor priorities was beginning to take place, affecting QAF's access to funding. New considerations had to be taken into account in the Fund's relationships with donors, as well as with its own operational methods in general. Two different yet interconnected threads underpin this section. Firstly, there is the linkage between the economic and political dimension of the New Policy Agenda, through which donors promoted democratization and liberalization alongside economic reform, good governance and market competition. Influenced by the international conferences of the 1990s, governments and NGOs increasingly focused on broader development issues such as population growth, the environment, gender equality and human rights. The changed donor agenda of this decade impacted at the local level on partnerships and projects, as well as on funding allocations. Consequently, whereas in the 1980s and early 1990s the Fund's programmes were mostly geared to service provision and income-generation, from the second half of the 1990s QAF began to concentrate more on issues related to the sustainability of projects, as well as the sustainability of the organization itself. Secondly, following the Gulf crisis and the reduction in levels of assistance from the Arab region, QAF, like the country as a whole, became more reliant on funding from Western donors. Arab funds received by QAF were mostly in the form of unconditional grants. But the new international donors had their own priorities and conditions, as well as their own approaches. Cooperation with such donors implied that mediation, and in some instances a reinterpretation of approaches was required of the Fund in order to adapt donor priorities to local realities.

An example of how the Fund was able to strike a balance between achieving its objectives and catering to the interests of its donors, as well as the needs of its local partner, is the Eco-Tourism project. The project, initiated in March 1996, was carried out in cooperation with Fundaçion CODESPA, a Spanish NGO, and funded by the Spanish government. QAF was initially approached by CODESPA with the idea of launching an environmentally-friendly project that would offer tours in Wadi Rum. Although the Fund's mandate did not focus specifically on the environment or tourism, the project would provide much needed job opportunities, and was therefore in keeping with the goal of economically activating communities in rural areas. After discussions with the Spanish NGO and the local community, a social development component was also added (QAF, 1997e). The open negotiations and successful partnership between CODESPA, QAF and the local community led to the project becoming fully sustainable after three years (al-Ustah interview; JOHUD, 2000d). Furthermore, the flexibility of the partnership between the Spanish NGO and QAF, which allowed for a new component to be added to the project, created a comprehensive development approach which had a favourable outcome for the local inhabitants.

Working with Northern NGOs

As many bilateral donors began to channel their aid through NGOs, the opportunities for cooperation and partnership among Jordanian and foreign NGOs increased. For the Fund, one of the main advantages of working with Northern NGOs (NNGOs), as opposed to working directly with bilateral donors, was that NNGOs understand the agenda and conditions of their donor counterparts and are able to lobby effectively to secure funding. In the Fund's experience, this kind of relationship 'has been very successful, its advantage is that it expedites the process. It's much faster than bilateral cooperation' (Zakhary interview).

In 1994 the Fund entered into partnership with EuroCom (Gesells-chaft für Europäische Kommunikation e.V.), a German NGO, to carry out a training and technical assistance project (JETT) for a wide range of Jordanian NGOs. The relationship with EuroCom 'facilitated the process of reporting and getting funding as European NGOs are familiar with the European Union policies and requirements' (Haj-Issa interview b). EuroCom submitted a proposal to the EU for a second phase (1996–1998), emphasizing QAF's need for continued support and stating that additional time was required to transfer technical skills and concepts to project participants (EuroCom, 1996). Having used this justification in its 1996 report, EuroCom was able to convince the EU to grant funding for the second phase. A third extension was given later to accommodate delays in project activities (EuroCom, 1998).

Despite the advantages of cooperation with foreign NGOs, certain disadvantages can also arise in the form of uneven working relationships. The Fund is often required to submit detailed work plans and budgets to a foreign partner. However, there is no reciprocal transparency, and the Fund's inadequate knowledge of the internal workings of its partner has sometimes compromised its own position with local counterparts in the field. For example, in March 1998 the Fund submitted a proposal for a Reproductive Health and Community Development initiative to a leading US-based organization subcontracted by USAID to conduct family planning programmes in Jordan. After two revisions of the proposal, numerous meetings with Amman representatives, and fax communications concerning budgetary refinements (QAF, 1998e), the Fund was given a verbal agreement to prepare the target community in al-Tafila. However, as the selection of local social workers was about to begin, QAF received notification from the NGO's head office that the project was rejected 'due to budgetary constraints' (QAF, 1998f). In such situations, with expectations raised at the local level, organizational credibility is diminished, and time and energy must be spent to regain the trust of local partners in the field.

The dilemma of funding

The link between the promotion of a dynamic civil society and the New Policy Agenda was reflected in Jordan by increased donor interest in civil society institutions which target areas such as human rights, women's advocacy and the environment. Not only did NGOs involved in such issues have direct access to donors as a result of specific government agreements with multilateral donors such as the European Union (see chapter 2), but donors have more actively sought out a wider range of local NGO-partnerships: 'I heard this from a donor myself, "We are a democratic nation and we need to work to enhance everybody's role in this country. So we need to move onto financing small NGOs"' (Zakhary interview). While this trend has led to a national debate over whether or not elements of Jordanian civil society were being co-opted by Western agendas (see chapter 2), the level of competition among Jordanian NGOs also grew, putting larger organizations such as the Fund in positions of greater financial vulnerability.

In the past it seemed that donors had certain 'systemic biases favoring the development of intermediary organizations' as part of the process of 'scaling up' and increasing institutional capacity to manage large volumes of aid monies (Davies, 1997: 614). By the late 1990s, however, in Jordan at least, this view had changed in favour of supporting smaller NGOs. In contrast to the period from the early to mid-1990s, in which donor coop-eration had helped to scale up QAF's operations, during the late 1990s the Fund has faced a challenge to its institutional sustainability as aid money was diverted to other areas to satisfy new conditions and agendas.

The hard reality for the Fund in 1999 was that donor support had decreased in overall terms, was less accessible and came with more strin-gent conditions. Not least of these was that even with projects that had found donor support, the Fund was contributing, in cash and in kind, anywhere between 20–40 per cent of the total costs.

Partnerships with Western donors had other implications for the Fund, in terms of relationships with the Fund, and also between the Fund and its clients in the field. In order to secure project funding and to be able to work collaboratively with its donor partners, the Fund had to demonstrate a willingness to hire additional English-speaking Western graduates with specialist skills who require higher pay than locally trained Arabic speak-ers. For example, in November 1996, the Fund signed an agreement with USAID to establish a Marketing and Export Development Unit for its ceramic projects. Six staff with marketing and production management skills were recruited at salaries above those offered by QAF for this level. In this instance the rates, competitive with the private sector, were budgeted within the line item and therefore did not lead to additional costs for the Fund (QAF, 1997f; JOHUD, 1999c). However, although it is recognized that projects of this kind are not open-ended, and their staff are only contracted for specific periods, the fact that those paid by USAID project funding received much higher salaries than the Fund's own staff created sensitivities within the organization. In another instance, on a CIDA-funded project two externally recruited business advisers were recruited upon the international manager's recommendation and offered salaries nearly double that of a staff member at the same level who had been with QAF for three years (QAF, 1997g). Again, while this may have been necessary to secure staff with the required skills, the wage differential affected the morale of other personnel. Moreover, in this particular case, the salaries were part of the Fund's in-kind contribution. The added financial burden was more than the organization could afford given that the project itself was not yet sustainable. In these situations, the Fund would have preferred to allocate a member of its own staff to undertake the responsibility on a part-time basis thereby cutting costs and reinforcing the Fund's drive towards organizational sustainability. The involvement of foreign project managers or consultants in hiring practices can sometimes blur the lines of authority and infringe upon the Fund's own internal operations (Nusseir interview b).

Overall, these new processes, designed to accommodate donor considerations, may result in the Fund's organizational culture moving closer to that of its donors, and further away from its own cultural base (Edwards and Hulme, 1995). Here we come face to face with the issue of 'he who pays the piper calls the tune' (Hulme and Edwards, 1997: 8). At the same time, it must be asked how far a local NGO should go to secure funding at the expense of maintaining its organizational equilibrium? Our experience has shown that when donors channel funds through the organization, their expectations also increase. Donors stress the need for organizational sustainability, including the sustainability of development projects and the Fund is working to achieve these goals. However, these objectives cannot quickly be achieved, especially in view of reduced financial support and project demands such as staffing criteria.

For the most part, QAF has managed to balance donor conditions and approaches with the values and needs of the grassroots it serves. This has required an ability to work with a variety of approaches without losing touch with the goals of the organization. However, in some situations time has been needed to understand and negotiate donor conditions, especially when doubts are cast on tested development methods. The following case study highlights this problem by examining microfinance 'best practice,' introduced to Jordan in the mid-1990s and the response of the Fund to this donor-driven approach.

The Microfinance Case Study

The concept of sustainable microfinance, also referred to as 'best practice,' was presented nationally for the first time in Amman in March 1997 at the Jordan Microfinance Conference sponsored by the World Bank, UNDP, USAID and European Union, six weeks after the Microcredit Summit in Washington. The goal of the conference was to 'promote dialogue among micro-finance practitioners and donors with the aim of building a sustainable micro-finance practice in Jordan' (*Jordan Times*, 1997b: 8). QAF staff members attended the conference, together with representatives of government and non-government organizations and local banks. At the national level, Jordan had recently launched the World Bank-proposed Social Productivity Programme (SPP) to combat poverty and unemployment. Part of the SPP package included a strategy to develop micro and small enterprises by a variety of means, including technical assistance to microfinancing intermediaries (JOHUD, 1999d). The design and implementation of the microfinance component was in accordance with donor-defined microfinance best practice (ibid.). This component, primarily financed by USAID, was implemented through such endeavours as the Sustainable Microfinance Initiative (SMI) of the AMIR programme[10] and would also involve the participation of NGOs and other institutions.

While there is no set definition of microfinance best practice it is understood to include different approaches to credit that ensure effective outreach and sustainability, both operational and financial. Some best practice principles include charging an interest rate that covers operational and financial costs including loan defaults; achieving a certain scale through the number of active clients and by means of small-size short-term repeat loans; promoting wide outreach and quick accessible credit; and separating social programmes and microfinance services (Brandsma and Chaouali cited in Dhumale et al., 1999: 4; UNDP, 1997c).

Some argue that the Middle East and North Africa is the region 'least exposed to microfinance best practice' with most of the microfinance programmes lodged in larger parent organizations that provide social services (Dhumale et al., 1999: 1–3). Since the concept of sustainable microfinance was relatively new to Jordan, doubts were raised among some development practitioners about its suitability within an Arab/Islamic culture. To some, the experience of Asia and Latin America where

10. The Access to Microfinance and Improved Implementation of Policy Reform (AMIR), a four-year project for Jordan funded by the U.S. Agency for International Development (USAID), was launched in 1998.

women micro-entrepreneurs sold items on the street was 'inappropriate for our society' (Nusseir interview a). However, others were 'one hundred per cent convinced that it (microfinance best practice) can work in Jordan' and that 'the economic situation in Jordan is making people more accepting of otherwise unacceptable practices' (Sharaf interview). The main regional institution held up as an example of successful microfinance was the Alexandria Business Association in Egypt, and in Jordan the primary experience was with the Jordanian Women's Development Society (Wade interview).[11]

By the late 1990s, the Fund was operating a large portfolio of subsidized credit schemes amounting to nearly JD 4 million in accordance with the criteria and conditions of their extenders.[12] The portfolio targeted various groups such as women, farmers, potential small entrepreneurs, the handicapped, and the poor in general (QAF, 1997d; JOHUD, 2000f). In late 1996, QAF established the Small Business Development Centre (SBDC) in association with Organisation Canadienne pour la Solidarité et le Développement (OCSD) and with funding from the Canadian International Development Agency (CIDA). The aim was to provide financial services, primarily credit, and non-financial services such as training and consultancy to low-income entrepreneurs, with a particular emphasis on women (QAF, 1997h; JOHUD, 2000f). It was also envisaged that, in the long term, all of the Fund's lending schemes would be consolidated under one umbrella through SBDC (QAF, 1998g; JOHUD, 2000f).

The introduction of new microfinance techniques to Jordan as part of a donor-led approach to alleviating poverty through credit was aimed at stimulating the economic involvement of those defined as 'the entrepreneurial poor.'[13] The premise of donor aid had begun to reflect a leaning

---

11. JWDS began its operations in 1996 by taking over Save the Children's Group Guarantee Lending and Savings pilot programme, and was offering women micro-entrepreneurs small repeat loans using group guarantees. In December 1999, JWDS operations were transferred to Microfund for Women, a non-profit company registered with the Ministry of Trade and Industry (Microfund for Women, 2000).

12. From January 1992 until June 1999 QAF disbursed JD 3.8 million worth of loans (Jordan, 1999b: 31).

13. Although this term is problematic, according to Garson there are two categories of poor: the entrepreneurial poor who with appropriate assistance could create economic activities that would bring them closer to or above the poverty line; and the non-entrepreneurial poor who either lack the skills, capacities or means to conduct any 'meaningful economic activity' (Garson, 1996: 6–7).

towards the values and practice of the business sector (Fowler, 1998). As the case study reveals, this shift created different dilemmas for the Fund in operating its credit schemes. First of all, the specific focus of certain donors on non-subsidized credit or microfinance 'best practice' to the exclusion of other approaches created a concern within the organization that donor conditions for credit funding would undermine the Fund's own integrated approach to development. While adopting the prevailing donor trend could lead to greater funding opportunities, there could be a cost both to our partners in the field and to the organization's own comprehensive development programmes, of which credit was just one component.

The new approach based on 'best practice' maintained that the provision of credit to any poor person who was able to repay a loan was a sufficient intervention to combat poverty (Rogaly cited in Garson, 1996: 10–11). However, in different ways, this assumption conflicted with the Fund's established income-generating approach which viewed credit as a means to an end, rather than the only way of promoting activities which increased the income of the poor. A similar view is put forward by an international development specialist who has worked with the Fund:

> I don't believe that if you are poor, you are already a potential entrepreneur. This parallelism doesn't exist for me. If you are poor, you need to be helped … The philosophical principle which is behind microcredit is that money is the only solution: 'if you are poor it is because you don't have access to money – if you have money you will solve your own poverty'. This is a new economic liberalism. And history tells us this is not true (Rodriguez interview).

Staff in QAF were split on the issue of whether one method should be adopted to the exclusion of another, or whether both subsidized and non-subsidized credit schemes could be successfully implemented by the organization either with or without the creation of a separate microfinance institution (MFI).

The microfinance divide

While the sustainable microfinance approach had its proponents in Jordan, it was also perceived to be biased in favour of those described as 'the entrepreneurial poor' who have the skills to start and sustain a micro-enterprise and repay high interest rate loans, as opposed to 'the non-entrepreneurial poor' who require a different kind of assistance: 'During the USAID presentation on their micro-finance programme in

Jordan, I raised the issue of the business approach and the development approach to micro-lending, and said that USAID is promoting the business approach as the only viable one. I am afraid it is not the only viable approach' (Bahous interview). The position taken by Jorgen Lissner, the UNDP resident representative in Amman at the time, was that while microfinance should be seen as a feasible option, it was not necessarily suited to all situations and therefore other credit approaches should not be discounted: 'What I am saying is the sustainable microfinance approach is respectable and acceptable in a society if it is seen as an option ... But the moment you begin to cast aspersions on the subsidized approach and the grant approach – I mean there are people below the poverty line for whom sustainable microfinance is simply not the option' (Lissner interview).

The Pilot Study conducted in 1997 revealed that QAF's field staff and beneficiaries had clear opinions about loan programmes. Whether with regard to beneficiaries, the size of loans, interest rates or other issues, there was an obvious bias in the field towards offering poor people loans. In responding to a question about the selection of potential beneficiaries of loans, one rural leader said: 'The poorest who are needy, but at the same time the ones we feel are willing to sustain a project' (QAF, 1998b, Rural Leader interview, Rawdat Basma 2: 212). There was also a clear preference in the field for larger-sized loans. A member of an NGO which runs one of the Fund's centres stated: 'You give someone two thousand dinars and tell him to make a project ... we are fooling ourselves! Just as if you are giving someone a hundred dinars and telling him "go buy a car!" Is it possible that you can get a car for a hundred dinars?' (ibid., Member of NGO interview, al-Zubairiya 10: 169). Interest rates were also a major area of concern in the field: 'People in rural areas shun what is called *riba*, because they consider it taboo, it is sinful' (ibid., Head of NGO interview, al-Zubairiya 10: 143).

Among QAF staff at headquarters there were also differing opinions. Some felt that the Fund's current target groups could not afford high interest loans,[14] and should not be abandoned in favour of a business approach simply in order to meet donor conditions. There was also apprehension that in the future the Fund might eventually be asked by donors to give up subsidized loans once they adopted best practice. Considering the large portfolio which the Fund was operating through subsidized credit, such

---

14. For example, some institutions in Jordan charge an annual flat interest rate of 22.8 per cent and 24 per cent (Cooperative Housing Foundation, 2000; Microfund for Women, 2000).

a change would have serious ramifications for the majority of QAF's borrowers. Others felt that, even if the Fund implemented both approaches and targeted different groups, it was still questionable whether the 'best practice' methodology of separating financial services from other development interventions could reduce poverty and serve overall development goals (Abu-Rish interview a). Views outside the Fund also concurred that it was 'a mistake to believe that microfinance, especially when we are talking about microcredit, is a solution to poverty. I don't believe it ... This is only one instrument, one single instrument inside the overall fight against poverty. We don't believe that health and education, and social activities can be solved by microfinance' (Rodriguez interview).

In fact, some of the literature suggests that a single intervention such as credit may be less successful in poverty reduction than a simultaneous intervention of credit, primary health and education, depending on the nature of poverty in a specific context (Lipton cited in Johnson and Rogaly, 1997: 14). 'There was a lot of talking and controversy about microfinance at the Fund itself. We had a meeting and there were two lobbies; a lobby saying no we should not enter into microfinance because we are working in development, and the target groups we are working with need development loans. The other people who had gone and attended some microfinance sessions were really sold on the idea' (Nusseir interview a). As one advocate of best practice within the Fund stated: 'My first reaction was this is a business opportunity. It can be about development and in alignment with the Fund's strategy and objectives. But it is a business opportunity. Let's go for it' (Haj-Issa interview a). The realization that donor funding could eventually dry up was also a consideration, 'I would say the Fund needs to sustain itself. It needs to look at its own needs. I look at (best practice) from a business and funding angle to ensure the sustainability of the organization' (Fariz interview).

Other objections came from QAF field workers (al-Shahwan interview a) and from the head of its social development department who was concerned about the socio-economic impact of new microfinance methodologies on targeted communities (Abu-Rish interview a). These apprehensions echoed the issues raised in the literature: that the impact of microfinance had not been fully analysed (Hulme, 2000); that, contrary to current opinion, credit might not actually empower women as many of them do not control their own loans or receive the income generated from their microenterprises (Dawkins Scully, n.d.; Goetz and Sen Gupta, 1996); the concern that development funds were being reallocated into microfinance programmes and away from promoting basic health and education (Oxfam, 1997); and that the centralized manner in which microfinance was being developed globally as an anti-poverty tool could lead to 'too much uniformity of approach at the expense of local adaptation and programmes' (ibid.).

Some staff at the Fund held the view that a non-subsidized approach to credit could detract from the needs of local communities, for whom it was important to provide options: 'What we are saying is that it differs from one area to another, even within Jordan which is a small country ... We have a small village right now that is refusing either to deal with interest, with Islamic profitability, or administration fees (with regard to credit) ... And it is a problem' (Abu-Rish interview a). The significance of recognizing local diversity was clearly reflected in the 1997 Pilot Study by the director of one of the Fund's main centres: 'In the governorate of al-Karak you find each area different from the other, as if we are not in the same governorate ... Mu'ta differs from al-Qatrana, al-Karak city differs from the Jordan Valley' (QAF, 1998b, Director of CDC interview, al-Karak 7: 17).

Those in favour of a more businesslike approach, however, contended that the Fund's subsidized credit programme had been unsuccessful due to a limited outreach (JOHUD/UNDP, 1999: 23), as well as the 'social work attitude of the loan officers who see credit as a means of helping the poor, and not as a tool for establishing an income-generating business. There is also an attitude among the borrowers that if they take a loan from the Fund, it is okay not to repay' (Fariz interview). Donor agencies promoting sustainable microfinance expressed similar concerns. For example, according to Lewis Lucke, the Director of USAID at the time training programmes for microfinance practitioners in Amman were first launched: 'Charity-based or subsidized credit approaches have proven ... to increase a culture of dependency' (*Jordan Times*, 1999: 3). There was, however, also a view that subsidized credit could lead a poor non-entrepreneurial borrower into further debt: 'Loans don't work for the poorest of the poor. We need to give them grants or a job' (Fariz interview).

As shown by this discussion, within the development field in Jordan, and more specifically within the Fund, ideologies differed regarding the linkage between credit schemes and development in general. A variety of questions were raised, including whether non-subsidized credit approaches were effective in helping the poor start or sustain micro businesses, whether credit alone could help combat poverty or whether it should be seen as one component within an integrated development approach. Another issue raised by such debates was whether, by switching to best practice methodologies that mostly targeted the so-called entrepreneurial poor, a development organization like the Fund could adequately serve the non-entrepreneurial poor, its main target group. These questions reflected a growing debate within the development community as a whole concerning the need to move beyond the economic towards a more holistic understanding of the process, as espoused by the proponents of sustainable human development. These were among the dilemmas which the Fund endeavoured to resolve as part of its response to the microfinance challenge. However, just as different perspectives in development discourse led to what was aptly called 'a microfinance schism' (Morduch, 2000), the divided positions within the Fund were also real and difficult to reconcile.

Options in a period of transition

In the autumn of 1998 a series of lengthy informal brainstorming sessions were held by QAF board members and management, together with representatives of international agencies, including the resident representative of UNDP and the Director of the British Council. The purpose of these meetings was to discuss the situation of microfinance in Jordan and how the Fund could best accommodate the different approaches that were being used (QAF, 1998h): 'I thought that the Fund was painfully aware of the dilemmas and therefore was an excellent candidate for doing both [subsidized and non-subsidized microfinance]' (Lissner interview).

These sessions came at a time when the Fund had embarked on a process of internal reform which involved re-examining its approach to development by focusing on issues such as decentralization and sustainability and was seeking to empower itself from within, as well as to respond to issues emerging from the new donor agenda. In contrast to the loss of control that the Sarvodaya movement in Sri Lanka experienced when donors became actively involved in internal decision-making, the process of self-examination undertaken by the Fund, with valuable input from donors, helped it not to rush into hasty decisions. Instead there was an attempt to come up with strategies that would move the organization forward without compromising its development goals.[15]

The decision that came out of these meetings was to initiate a consultancy sponsored by UNDP 'to assess and identify QAF's current

---

15. See the discussion of the Sarvodaya movement in chapter 1.

programme and management capacity in microfinance service delivery and ways in which to apply microfinance best practice' (UNDP, 1998: 2). Upon completion of the technical assistance component, QAF would receive a capital fund for on-lending to micro-borrowers as part of an already agreed UNDP-sponsored Poverty Alleviation Initiative signed in 1997. The aim of this pilot project would be to enable QAF to 'become a more efficient micro-finance intermediary, thereby increasing its eligibility to receive capital funds from other donors' (QAF, 1997j). This was viewed as part of a transitional phase in which the Fund could prepare itself and its target groups for a new approach: 'We did not want to jump into an operation that we really didn't have much information about. The second thing was that we wanted to go through a transition period where we could change attitudes and train our people to build their capacities, establish a system and then go into microfinance (best practice)' (Haj-Issa interview a).

The loss of a funding opportunity

In December 1998, the Terms of Reference of the AMIR grant were made available, and the Fund set about preparing its business plan for submission by 31 January 1999. Part of the AMIR eligibility criteria for the Microfinance Innovation Programme was the requirement to set up an operationally and financially autonomous microfinance institution 'to provide access to financial services for small and micro-scale borrowers on a sustainable basis following Best Practice methodologies' (AMIR, 1998). In effect this would separate social and training components from financial services: 'The theory is that the same institution cannot provide grants and subsidized loans, and at the same time do sustainable microfinance. Therefore you need to create a subsidiary, that is the spin-off' (Lissner interview).

The Fund's proposal included a letter of commitment to the principles of best practice but did not specifically indicate the Fund's intention to create a separate microfinance institution that would provide financial services separate from training and consultancy (QAF, 1999b). The proposal did not meet the AMIR eligibility requirements (QAF 1999c; JOHUD/UNDP, 1999: 33). As a result, QAF lost a major opportunity to play a substantial role in the area of microfinance best practice: 'The proposal that came in from the Fund made it clear that it wasn't really a serious decision to get into this industry ... In contrast, the other three organizations did express that and did make moves and did start to form companies … I think this demonstrated a huge level of seriousness that was quite different' (Wade interview).[16]

Subsequent meetings were held with representatives of USAID and AMIR, in which the Fund explained its need for a transitional phase for further assessment of the required approach 'to see what the effects are and how it could impact development work done in Jordan' (Nusseir interview a). However, it was not possible to negotiate such a period of grace since 'AMIR have a condition from USAID. They have three years to implement this project, and so they couldn't wait for us … to go through a transitional period, especially when they have goals themselves' (Haj-Issa interview a).

A new direction: The Microfinance Pilot Project

While some staff at the Fund had no regrets over the loss of the AMIR funding, others felt that 'we missed an opportunity' (Haj-Issa interview a). Those who were committed to microfinance best practice came to the conclusion that the organization was not ready for such an initiative, because it would require a shift of attitude 'to the way business is conducted … The Fund takes up too much time thinking rather than acting' (Fariz interview). However, as the 1997 Pilot Study reveals, another consideration was that many of the staff, volunteers, and loan officers at the CDCs viewed credit in social rather than business terms: 'Basically, the goal of these loans is social, the policy of these loans is actually a social policy … We do not make profits like banks or any other governmental or non-governmental institutions. Ever since we started, our goal, our noblest goal, has been social. We give loans to poor people who need them' (QAF, 1998b, CDC Loan Officer interview, Madaba 5: 19). This perception was noted in an evaluation of the Fund's capacity to take up microfinance best practice: 'It is also difficult for staff steeped in traditional development work to accept and adopt more businesslike attitudes and methodologies in their day-to-day work' (JOHUD/UNDP, 1999: 2). Clearly, the Fund needed to address numerous issues in order to decide the most appropriate course to follow regarding credit programmes. However, one

---

16. In April 1999, the AMIR programme awarded grant agreements to the amount of JD 3,976,141 ($5,603,017) to JWDS and two newly-created microfinance institutions, the Ahli Microfinancing Company (AMC), a company created by the National Bank of Jordan, and the Jordan Micro Credit Company (JMCC), a subsidiary of Noor al-Hussein Foundation (AMIR, 1999; *The Arab Daily*, 1999).

way of facilitating the Fund's entry into sustainable microfinance would be the pilot project sponsored by UNDP, as a result of joint consultations earlier described.

The pilot project was launched through SBDC during the second half of 1999 in the district of al-Hashimi al-Shamali in Amman. As a highly-populated, low-income area where, typically, credit programmes tend to thrive, this location was thought to be well suited to building the Fund's experience in microfinance best practice (ibid.: 38). By entering into sustainable microfinance through the pilot project, the Fund sought to achieve several objectives. Firstly, management and staff would be able to test whether or not micro-lending programmes would be successful using best practice methodology. Secondly, since the pilot programme was small and restricted to one area, the process of testing new ideas would mean less risk to existing schemes. Thirdly, the project would allow the Fund the necessary transitional time to assess the strengths and weaknesses of such an approach, and enable it to identify areas where institutional changes were also required (ibid.: 56): 'What UNDP is trying with the Fund is to have one locality where we try to do sustainable microfinance, far removed from any other schemes which are subsidized, and to see how that works' (Lissner interview).

Another dimension of the pilot project envisaged by UNDP was to help develop the capacities of the Fund 'through a slow but thorough process, in order for them to catch up with the rest of the organizations working in microfinance (best practice)' (JOHUD, 1999e). After a thorough study of the target area to design the loan product and prepare a business plan SBDC staff, and more specifically loan officers, were trained in microfinance best practice methodology. The first loans were to be given out in July 2000 (JOHUD, 2000g). Staff at SBDC were optimistic about the potential success of the pilot project, and the possible impact it could have on making credit delivery at the Fund more efficient 'as a first step to channelling other loans towards this microfinance methodology' (Fariz interview).

While it has been acknowledged that, in adopting microfinance approaches, NGOs may be moving away from their own priorities and activities (Hulme and Edwards, 1997: 9), there was an argument for the Fund's slow embrace of sustainable microfinance as more in keeping with the home-grown development approach which it had consolidated over many years. In this sense a transitional phase was important for a number of reasons. To have suddenly taken up microfinance best practice, including conforming to the conditions of AMIR, would have implied a radical change in direction for the organization, as well as for its clients. There was also concern about the impact of a swift change on the relationship between the Fund and its target groups, especially when borrowers were accustomed to much lower interest rates and longer repayment periods. A transitional period was also required to resolve other issues: switching to non-subsidized credit not only implied cultivating a different client group, but also setting policies to determine whether subsidized credit for the majority of borrowers served by the Fund would either be continued or eventually phased out.

Problems and prospects

The dilemma the Fund faced in responding to the microfinance debate was perhaps indicative of many organizations' experiences when faced with external factors pushing for rapid change. As an issue of transition, the microfinance argument reflected the tensions which were part of the Fund's overall process of reform. Nevertheless, beyond organizational resistance to change there was a genuine concern that, as a development agency, the Fund was having to choose between 'doing business' and 'doing development.' Ironically, the whole debate concerning microfinance took place while the concept of 'sustainability' itself was under review. Environmental sustainability had been placed within a broader paradigm with the articulation of the holistic and participatory model of sustainable human development. By the late 1990s, this model was being adapted and emerging as the 'sustainable livelihoods' approach. This took the paradigm one step further, challenging the narrow economic focus of microfinance, and noting that access to increased finance might also damage the long-term asset base of poor people and weaken their livelihood strategies. On this point, at least, the Fund seemed clear: it would not compromise its development efforts but seek a slower and more moderate path: 'At least as a development organization we really stuck to our logic in terms of the development work, the transition period, and the project that we are implementing on a much smaller scale through UNDP funding. We are taking into consideration the needs of the local communities … Hopefully, if this works I think we will be in a much stronger position to … utilize the microfinace programme in Jordan to the benefit of development goals' (Nusseir interview a).

While the results of the pilot project were awaited, the Fund still had to deal with the decisions concerning microfinance. It was also faced with having to negotiate subsidized loan schemes, which in themselves were subject to differing donor criteria.[17] The fact that such lending programmes were neither aligned with microfinance best practice nor with SBDC posed an additional problem. However, in spite of these challenges, within the context of reform and the Fund's overall drive towards sustainability, credit schemes came to form a major component of the Fund's work.

In 1999, looking at the experiences of microfinance institutions in the region, and particularly in Jordan, it was still too early to predict how successful they would be, and whether or not they would attain their desired goal of sustainability. When asked about the level of sustainability of credit programmes in her institution, Niveen Sharaf responded: 'We are on the way to sustainability. Usually it takes five to seven years to reach sustainability' (Sharaf interview). However, the findings of a 1995 USAID study of eleven microfinance programmes from a range of geographical locations showed that only five of them had reached full self-sufficiency (USAID, 1995: viii).

In the microfinance industry many variables and uncertainties existed to prevent an NGO from making clear and informed decisions for the future. For instance, it was conceivable that financing for subsidized loans could decline as donor priorities changed. At the same time it was too early to predict whether microfinance best practice could alleviate poverty and contribute to sustainable development goals. Different donor approaches, coupled with conflicting views within the Fund's management, left the situation unresolved. It still cannot be ascertained whether the organization made a mistake by taking time to embrace microfinance best practice, or whether the transitional approach indeed reflected the wiser option. Thus, while the controversial issue of 'from aid to business' persisted, the Fund was obliged to continue to straddle the transitional line.

Embarking on Internal Reform

It has been noted that NGOs go through a range of experiences which to a great extent reflect their level of development and maturity. Thus, the life cycle of an NGO can loosely be classified as four organizational stages, namely: 'start up; expansion; consolidation; and close-out' (Avina, 1993:

17. A Spanish NGO recently requested as part of an integrated agricultural development project, to give grants rather than loans according to funding conditions; while an Italian NGO proposed a 3 per cent interest rate on agricultural loans as part of their government's policy to subsidize loans to farmers (Abu-Rish interview b).

455). Drawing on this classification it can be said that by the late 1990s the Fund was entering the stage of consolidation in which 'an NGO analyzes its performance to better align its operative capacity to its external reality' (ibid.: 466). Within the Fund it was increasingly felt at this time that, to be able to cater to the requirements of the country's transition, organizational change was necessary. This realization was heightened not only by the overall reform measures which were being promoted at national and international levels, but also by the demand from the field. Thus, in response to changes in its external environment, the Fund adopted a new course of action based on re-evaluation and reform of its operational procedures, its development approach and its relations with the field.

The national and international context

A number of considerations contributed to the Fund's strategic decision in 1997 to begin the process of internal reform. The climate of political liberalization was opening up the country to greater democratic principles and a strengthening of civil society. The comprehensive plan for public sector reform, set in motion in 1996, also sensitized national institutions such as QAF to the need for better service delivery, decentralization and a tightening of internal procedures. Furthermore, by this time not only had the Fund grown in size; it was also experiencing many of the difficulties associated with large bureaucratic organizations (Brown and Covey cited in Stewart, 1997: 14). As one observer remarks: 'I think that QAF was sidetracked in the sense that it became an institution, and began growing as an institution, and not taking into consideration the goals that it was created for … The whole administration is very bureaucratic … It really doesn't differ from the Ministry (of Social Development)' (Nassir interview).

Another factor affecting the Fund, as well as other NGOs in Jordan, was the increased demand by the donor community for greater transparency and accountability, especially where financial and project management were concerned (QAF, 1998a). The heightened emphasis on the quality of aid rather than its volume, and the concentration on procedures such as monitoring and reporting, was a reflection of donor concerns (Archer, 1994). As observed in relation to Jordanian NGOs: 'The one complaint I hear in the donor community is the reporting … I think it's endemic that the reporting on projects is poor' (Lissner interview).

QAF was well aware of its inadequate system of monitoring and reporting and knew that it had to become more systematic in order to optimize its access to increasingly scarce funding. It therefore sought to address this weakness as part of its reform (QAF, 1998j). The Fund recognized as well that international agencies were becoming more interested in its internal structure. The existence of a clear and well defined mission statement and strategy, in addition to good management practices, were important factors for receiving funding (JOHUD, 2000h).

The voice of the field

The process of reform within the Fund was also directly influenced by the conditions of its partners in the field, many of whom had been affected by Jordan's economic recession and subsequent adjustment policies. Meanwhile, political liberalization had heightened the climate of openness and people were expressing their desire for change: 'They were demanding that more freedom be given to them, more responsibility and particularly more funding ... I think they really wanted to become major players in the design and implementation of their affairs because they were feeling ... that they were being excluded and that their economic situation could not wait anymore' (Abu-Rish interview b). As previously noted, social and political democratization bring opportunities for new forms of social or community representativeness to emerge (Marzouk, 1997). Thus, among QAF's partners there were calls for greater involvement: 'If you, as the Fund, did not have confidence in me [as an NGO], you would not have given me the centre to operate. Fine, on the one hand you give me your trust, yet on the other hand you – let's spell it out – you pull all the strings, you decide the policies you want, and that's it! Why don't you delegate authority? By God, this system is wrong' (QAF, 1998b, NGO Treasurer interview, Rawdat Basma 2: 197). However, not everyone in the field expressed such desire for greater autonomy: 'We simply cannot separate from the Fund. They are the cornerstone, we are only a part and we cannot split from the whole. It is impossible to be uprooted. Their aim is to encourage the centres to have their own projects, nevertheless, they will always be the beginning and the end' (ibid., Rural Leader interview, al-Hisa 8: 76).

The voice of discontent, revealed in the meetings which took place at that time with local partners and CDCs, was growing stronger. This was seen, for instance, when headquarters staff and rural leaders met in 1997 at al-'Aqaba to discuss issues such as planning, programmes, administration and finance. Some of the rural leaders pointed out that planning was centralized and that they were not involved in the process. Furthermore, planning took into consideration financial resources but not other resources. There were also criticisms of the Fund's programmes which were described as uninventive, mostly centrally imposed and too limited to cover all the local needs. Furthermore, the administration of the centres, both centrally and locally, was inefficient and staff lacked proper training in administrative skills (QAF, 1997k). The 1997 Pilot Study revealed similar criticisms. For example, a respondent took the Fund to task for its centralized approach with these words: 'The problem is our relationship with the Fund. We are tied to it, we cannot move beyond. Just like our relationship with the Ministry of Social Development. We are tied to the Ministry, we are tied to the Fund. We cannot do anything until we have consulted with the Fund' (QAF 1998b, NGO Member interview, Rihab 3: 275). Another respondent who made the same point nevertheless believed there was hope of improvement: 'If channels between us, the main centre and the Fund headquarters in Amman were open, things would definitely be better' (ibid., Deputy Head of NGO interview, al-Za'tari 3: 300).

In contrast to the criticisms levelled against the Fund's centralized approach, there were those in the field who felt that it should be more involved and concerned with the work of the CDCs: 'The relationship between the centre and the Fund is very, very weak. There is no coordination, no organization and no follow-up' (ibid., Rural Leader interview, al-Ba'ij 1: 24). Complaints of this kind were usually aired by rural leaders, who obviously felt that they needed stronger support from the Fund: 'Things are only happening through God's grace. I manage the centre the way I want. Hardly anyone comes to tell me do this or that. I run the centre with my own management and skills ... they visit me once a year' (ibid., Rural Leader interview, al-Sheikh Hussein 4: 20).

The rural leaders were also the most affected by any kind of tension that occurred between the Fund and local NGOs in charge of running the CDCs: 'As I know and hear, the NGO and Fund are complementary to each other, but I don't know which one is the more important ... I don't know what to do, who is directly responsible, the Fund or the NGO? Each wants to have the primary responsibility. Either they should join into one entity or each work on its own, take their own way (and stop telling me) "don't do this," "don't do that"' (ibid., Rural Leader interview, Bsaira 8: 39). Many expressed the need for change and felt that the responsibility for this change lay with the Fund. As one field respondent aptly put it: 'There is some kind of commitment (from the Fund), but it should be more if the centre is to succeed. The reputation of the centre is, in the final analysis, the reputation of the Fund. So if the centre fails, the Fund fails' (ibid., Head of NGO interview, al-Ba'ij 1: 38).

The 1996 study on the impact of QAF's programmes revealed the generally low participation of the women's committees in the planning of the centres' activities, although the level of participation differed from area to area (QAF, 1996a). This variation raises questions about the impact of different administrative structures, and the role played by centre directors in fostering local involvement. The various administrative arrangements for running the CDCs might have been expedient while the Fund was expanding its network, yet by the late 1990s they seemed to have become a liability. Both staff and community members at the satellite centres expressed their discontent: '[They don't tell me about meetings], they consider that Irbid [main centre] represents me. Irbid does not represent me and I told them as much ... They say you are a satellite centre and they [Irbid centre] are a main centre. On what basis and how am I a satellite centre and they are a main centre?' (QAF 1998b, Rural Leader interview, Jarash 4: 38–39). Complaints aired in the 1997 Pilot Study were even harsher towards main centres than they were towards the Fund itself: 'The problem would be easier if they would only respond to the letters I send. Poor Abu Mohammed, I sent three letters (asking for a loan for him), they did not answer. If only they would answer, two words only, to say "we cannot"' (ibid., Rural Leader interview, al-Sheikh Hussein 4: 37).

From the perspective of the field, then, decentralization was clearly necessary if a greater degree of operational competence, at headquarters as well as at the local level, was to be achieved. For the CDCs had reached a stage of maturity which necessitated an overall revision of their linkages with the Fund. From the comments which have been highlighted, it can be said that in many instances QAF's partners in the local communities had a more realistic understanding of their needs and priorities than the central office, which had seemingly grown out of touch.

The economic circumstances of the 1990s, together with the process of political liberalization, had created a new set of perceptions among people at the local level which the Fund needed to take into account in its dealings with the CDCs. While taking these issues on board, as part of the process of decentralization the Fund also had to identify new methods to build the capacity of its partners in local communities in order for them to manage and sustain their own affairs. Consequently, in keeping with the national trend of reform, and while responding to the voice of the field, the Fund embarked on a process of organizational consolidation and restructuring, leading to the creation of a new strategy.

Consolidating and restructuring the Fund

During the early to mid-1990s, QAF had made a number of attempts to strengthen its organizational structure and operations with inputs from foreign consultants who worked with a small select group of the Fund's administration (JOHUD, 2000h; CEDC, 1992; QAF, 1994f). However, while the recommendations of consultancies were quite valid, they did not necessarily produce the desired results. This may have been because of a perception that they were externally imposed and thus not always in keeping with QAF's organizational culture. As an organization, the Fund could be described as a community with its own culture (Handy, 1988) which reflected its specific experience in solving problems related to its own history (Schein, 1989). Consequently, for organizational reform to succeed, it would have had to be internally motivated, based on QAF's own knowledge, experiences, and values and led primarily by its own managers.

In December 1997, a meeting was called by the Chairperson of the Board of Trustees with the Fund's top management to announce the formation of a task force. Its mission was to examine the organizational structure of the Fund and to prepare a new strategy. The principal themes would be to promote decentralization and greater organizational sustainability and to consolidate the Fund's role as a leading national organization working in development (JOHUD, 2000h). Eleven members of QAF's top administration were involved, a number of whom had participated in meetings in the field and could convey the concerns of the grassroots to their colleagues. The limited size of the task force posed a dilemma for a truly participatory strategic planning process; but to have involved more people in the discussions would have made the process cumbersome and lengthy. There are, nevertheless, inherent paradoxes in a high level planning process conducted in the interest of enhancing participation; indeed this reflects the challenges that all large organizations encounter when attempting to decentralize.

The task force embarked on a series of lengthy brainstorming sessions in which members discussed a range of issues related to the Fund's development approach. Methods of achieving institutional sustainability were considered in light of the fact that many of our activities and income-generating projects were not financially sustainable. Some members believed that the continued dependency of the CDCs on QAF to sustain local operations was contributing to a depletion of the Fund's own resources – a vulnerability that needed to be addressed (ibid.). This reinforced the observations of the 1997 Pilot Study since many of the field staff, NGO partners and even community members, viewed the Fund primarily in its capacity as their main financial provider: '... it is the one and only funding source' (QAF, 1998b, Community Member interview, al-Zubairiya 10: 178).

With overtones that resemble those of the microfinance debate, there were differing points of view among task force members over how to achieve the interrelated goals of decentralization and financial sustainability. Again this mirrors the broader development debate which placed greater emphasis on promoting local ownership and full participation of the people as an essential component of sustainable human development. Some argued that for the CDCs to become financially sustainable they would need to operate successful projects that would cover costs and later generate an income to sustain the centres' activities. Another group believed that those of QAF's income-generating projects that were not giving positive returns and had a minimal social impact should be closed down and funding diverted to other more socially and economically viable projects. Yet others were concerned about the human dimension of development and the Fund's obligations to its partners. They argued that even if a project made a loss, QAF should continue to support it and supplement the difference as its contribution to community development (QAF, 1998k). A decision was subsequently taken to evaluate some of the income-generating projects in order to determine which were successful and could be managed locally, and which projects required an alternative solution (QAF, 1998l).

Through this process of self-evaluation, the task force was able to gain greater clarity and insight in order to make the required adjustments to the Fund's operational approach. Meetings sometimes drew on the experience of the Director of the British Council in Amman during that period, whose knowledge of the country as well as of the Fund, particularly in this context, was helpful. For an organization like QAF this was a lengthy process and the work of the task force took the better part of a year. QAF's Executive Director nevertheless concluded that the experience 'was a healthy one' (Nusseir interview b). A similar view was also voiced by the resident representative of UNDP at that time, who was well acquainted with QAF: 'What is so encouraging about the Fund is that they are inviting the debate into their own chambers, and that sets the dynamism in motion which I think will eventually end up making the Fund more attractive to the donors' (Lissner interview).

A new strategy

Once the organizational structure of the Fund had been thoroughly revised, a smaller group from the task force was assigned to formulate its strategy and work plan for 1999–2002 (JOHUD, 2000h). As part of the strategy, a new mission statement was developed which positioned the Fund: 'To play a leading role in advancing comprehensive and sustainable human development through the enhanced participation of Jordanians.' The Fund would strive 'to impact best development practices at the national level, drawing on its experiences and local presence …' (JOHUD, 1999f: 1). A reflection of these new directions was the focus on sustainable human development. The CDCs were recognized as playing a central role. Hence, the Fund would support this objective by building the capacity of the CDCs to deliver services which contributed to the sustainability of local community development. Efforts to incorporate current best practices in the Fund's operational approach would therefore be furthered in order 'to ensure optimum support services at minimum costs' (ibid.: 3).

The strategy was ambitious and it implied promoting a continuous process of change. At the same time, however, it recognized the distinction between elements of the Fund's agenda which addressed differing levels of achievement within its overall sphere of activities. The Fund needed to emphasize such elements in conveying the new strategy to the field. For, as the 1997 Pilot Study had shown, at the local level varying understandings existed even about the concept of development itself. Some people in the field believed 'development' to be synonymous with the Ministry of Social Development, which they associated with welfare: 'Helping the poor and needy … I know many poor people who go to "Development," they help them because they are poor' (QAF, 1998b, Member of Women's Committee interview, al-'Aqaba 11: 28). Another respondent reiterated the same perception: 'As I told you, "Development" is only about giving assistance to the people and needy families.' When asked for her opinion on what the negative impacts of development were, she countered: 'As it is, I could not even explain what development is in the first place' (ibid., Rural Leader interview, al-Khalidiyya 2: 132). Given the fact that the CDCs' programmes focus largely on women, some thought that the concept of development as a whole targeted women. In explaining her own understanding of development, one respondent stated: 'Here we are a social services centre. Social services attempt to deliver services to women in their communities, to improve their work and train them so that they can improve their financial and living conditions' (ibid., CDC Vocational Trainer interview, al-Mafraq 1: 1).

Other partners in the field had a quite different perception of the concept of development: 'I have a humble understanding [of the concept], it might be right or it might be wrong. I can say that development is the advancement of society ... when the local community reaches an advanced stage' (ibid., NGO Treasurer interview, Rawdat Basma 2: 192). Or, as another partner said: 'Of course, development is opening up, interaction and involvement' (ibid., Women's Committee Coordinator interview, al-Khalidiyya 2: 159). It is also encouraging to note that even before the Fund adopted its new strategy, one of its CDCs' staff said: 'My understanding is a little different. Development to me means human development. I am concerned with humans, the human element that I work with, and through my work there is development of thoughts and of attitudes, then there is behavioural change towards many of the social development issues that we have to deal with' (ibid., CDC Director interview, Sahab 6: 1).

These different perspectives serve to highlight a question which has always been central to the approach of the Fund: namely, how to further development efforts while taking on board the diversity of understandings and levels of readiness for various interventions in the field. The diversity of local understanding of development reflects the changes which have occurred in development theory and practice as discussed in chapter 1, and emphasizes that any development approach has to consider the complexities of poor people's livelihood strategies and go beyond the simply economic. Twenty-one years had passed since the Fund formulated its initial set of objectives in 1978. While in some areas significant progress had been made, challenges in others reinforced the need for a revised approach by the Fund, as promised by its new strategy in 1999. However, as in the early phase, the major test for the Fund remained how to translate discourse into concrete achievements within the challenging circumstances of the field.

By contrast to the objectives set out in 1978, whose basic purpose was to define QAF's role (see chapter 4), in 1999 the primary strategic objective for the Fund was to 'consolidate' its role 'as a key partner and reference in the formulation of national development initiatives' (JOHUD, 1999f: 3). Thus, in drawing up the Fund's new strategy, task force members had to take into account local needs and perceptions as well as national and international trends. Accordingly, they focused on priority areas at the national, community and internal levels. These areas were to be addressed through specific strategic objectives and measures that emphasized the importance of human capacity-building, institutional sustainability, transparency and decentralization (JOHUD, 2000h). In order to start the decentralization process, the Fund would strengthen the institutional capacity of local management at the CDCs, and within the voluntary committees and NGOs. Thus, the CDCs would be enhanced as 'focal points' for human development at the community level. In a bid to strengthen its operations and to 'ensure optimum use of the Fund's resources,' particularly with regard to project management, the Fund would carry out 'technical and financial assessment' of projects (JOHUD, 1999f: 6). This responsibility would be undertaken by the newly established Monitoring and Evaluation Unit.[18]

One means of operationalizing the strategy, it was envisaged, would be by presenting it to staff at headquarters, as well as to directors of CDCs, rural leaders and the Fund's NGO partners through workshops and discussions, so that a common language and approach to development could be cultivated. Staff at headquarters and in the field would also require continuous training and capacity-building to enable them to become more effective in the implementation of the strategy by 2002 (Nusseir interview b). Part of the organization's new goals would be to strengthen the capacity of its partners from the private and public sectors, as well as NGOs. The Fund would emphasize the national importance of human resource development through the Zein al Sharaf Institute for Development[19] which would act as 'its primary training provider' (JOHUD, 1999f).

The Queen Zein al Sharaf Institute for Development

The Fund's increased emphasis on capacity-building was reflected in the role it gave to the Queen Zein al Sharaf Institute for Development (ZENID) in its strategic plan. Indeed, the evolution of ZENID from a Compound for Training and Social Development (see chapter 5) to a national institute specialized in development training, consultation and information provision corresponded with the Fund's strategic planning process. Although the Compound had been originally created to serve the training capacity requirements of both the Fund and other development agents, its role had clearly become broader.

---

18. The Monitoring and Evaluation Unit was established in April 1998.

19. The Queen Zein al Sharaf Compound for Training and Social Development changed its name to the Queen Zein al Sharaf Institute for Development in 1999.

The increasing role that ZENID began to recognize for itself was con-current with the Fund's own realization of the need to review and reap-praise its functions and performance. As the Fund sought to consolidate its position as a key authority on development issues, and not merely as a service provider, the Institute became the logical entity through which the Fund's knowledge and experience could be made available. The Fund's strategic plan stated that ZENID 'would assume a key role in the process of building the capacity of the Fund's staff and its national network, to assist them in applying contemporary best practice in all aspects of their work and services.' It would also draw on the Fund's experience and know-how 'to meet the increasing training needs on both national and regional levels' (JOHUD, 1999f).

A British government-funded capacity building project, launched in 1997, played a significant role in the growth of ZENID. The three-year project was later extended for a further three years, thus illustrating the expansion of the Institute's role both in the internal capacity building of the Fund's staff and at the national level (DFID, 1999). ZENID's own mission shows a clear progression from its original mandate of providing and facilitating training to 'acting as a resource and providing services which enhance the skills of those involved in development' (ZENID, 1999). A major contribution of ZENID was that it helped JOHUD to analyse its own operations within the international debates concerning 'good practice.' JOHUD was better able to understand, for example, its internal conflicts concerning microfinance, or the need to devolve responsibility to the field as a reflection of a growing challenge to top-down, narrowly-focused models of development. JOHUD's own determination to propose a slower path, in line with Jordan's long-term interests, were better understood within the emerging debate concerning the sustainable livelihoods approach to development. Thus, ZENID was to become the central means through which the Fund could provide expertise nationally and regionally through training, research and the dissemination of information on development. By enhancing ZENID's role, the Fund would in effect be repositioning itself at national level as an authority on development.

Reflections on the Fund in Transition

Parallels may be drawn between the complexities of Jordan's transitional process in the 1990s and the smaller, yet similarly difficult, transitional efforts of national institutions such as the Fund. For both the state and non-governmental actors the push for change – the benefits of which are often intangible and essentially long-term – had in various ways created tensions whether in sustaining the overall course of change or the often unpopular dimensions of reform. However, as already noted, it is generally too early for either state or non-governmental bodies to evaluate with clarity the impact of the measures and approaches promoted during this period. In this chapter, analysis has centred on particular issues which have defined the Fund's directions in the 1990s, including its attempts to consolidate earlier efforts. Thus, it is relevant at this stage to reflect on a few of the most important problems that the Fund continued to face as it renegotiated its place within the changing national setting and within a context of newly emerging international development trends.

As discussions have shown, during its own process of transition the Fund was increasingly obliged to play a mediating role between the needs of the grassroots and the priorities of donors. Moreover, being placed in a 'middle' position, the Fund met a variety of challenges, which even now it is still trying to address. In other ways, the internal reform process gave the organization greater clarity and confidence with which to mediate the paradoxes of this period. Yet, despite some positive changes within the organization as it entered a new phase in 1999, sustainability remained the most pressing issue facing the Fund. Clearly, as the organization had grown in size, its need for funding had increased and to address its financial vulnerability, efforts had to be made to introduce tighter fiscal control and accountability.

The Fund had to balance the need to become organizationally sustainable and ensure the sustainability of its projects in the field while maintaining its original people-centred development orientations. Herein lay the dilemma: increasingly in the context of economic hardships, a large majority of its target groups relied on the Fund's often subsidized approaches. And yet, the pursuit of organizational sustainability, including greater financial self-reliance for partners in the field, possibly required a more radical shift to business methods. As noted by one observer: 'Some of the production, the ceramics, rugs, some of that stuff is very good, and probably could stand on its own. If they run it as a business it could probably do very well. But I think most of the work that they do is not sustainable in its present form, and therefore they've got to figure out. I think there is a legitimate role for what they're doing. They just have to identify that role much more carefully' (Khouri interview).

Consequently, for the Fund to survive and succeed in the future, it would have to keep re-evaluating and negotiating its role locally, nationally, and with its international partners. Yet a pertinent question remained: How far the Fund could extend itself as a development organization while promoting a more business-oriented focus? Moreover, what new dilemmas might emerge in the field if the emphasis were placed too squarely on financial sustainability at the expense of the human dimension within the process of change? In addition to these internal concerns, the Fund as a national NGO was having to consider issues which were emerging within the national context. For example, as seen with the national debate about the role of Jordanian NGOs (see chapter 2), concerns were raised over whether civil society was being shaped from within or whether development processes in Jordan were being primarily defined by external influences.

According to Dr Mustafa Hamarneh, Director of the Centre for Strategic Studies, one of the main obstacles to the advancement of the Jordanian NGO movement is the fact that resources within the country are minimal. Therefore: 'If anything is to develop in a formal sense, a strong reliance on foreign funding is the order of the day' (Hamarneh interview). In some respects the reliance on external aid raises concerns for the Fund, similar to those expressed by the national debate. For over the years the Fund has managed to cater to different needs and priorities within the local context largely through a home-grown approach. The value and experience of such indigenous models, which work primarily because they have been gener-ated from within, may well be eroded as NGOs try to accommodate the conditions and methods of external donors. Here the following question is of relevance: 'Do we really address our needs as we see them or as our needs are seen from the perspective of Washington, Ottawa or Brussels? Monies are diverted into these areas as a result of that strategy. Then, of course, the result is a society with sectors linked to the outside world, some of them quite advanced and others not. This is an age old problem' (Hamarneh interview).

Another view which perceives Jordanian NGOs to be playing a more pivotal role at this transitional time maintains that they must evolve according to their own environment and context:

> The way society is structured here is very different from the West. I think it is very dangerous to just take some of these Western models and assumptions. Some of them fit and some of them don't ... I think we have a whole different concept of society here that has to evolve according to its own standard. I mean what you have here is the strong family tribal base. You have this incredibly strong religious element ... I just don't think we're going to follow the same model as the West, at least not in the short-term ... My guess is the evolution

here of civil society is going to be different … And I think it's the NGOs, in a way, that straddle that space between the traditional and the indigenous, versus the Western or foreign and the modern. And I think the NGOs are starting to make that transition slowly … So again they go right across the board of the indigenous forces in society. My guess is that they will become more and more credible players (Khouri interview).

As the country at large continued along the path of political liberalization and economic reform a growing need and desire has emerged for greater dialogue about the roles which different actors, including NGOs, would have to fulfil. In assisting this process, the Fund would have to be discerning as it examined its own role and its impact on the ground. For in essence, by sustaining the process of self-evaluation and adjusting to the ebbs and flows of a transitional period, the Fund might be called upon to bring its experience into a larger national reflection within the Jordanian setting, and possibly even beyond.

Epilogue:
The Beginning of a New Era

Twenty-two years ago, His Majesty King Hussein, entrusted me with the creation of the Queen Alia Jordan Social Welfare Fund.

Since the Fund was established in 1977, the concept of development both internationally and in Jordan has changed considerably. We have moved into the era of sustainable development, which seeks to empower people to become active participants in the development process, from the identification of needs, to the planning and implementation of programmes and projects.

Over the last two decades, the Queen Alia Fund has played a pivotal role in Jordan's development scene. Our approach has evolved in stages, according to prevailing social and economic conditions, and the needs of our community-based partners, in consistency with international definitions and priorities, which have placed an increasing responsibility upon NGOs to become key partners in the development process.

Our beloved leader, His Majesty King Hussein, one of the great humanitarians of our time, believed that 'People are our most precious asset,' and thus dedicated his life to ensuring the dignity and well-being of our Jordanian family. Both His Majesty's vision of a people-centred development, and his determination for the most disadvantaged groups to be integrated into society, has inspired and guided our work over the last two decades.

And, as we move collectively into a new phase of development, we honour His Majesty's memory by commemorating our national achievements. With this aim, we have decided to consolidate the work of the Queen Alia Fund, and pay tribute to the leadership which has inspired its progress over the years, under the new title: 'The Jordanian Hashemite Fund for Human Development' (JOHUD).

Under its new title, the Jordanian Hashemite Fund for Human Development seeks to reflect our national pride as Jordanians, and our pledge to develop the potential of the country's most valuable asset; its people. Through this initiative, we shall also uphold international principles which place human needs at the heart of the development agenda.

The Jordanian Hashemite Fund for Human Development shall thus be a testament to our continued commitment to human development, in the spirit of dedication inspired by His Majesty King Hussein.

The organization, as a result of this change in title, will not differ radically in its function from the organization you have come to know, trust and support. However we will continue to advance the process begun last year, which focuses on a comprehensive review of our structure, approach and priorities. We believe such a process to be essential to ensuring appropriate changes, geared not only to improving our own performance, but also enhancing the effectiveness and efficiency of our partners in the field.

I would like to take this opportunity to thank you for the support and interest you have shown the Fund over the years. I know that the Jordanian Hashemite Fund for Human Development will continue to draw on your friendship and help in the years to come, in facing the challenges of the future and honouring the legacy of His Majesty King Hussein's vision.

Yours sincerely,
Princess Basma bint Talal
Chairperson, Board of Trustees
21 March 1999
Reference: 1/1/775[1]

It is well recognized that the course of people's lives can be shaped and even determined by the impact of certain events. There are times when events of this kind can take on a life of their own, 'and people's lives, their cultures and the world are never again quite the same' (Salzman, 1999: 10). For Jordanians, the death of King Hussein was such an event. In the aftermath of February 1999, as Jordan sought to come to terms with its great loss, people were united in their resolve to uphold the king's legacy by taking forward the country which he had built and nurtured over close to five decades. It was a time for me to also reconsider the role of the organization which had been created by His Majesty's original vision. I sensed that we had reached a turning point. The way ahead, I felt, was to honour the lifelong belief of His Majesty King Hussein, which placed the well-being of people at the heart of his efforts, and also to symbolize the Fund's renewed commitment to the future. It was in this spirit that I

---

1. The announcement of the Jordanian Hashemite Fund for Human Development (JOHUD) to international associates by the Chairperson of the Board of Trustees.

decided to send a proposal to parliament to change the name of the Fund, and on 16 March 1999 an amendment to the law was approved, naming The Jordanian Hashemite Fund for Human Development (The Official Gazette, 1999).

In this book I have attempted to demonstrate that development is a continuously evolving process subject to varying economic, political, social, and cultural forces and interests. These forces and interests exert pressures of their own and are, moreover, often in opposition to one another. I have traced the path of Jordan's development which has been shaped by a process of mediation and compromise to accommodate these political and economic forces at the local, regional and international levels. The story of the Queen Alia Fund tells of similar challenges as the organization responded to the world around it, and sought to accommodate the numerous facets and divisions which it came to embody, culminating in the decision to change its name to the Jordanian Hashemite Fund for Human Development.

For the Fund, and for the country as a whole, the arrival of the new millennium was a significant moment in Jordan's development. A growing spirit of optimism was emerging once again with high expectations of social change and economic growth. And yet there was still the awareness of vulnerability, learnt from the experience of development as a process of mediation and compromise and the knowledge that external forces impact significantly on the development choices a nation can take.

This book has traced the history of this experience by analysing the different phases of international development policy from the 1950s to the end of the 1990s, and by examining the challenges that countries like Jordan have faced in their attempt to keep pace with frequent shifts in donor discourse and approaches. In Jordan, the pressures on the development process were also exacerbated by the need to balance a particular combination of political and economic factors which in turn were affected by both internal and external conditions. From the analysis, it is clear that Jordan's efforts to promote its own political and economic interests have necessitated a frequent redefining of national strategies in order to respond to and sustain the country's priorities and needs. Within this context, the chances of being able to maintain a particular, desired, course of development have sometimes seemed remote. Indeed, at various junctures, the pursuit of such goals has been severely interrupted by events largely beyond the country's control. Hence, when considering 'development' in the broader sense, whether from the viewpoint of a developing country, or from a practitioner's perspective, the question arises: to what extent do international development policies take into account the diverse factors that influence the development process at any given time?

What is often not sufficiently recognized by policy-makers, at international and state levels alike, is the fact that development is a people-centred process, which requires explicit consideration of the human component. In Jordan, for example, over each of the phases of development outlined in this book, problems were encountered in trying to help people to adjust to the country's serious economic situation. With the introduction of structural adjustment measures from 1989 onwards, the Jordanian state was obliged to try to address complex issues concerning the problems of poverty and unemployment. Many of these derived from the culture of dependency previously created by the patron state approach. Consequently, government reforms faced resistance from many of those who relied on the state as a provider of job security, services, subsidies and emergency funds. Clearly, a change of attitude was needed in order to create greater self-reliance. Yet the problem was compounded because, as people experienced increased economic hardship, they became more vulnerable, and the capacity and resources needed to become more self-reliant were increasingly difficult to muster. Alongside the structural adjustment measures, a parallel process of political liberalization created its own tensions, as well as opportunities, as the roles of state and civil society were reshaped at the critical time of transition leading up to the end of the 1990s.

Given the country's heavy reliance on external aid, the international donor agenda also had its effect on the prevailing climate of change. The political conditionality of the New Policy Agenda, emerging in the 1990s, required that various concepts such as good governance and democratization should be promoted. However, it must be recognized that democratic processes are characterized by the specific historical conditions under which they emerge (White, 1995). The significance for Jordan of contexts and historical timing has been highlighted in this book with reference to the complexities and fluctuations of the state-civil society relations which underpin economic growth. In the context of Jordan's political and economic transition, the paradoxical issues facing both sectors are still proving difficult to resolve. Within the climate of structural adjustment, economic conditions put social stability to the test. Furthermore, in the late 1990s, while the country was striving to join the global economy, it was also severely affected by regional factors, including the ongoing Arab-Israeli conflict. Political circumstances thus provoked varying reactions which, in an environment of political liberalization, were sometimes heatedly expressed. On the other hand, to foster a good investment climate and improve the country's economic situation, political and social stability had to be maintained. The challenge arising from these contradictory demands cannot be underestimated in view of regional tensions and internal economic strains.

From the late 1980s onwards, Jordan has had to grapple with the complexities of such interrelated factors, and to understand the extent to which the effects of structural adjustment could be tolerated, particularly when so many people felt that the only transitional change was that things were getting harder. In conditions of rising poverty and unemployment, good governance policies created additional pressures, while reforms such as downsizing implied that the security of state jobs was becoming even less assured.

Even as Jordan was having to contend with its own specific circumstances, the advent of globalization created additional uncertainties. Globalization was greeted with scepticism in the international development community, with concerns raised about issues of ownership of the process and fears concerning its potential impact on the specific realities of developing countries. The world, as we were constantly reminded, had become a 'global village;' but the Western understanding of 'globalization,' and its implications were still not clear. In 1999 globalization was still unfamiliar ground for Jordanians, as yet a distant idea rather than a reality of life. Regardless of whether it would eventually prove to be an opportunity or a threat, it was already clearly imposing significant change on the Jordanian development path.

Between the arguments of those who believe that the liberalization of markets has the effect of encouraging growth – which means a better standard of living – and those who see globalization as the cause of the widening gap between the rich and the poor, the continuing uncertainty surrounding the process makes it imperative to find ways and means to lessen disparities between countries and to promote measures to enhance inclusiveness, equity and democracy among nations. Globalization continues to be the reality of our world today, yet we should not accept its consequences as a predestined course of events. Globalization is the result of a conscious political and economic strategy emerging from a particular historical, economic and social context, and as such it can be countered by political means.

Given the feeling of insecurity and inequality inherited from an earlier age, many parts of the developing world believe that they are being further marginalized or victimized by the overall drive to globalization. This sense of helplessness is further exacerbated by the intensifying invasion of a global culture to which they must submit. Proponents of globalization must recognize that diverse cultures, languages, religions and interests, as well as different levels of development, make up the global village – and can make it work. The dialectic between diversity and globalization has not, however, been successfully addressed so far.

Throughout the country's development processes, the Jordanian NGO movement has also steadily evolved, influenced by shifts in development thinking and directly affected by changes in donor funding. By the 1990s, local NGO initiatives had left behind their early charity-based efforts and moved to a more development-oriented approach. Since the advent of political liberalization, there had been both a marked increase in the number of local NGOs and a diversification in NGO activities. In the context of the country's transition, the dilemmas faced by Jordanian NGOs mirrored the numerous problems which the state also faced. In both cases, the contentious issue was the dichotomy which exists between the need to promote and sustain change on the one hand, and the need to respond to the problems which are often magnified by the process of change itself on the other. A perception that these new directions were externally imposed, exacerbated the situation. For instance, when bread subsidies were lifted in 1996, state policy appeared to be less sensitive to people's hardships than to the conditionalities of structural adjustment, and riots ensued. A similar, if smaller, example is the Fund's experience with microfinance and the conflict which it precipitated within the organization, although in this case the option of choosing a less difficult course of action was available.

For the Jordanian Hashemite Fund for Human Development, as the Fund became known in 1999, the need to find a balance between accommodating donor priorities and maintaining the largely home-grown dimensions of its development approach remained a predominant concern. While donor contributions are a lifeline to sustainable development projects, their approaches need to show sensitivity and consideration to the varying local cultures which dictate the pace and methods of implementation, and to recognize the need to build on existing knowledge instead of replacing it. With its community-based presence through the CDCs, the Fund's interventions have shown that change has its own momentum and is more readily fostered when internally motivated than when externally imposed. This is most clearly seen in the area of women's advancement. Through its work with the women's sector, the Fund's experience has shown that women themselves have different priorities and ways of participation, all of which must be accommodated within the continuum of practical and strategic needs. The Fund's programmes and projects have always been gender sensitive, more from a pragmatic recognition than through theoretical discourse. Accordingly, its 'Gender and Development' approach to activities concerning women has been shaped by local realities rather than a particular development trend.

While recognizing that the inherent value of initiatives which have been promoted from within must be preserved, the Fund has had to assimilate other methods and approaches in order to keep pace with the overall process of change. During the 1990s, donor interest in Jordanian NGOs heightened, and in view of diminishing local resources the Fund wanted to ensure its share of international donor support. However, the kind of projects which were being sponsored by donors at this time meant that the Fund had first to build its own internal capacities. In trying to access new funding opportunities, concentration was shifting to accommodate donor priorities, often at the expense of attention to the field. Significantly, while laying the ground for new directions, the Fund was inadvertently distancing itself from the very target groups its efforts were preparing to address. Hence a gap began to develop between the Fund and the Community Development Centres and local partners felt increasingly marginalized by their own organization. Despite the climate of liberalization, at which time people in the field were becoming more vocal in articulating their feelings, the Fund was often slow to respond.

The Fund may well have occupied what has been described earlier as a 'middle position' between the needs of the grassroots and the priorities of donors; but that does not mean it was always able to stand the middle ground. The varying interests and perspectives which donors and grassroots embody each exert a powerful pull and they inevitably swayed the Fund. Within this equation, however, lie the needs of the field which the Fund is largely reliant on donors to enable it to meet. Thus, to be able to mediate effectively between the two, the Fund must continue to draw on its experience and enhance its capacity to become a strong and effective partner with each.

As a significant actor within the national development setting, JOHUD clearly had a valuable contribution to make as the country entered a new century and a new era. The maturity which the organization had acquired, combined with a receptiveness to change, were strong assets. Accordingly, the key to shaping the progress of JOHUD in the future would lie in the capacity to address new changes as they arose and to undertake further self-evaluation. While answers to the questions raised in this process would not always be found, and while some agonizing was likely, greater clarity for the way forward could be achieved. These comments on the future of JOHUD, identified in 1999, continue to apply right up to the present.

Like other Jordanian institutions which are undergoing processes of reform, the challenge for JOHUD is to develop an approach to problem solving which allows it to become more innovative and resourceful in the face of shrinking budgets and growing constraints. This requires that JOHUD also pays careful attention to bridging the divide that change may bring. From a human dimension, for example, the 'professionalization' of development has meant that a cadre of increasingly Western-educated and Western-trained individuals are being brought into the organization. Whilst the contribution of these skilled professional cadres has to be recognized, the process has also led to a widening gap between JOHUD and the people it seeks to serve. JOHUD, as a development organization working in local communities, cannot afford to neglect the value of indigenous knowledge, which is essential to making things succeed.

While seeking to balance external pressures and trends with local conditions and needs, programme revision within the CDCs continues to merit serious attention. In the case of most centres, many of the programmes which started in the 1980s, when better circumstances prevailed, may no longer provide solutions for the economic problems of most target groups which have since intensified. Microfinance can play an important part; but present conditions continue to necessitate some emphasis on basic needs.

The establishment of the CDC network has been one of the Fund's most significant achievements and in taking forward the process of reform a priority is to identify ways to activate the role of the CDCs within the emerging context. JOHUD needs to forge a new understanding from the perspective of its partners in the field. Decentralization, which forms an important aspect of the Fund's new strategy, is a lengthy and complex undertaking. Only by moving from the rhetorical to the practical can the full implications of this process for JOHUD, as well as for the CDCs, be grasped. Fundamental requirements such as costing and building technical and administrative know-how need to be addressed in detail in order for the CDCs to be able to sustain efficient operations. Furthermore, JOHUD itself must re-examine its administrative linkages with the centres, particularly in relationship to its own bureaucracy which has been known to delay work on the ground.

A basic component of the process of decentralization is participation. Hence in seeking to decentralize, a greater level of participation needs to be incorporated within the approaches of the Fund, as well as in the CDCs. However, the question this poses is to what extent participatory and democratic methods can be effective when development is in itself a value-laden process? Moreover, in demanding greater participation, people must themselves recognize that their own attitudes need to change. As the CDCs grow more autonomous, greater accountability within their internal administrations will be required. Otherwise, decentralization will bring new problems in its wake, such as nepotism and the transfer of authority to local elites.

For JOHUD sustainability has become a major concern. From a long-term perspective, and in theory, development organizations should eventually write themselves out of the field. In this respect, questions have to be raised about the future of development NGOs like JOHUD, and indeed the future role of such organizations in civil society. In the medium term and in practice, the Fund has to contend with the innate paradox that in order to become a self-sustaining body it has to adopt sometimes unsustainable short term strategies to attract donor funding. As a result, the Fund has often had to operate as an output-oriented mechanism delivering funding and programmes to the field. Hopefully this stage is one of transition. Ideally, if JOHUD could reach a stage at which its financial sustainability, and hence its continuity, was no longer an overriding concern, greater emphasis could be placed on the personal and human dimensions of organizational development, and staff would be in a position to transmit a new dynamism to the field. A key dimension of the Fund's new outlook is embodied by the Queen Zein al Sharaf Institute for Development. ZENID will have to play a leading role in advancing the Fund's strategic objectives, particularly in relation to human capacity-building. Here, one of the main challenges it will need to address is how to stimulate the attitudinal shifts which genuinely reflect a strategic commitment to change.

It has been argued that QAF, and now JOHUD, is not representative of civil society and grassroots organizations because of its association with the monarchy. The Fund, some might say, was empowered and able to sustain itself with resources that would not necessarily have been available to other NGOs and enjoys closer relations with state organizations than other elements of civil society. Equally, its patronage and connections might be considered to have restricted its ability to challenge certain aspects of the status quo, or of systems in the country. These are valid issues. Legitimacy and authenticity are important and the debate that surrounds NGOs with royal patronage certainly points to the way in which organizations with such links can, in fact, operate with their own interests.

I would, however, maintain that certain of these concerns call into question some of our notions of civil society and grassroots mobilization, for classifications and distinctions of what constitutes 'grassroots' activism, or how it can originate, are sometimes oversimplified. Development and the experiences and processes which it embodies is never straightforward, but rather the result of highly complex and intertwining interests and the agendas of diverse social groupings at local, national and international levels. The parameters of these groupings are always fluctuating, so that the interests they embody can vary, and can change those whom they represent. We must also understand that participation (in its current definition), now and then needs to be nurtured and that grassroots involvement is, at times, the result of centralized initiatives.

The challenge for the Fund is to recognize how its connections and relationships have shaped its growth over the years and to promote the best conditions for civil society to thrive. The Fund itself is not a monolithic whole, but a combination of different elements, extending from community counterparts to executive management levels in the central organization. The enhancement of participation is therefore also linked to issues of organizational governance within the Fund itself. Numerous processes of devolving responsibility must be undertaken at all organizational levels in order to ensure that the environment at the community level becomes more conducive to genuine participation. This is the difficult path that the organization must tread. Leadership and management are still vital, but they will, if the reform succeeds, be essentially altered.

The questions which this book has raised concerning some of the paradoxes of the Fund's experience, and considerations for the future, show that there is still much to be 'problematized' within the accepted body of development theory. There is a need to challenge and question many of the notions that we have come to accept, including issues related to participation, decentralization and decision-making. However, there are even bigger questions at stake about 'development' itself, not just the organizations that promote it. Of fundamental concern is the extent to which development interventions can complement national growth processes and validate their efforts within the context of globalization. Serious questions need in addition to be asked about whose interests it is really serving.

As a concept, development carries its own epistemological assumptions and values, derived from combinations of cultural attitudes, political agendas and economic interests. It is subject to interfaces of power that mirror the power relationships which characterize the modern age. Thus, deconstructing development means not only unveiling the inner workings and origins of the development paradigm, but challenging the very premise of the development agenda, and the linear process it advocates whereby people are engaged in a process of 'advancement' and 'improvement.'

Jordan's own development experience underlines some of the philosophical complexity that sits at the heart of development theory. Frequently the very steps that the country has undertaken along the path of development have created their own loopholes and barriers. It is therefore problematic to measure progress in a linear fashion because success is often not incremental but sporadic and difficult to assess. Just as development theories, approaches and paradigms are often imported, so too are the criteria for measuring its achievements. Even the earlier development efforts in Jordan cannot be underestimated, whether or not, in retrospect, they were as farsighted as they might have been. Jordan has demonstrated a resilience and an ability to cope with the unexpected and the inevitable. It has rebounded back and forth, from periods of grace to setbacks and stagnation. Any assessment of Jordan's performance and achievements from the perspective of the present day has to do justice to this dynamic which has been so vital to the country's survival. However, recognizing this dynamic also means recognizing the non-linear nature of social reality and survival. Understanding development means more than tracing a continuum: it means also acknowledging and appreciating coping strategies and reactions, as and when they emerge. The dynamics of development should be recognized and understood not merely in the context of current times, conditions and attitudes, but in their own context. These conclusions, originally drawn in 1999, still apply for the developing world in general, but, as subsequent events have proven, they hold a particular truth in the context of Jordan.

Bibliography

Interviews

Abu el-Ata, Abdullah. Director of the Social Development Department, QAF, 1978–1995; Director of the Queen Zein al Sharaf Compound for Training and Development, 1995–1999. Interviewed by Taghreed Abu-Hamdan, 14 June 1999, in Amman (in Arabic).

Abu-Jaber, Kamel. Executive Director of QAF, 1979–1980. Former Minister of Foreign Affairs and former Minister of the Economy. Former President of the Higher Media Council and former President of the Institute of Diplomacy. Interviewed by Nicholaa Malet de Carteret, 5 September 1999, in Amman.

Abu-Rish, Munif. Director of Social Development Department, JOHUD, 1997–2002 (joined the Fund in 1996 as Deputy Director of the Department). Interviewed by Nicholaa Malet de Carteret, 18 October 1999 (a), and 22 August 2000 (b), in Amman.

Abu al-Samen, Mai. Secretary General of the Jordanian National Forum for Women from 1997 till present. Interviewed by Taghreed Abu-Hamdan, 11 February 2000, in Amman (in Arabic).

Arabiat, Bashir. Former Director of Studies, Research and Development Department, Ministry of Municipal and Rural Affairs. Interviewed by Taghreed Abu-Hamdan, 6 January 1999, in Amman (in Arabic).

Bahous, Sima. Director, Communication and Information Division, Royal Hashemite Court. Former Executive Director, Noor al-Hussein Foundation. Interviewed by Nicholaa Malet de Carteret, 26 July 1999, in Amman.

Fariz, Reem. Director of Small Business Development Centre (SBDC), JOHUD, (joined the Fund in 1995 as Head of Marketing Section). Interviewed by Nicholaa Malet de Carteret, 30 May 2000, in Amman.

Haj-Issa, Basel. Head of Monitoring and Evaluation Unit, JOHUD, 1998–2001. Interviewed by Nicholaa Malet de Carteret, 10 October 1999 (a), and 3 August 2000 (b), in Amman.

Hamarneh, Mustafa. Director of the Centre for Strategic Studies, University of Jordan since 1992. Interviewed by Nicholaa Malet de Carteret, 1 October 2000, in Amman.

Hassanein, Hussein. Senior Trainer, Skills and Community Development Department, Queen Zein al Sharaf Institute for Development, 1994–2000 (joined the Fund in 1983 as staff member of the Social Development Department). Interviewed by Nicholaa Malet de Carteret, 10 November 1993, in Amman.

Hessa, Wijdan al-. Rural Leader, Ma'in Centre since 1987. Interviewed by Taghreed Abu-Hamdan, 13 June 2000, in Ma'in, Madaba (in Arabic).

Himsi, Maha al-. Project Officer, Protection and Early Childhood, UNICEF. Interviewed by Taghreed Abu-Hamdan, 5 March 2000, in Amman (in Arabic).

Hmeidat, Amneh al-. Rural Leader of al-Tayyiba Centre since 1986. Interviewed by Taghreed Abu-Hamdan, 5 October 1999, in al-Tayyiba, Ma'an (in Arabic).

Hussein, Omar. General Manager of GUVS for the Amman Governorate. Assistant Secretary General of MOSD 1996–1999. Interviewed by Taghreed Abu-Hamdan, 2 April 2000, in Amman (in Arabic).

Iss'iss, Ahmad al-. Member, Executive Council, General Union of Voluntary Societies. Interviewed by Taghreed Abu-Hamdan, 17 June 1999, in Amman (in Arabic).

Khatib, Abdullah al-. President, Executive Council, General Union of Voluntary Societies since 1982. Interviewed by Nicholaa Malet de Carteret, 27 July 1999, in Amman.

Khouri, Rami. Author and Political Journalist. Executive Editor, *The Daily Star*. General Manager of al-Kutba Publishers. Former editor of the *Jordan Times*. Interviewed by Nicholaa Malet de Carteret, 7 October 2000, in Amman.

Lissner, Jörgen. United Nations Resident Coordinator and Resident Representative of the United Nations Development Programme (UNDP) in Jordan, 1995–2000. Interviewed by Nicholaa Malet de Carteret, 5 June 2000, in Amman.

Mufti, In'am al-. Served on QAF's Board of Trustees 1977–1988. Former Minister of Social Development. Former Executive Director of the Noor al-Hussein Foundation. Interviewed by Nicholaa Malet de Carteret, 18 August 1999, in Amman.

Nassir, Sari. Chairman, Community Centres Association, 1997 to present. Former Head, Sociology Department, University of Jordan. Interviewed by Nicholaa Malet de Carteret, 10 August 1999, in Amman.

Nusseir, Shadia. Executive Director, JOHUD, 1999–2002 (joined the Fund in 1988 as Director of Coordination and Follow-up). Interviewed by Nicholaa Malet de Carteret, 10 October 1999 (a), and 18 June 2000 (b), in Amman.

Rodriguez, Carlos. Director of Development Programmes, Oxfam-Quebec, 1993–2001. Programme Director of Organization Canadienne pour la Solidarité et le Développement (OCSD), 1987–1993. Co-founder and General Secretary of OCSD 1983–1987. Interviewed by Nicholaa Malet de Carteret, 10 October 2000, in Amman.

Saqour, Mohammed al-. Minister of Social Development 1993–1995. Secretary-General of MOSD, 1987–1993. Assistant Secretary-General of MOSD,

1985–1987. Former Chief Technical Advisor, National Poverty Eradication and Employment Programme, UNDP Yemen. Interviewed by Nicholaa Malet de Carteret, 11 September 1999, in Amman.

Saudi, Huda. Rural Leader, Hisban Community Development Centre from 1984 till present (the first rural leader). Interviewed by Taghreed Abu-Hamdan, 16 January 2000, in Hisban, Madaba (in Arabic).

Shahwan, Samar al-. Head of the Women and Children's Section, JOHUD, from 1998 till present (joined the Fund as staff member of the Women's Committees and Family Education Programme in 1990). Interviewed by Nicholaa Malet de Carteret, 17 October 1999 (a). Interviewed by Taghreed Abu-Hamdan, 7 February 2000 (b) in Amman (in Arabic).

Sharaf, Niveen. Former General Manager, Microfund for Women. Interviewed by Nicholaa Malet de Carteret, 25 October 1999 in Amman.

Shawabkeh, Salem al-. Director of Madaba Main Centre, JOHUD, 1986–2001. Interviewed by Taghreed Abu-Hamdan, 30 September 1999 in Madaba (in Arabic).

Ustah, Hasan al-. Director of Development Projects, JOHUD, 1997–2001 (joined the Fund in 1991 as Coordinator for Support to NGOs Project). Director of Social Development Department,1995–1997. Interviewed by Nicholaa Malet de Carteret, 6 June 2000, in Amman.

Wade, Stephen. Programme Director, Access to Microfinance and Improved Implementation of Policy Reform (AMIR). Interviewed by Nicholaa Malet de Carteret, 18 October 1999, in Amman.

Women's Committee of Idoun, Irbid. Group interview by Taghreed Abu-Hamdan, 27 November 1999, in Idoun, Irbid (in Arabic).

Zakhary, Evelyn. Director of External Relations Department, JOHUD, 1997–2001 (joined the Fund in 1993 as Projects Coordinator for the Department). Interviewed by Nicholaa Malet de Carteret, 2 July 1999, in Amman.

Archives of JOHUD and QAF Housed in the Jordanian Hashemite Fund for Human Development

JOHUD. 1999b. Final Report on the Rural Women Groups and Credit Project in Jordan in cooperation with UNIFEM, by Samar al-Shahwan (in Arabic).

——1999c. A Memorandum to Samir Hudhud from Joy Lucke.

——1999e. Minutes of the TPR Meeting, 'Poverty Alleviation Initiative.' (JOR/93/119). 20 April 1999.

——1999g. Letter from the Chairperson of the Board of Trustees to international associates announcing the name change from Queen Alia Fund (QAF) to the Jordanian Hashemite Fund for Human Development (JOHUD).

——2000b. Figures of assistance provided by the Goodwill Campaign to individuals and families (in Arabic).

——2000d. Memorandum from the Director of Auditing Department to the

Chairperson of the Board of Trustees on Accounts for the Wadi Rum project, 2 April 2000 (in Arabic).

——2000e. List of Projects submitted for Funding. External Relations Department.

QAF. 1978b. Financial Aid to Schools in Remote Areas in Jordan (in Arabic).

——1979a. Minutes of Meeting of the Board of Trustees with the Prime Minister. 29 September 1979 (in Arabic).

——1979b. Rockefeller Foundation Task Force to Jordan. Amman: QAF.

——1979h. Minutes of Meeting of the Board of Trustees. 15 March 1979 (in Arabic).

——1981c. The Community Development Centres Project (in Arabic).

——1982b. Minutes of Meeting of the Local Committee for the Madaba Community Development Centres (in Arabic).

——1984b. Centres of Basic Social Services for Nomadic Settlements in Jordan (in Arabic).

——1984c. Job Description of the ra'ida rifiyya (in Arabic).

——1984d. Madaba Centres (in Arabic).

——1985b. Training for Pre-School Teachers (in Arabic).

——1985c. A Report on the Achievement of Madaba Centres, July 1984–December 1985 (in Arabic).

——1986a. Five Year Plan 1986–1990 for Queen Alia Fund. Amman (in Arabic).

——1986b. By-Laws of QAF Main Centres, Local Committee of Volunteers (in Arabic).

——1986c. Signed Agreement with Voluntary and Community Based Organizations (in Arabic).

——1986d. Personnel (in Arabic).

——1987a. Personnel (in Arabic).

——1987b. Training Programme for the Year 1987 (in Arabic).

——1988a. Personnel (in Arabic).

——1988b. Training Programme for Rural Leaders in Ma'an (in Arabic).

——1988d. Letter from Canadian Embassy to the Executive Director with a Contribution to the Rug-Weaving Projects. 20 December 1988.

——1989a. Personnel (in Arabic).

——1989b. Consultative Committee for the Pre-School Programme (in Arabic).

——1989c. The Queen Zein al-Sharaf Compound for Training and Social Development.

——1989e. Women's Committees in Community Development Centres and Voluntary Organizations. A concept paper prepared by Leila Qaqish (in Arabic).

——1990a. Support to Non-Governmental Organisations in Jordan.

——1990b. Consultative Committee for the Pre-School Programme (in Arabic).

——1990c. Pre-school Outreach Programme (in Arabic).

——1991a. Signed Agreement with Voluntary and Community-Based Organizations (in Arabic).

——1991c. Developing the Palm Plantation in al-'Aqaba Region (in Arabic).

——1991d. A Signed Agreement with the Industrial Development Bank (in Arabic).

——1991e. Revolving Loans Fund (in Arabic).

——1992c. Concept paper on the Revolving Loan Fund Programme (RLF).

——1992d. A Report from the Director of the Income-Generating Department to the Executive Director on the Rug Weaving Project in Mulayh (in Arabic).

——1992e. A signed agreement between QAF and Khsha' al-Slateen Social Development Society (KSSDS) (in Arabic).

——1992f. Revolving Loans Programme (in Arabic).

——1993a. Letter from the Ministry of Agriculture to QAF regarding the Ministry's contribution to the Goodwill Campaign (in Arabic).

——1993b. Letter from Amman Municipality regarding their donation to the Goodwill Campaign (in Arabic).

——1993c. *Zakat* Fund donation to the Goodwill Campaign (in Arabic).

——1993d. Proposal on the Rehabilitation of Poor Families in Jordan. Prepared by the Planning Department (in Arabic).

——1994b. Letters requesting assistance for villages in Jordan (in Arabic).

——1994c. Letter from the Central *Badia* Directorate, al-Muwaqar branch of the Ministry of Social Development requesting assistance for families in need (in Arabic).

——1994d. Letter from Haddad Sons Company with a donation to support the establishment of income-generating projects for families in need (in Arabic).

——1994e. Report on Income Generating Projects by Derek Reeves.

——1994f. Visit report by Derek Reeves to QAF. 18 October–17 November 1994.

——1995. Letter from General Union for Voluntary Societies on their contribution to the Goodwill Campaign (in Arabic).

——1996b. Letter from USAID to QAF. 10 November 1996.

——1997a. Report on the Development of the Community Development Centres (in Arabic).

——1997b. A Case Study on Kawkab al-Ghnameen, Rural Leader of al-Baq'a Centre in Ma'an Governorate.

——1997d. Report on the Loans Scheme by Munif Abu Rish.

——1997e. Agreement between QAF and Wadi Rum Committee. 1 June 1997 (in Arabic).

——1997f. Memorandum from Joy Lucke to the Acting Executive Director.

——1997g. A Contract Salary Agreement (in Arabic).

——1997h. Concept Paper: Small Business Development Centre (SBDC) at the Queen Alia Fund by Juliette Chateauneuf.

——1997i. Summary Report on the Task Force Meetings. 20 December 1997.

——1997j. Letter of Agreement between the United Nations Development Programme and Queen Alia Fund for Social Development for a joint Project on Poverty Alleviation Initiative in Jordan.

——1997k. Minutes of the Meeting between Social Development Department and Rural Leaders of al-'Aqaba centres, 30 October 1997, in al-'Aqaba (in Arabic).

——1998d. Circular from the Chairperson to QAF staff (in Arabic).

——1998e. Fax from Pathfinder International to QAF. 19 May 1998.

——1998f. Letter from Pathfinder International to QAF. 22 October 1998.

——1998g. Minutes of the Meeting of the Steering Committee, QAF, OCSD, CIDA, MOP. Amman, 5 May 1998.

——1998h. Minutes of Meeting with UNDP. Amman, 24 September 1998.

——1998i. Minutes of the Fundraising Workshop. Amman, 19 November 1998 (in Arabic).

——1998j. Minutes of the Task Force Meeting. Amman, 3 March 1998 (in Arabic).

——1998k. Minutes of the Task Force Meeting. Amman, 7 March 1998.

——1998l. Minutes of the Task Force Meeting. Amman, 25 February 1998 (in Arabic).

——1999a. Analytic Report on CDCs' Income and Expenditures (in Arabic).

——1999c. Letter from QAF Chairperson, Board of Trustees to Mr. Stephen Wade, Director of AMIR Programme. 31 January 1999.

Unpublished Reports and Studies of the Fund

JOHUD. 1999d. Social Productivity Programme (SPP), by Salem Ghawi.

——2000a. Donors' Shift from Government to NGOs, by Salem Ghawi.

——2000c. Report on the Income-Generating Projects, by Munif Abu-Rish.

——2000f. Background paper on Microfinance, by Reem Fariz.

——2000g. Small Business Development Centre: Aims, Services and Activities (in Arabic).

——2000h. Background paper on the Fund's Internal Reform by Basel Haj-Issa.

JOHUD/UNDP. 1999. Technical Assessment to Strengthen JOHUD (QAF) Capacity for Sustainable Microfinance Operations. 7 May 1999.

QAF. 1979f. A Preliminary Study of Rural Women in the Karak District.

——1992a. Fields of Activities and Achievements.

——1992b. Women's Socio-Economic Status in Rawdat Basma Village, al-Mafraq Governorate (in Arabic).

——1994a. Report on Achievements of the Social Development Department for 1994 (in Arabic).

——1996a. The Impact of QAF's Programmes and Activities on People's Participation in Social and Economic Activities, Women's Participation in Decision-Making and at the National Level.

——1998a. Trends of Jordan Development Policies, 1950s-1990s, by Salem Ghawi.

——1998b. Study on Management Versus Decentralization. Field interviews conducted between May and August 1997. 12 Volumes.

——1998c. Annual Report of the Social Development Department (In Arabic).

——1999b. Small Business Development Center Small and Micro Finance Program: Business Plan. Proposal submitted to the AMIR Program.

Published Reports and Studies of the Fund

JOHUD. 1999a. The Jordanian Hashemite Fund for Human Development: Where People Build the Future. Amman: JOHUD.

——1999f. A Strategic Plan, 1999–2002. Amman: JOHUD.

QAF. 1978a. Annual Report 1978. Amman: QAF.

——1979c. Annual Report 1979. Amman: QAF.

——1979d. An Evaluative Study of Voluntary Social Work in the East Bank of Jordan. Amman: QAF.

——1979e. National Survey of the Handicapped in Jordan. Amman: QAF.

——1979g. A Survey of Centres of Basic Social Services for the Nomadic Settlements in Jordan. Amman: QAF (in Arabic).

——1980. Annual Report 1980. Amman: QAF.

——1981a. Annual Report 1981. Amman: QAF.

——1981b. A Sample of the Study of the Socio-Economic Conditions of Rural Women in the Karak Region. Amman: QAF.

——1982a. Annual Report 1982. Amman: QAF.

——1983. Annual Report 1983. Amman: QAF.

——1984a. Annual Report 1984. Amman: QAF.

——1985a. Annual Report 1985. Amman: QAF.

——1986e. Annual Report 1986. Amman: QAF.

——1987c. Annual Report 1987. Amman: QAF.

——1988c. Annual Report 1988. Amman: QAF.

——1989d. Strategy. Amman: QAF.

——1989f. Annual Report 1989. Amman: QAF.

——1991b. Annual Report 1990/1991. Amman: Queen Alia Jordan Social Welfare Fund (in Arabic).

——1997c. Annual Report 1997. Amman: QAF.

Unpublished Government Documents and Reports

Jordan. 1977b. Registration Certificate No. 496. 10 April 1977. Amman: Department of Social Affairs.

——1978b. Letter from the Prime Minister to the Minister of Finance regarding a partial income tax exemption for citizens who donate to QAF. Ref. No. 13/9/7/16/2505, 6 March 1978. Amman: Prime Ministry (in Arabic).

——1979c. Data of the Housing and Population Census. Amman: Department of Statistics (in Arabic).

——1992b. Prime Ministerial Directive No. 4 for 1992. Amman: Prime Ministry.

——1995b. Administrative Development Plan. Amman: Ministry of Administrative Development (in Arabic).

——1998c. Proposal on Social Productivity Program. Amman: Ministry of Planning.

——1999b. Micro-Finance Sector in Jordan. Amman: Ministry of Planning. June 1999 (in Arabic).

——2000d. Unofficial Memo from Ministry of Interior. Amman: Ministry of Interior (in Arabic).

Government of Jordan Reports

JNPC (Jordanian National Population Commission). 2000. Population Challenges to Sustainable Development in Jordan, 2000–2020. Amman: JNPC (in Arabic).

Jordan. 1957. Report on the Work of the Ministry, 1956–1957. Amman: Ministry of Social Affairs (in Arabic).

——1959. Report on the Work of the Ministry, 1958–1959. Amman: Ministry of Social Affairs (in Arabic).

——1960. Report on the Work of the Ministry 1959–1960. Amman: Ministry of Social Affairs (in Arabic).

——1961. Ministry of Social Affairs Annual Report 1960–1961. Amman: Ministry of Social Affairs (in Arabic).

——1963. Ministry of Social Affairs and Labour Annual Report 1962–1963. Amman: Ministry of Social Affairs and Labour (in Arabic).

——1964. Seven Year Programme for Economic Development 1964–1970. Amman: Jordanian Development Board.

——1966. Ministry of Social Affairs and Labour Annual Report 1966. Amman: Ministry of Social Affairs and Labour (in Arabic).

——1967. Ministry of Social Affairs and Labour Annual Report 1967. Amman: Ministry of Social Affairs and Labour (in Arabic).

——1969. Ministry of Social Affairs and Labour Annual Report 1969. Amman: Ministry of Social Affairs and Labour (in Arabic).

——1970. Ministry of Social Affairs and Labour Annual Report 1970. Amman: Ministry of Social Affairs and Labour (in Arabic).

——1971. Planning Law No. 68 for the Year 1971. Amman: National Planning Council.

——1972. Annual Report 1972. Amman: Ministry of Labour and Social Development.

——1973. Three Year Development Plan 1973–1975. Amman: National Planning Council.

——1975a. General Budget 1975. Amman: Budget Department (in Arabic).

——1975b. Ministry of Social Affairs and Labour Annual Report 1975. Amman: Ministry of Social Affairs and Labour (in Arabic).

——1976a. Five Year Development Plan for Economic and Social Development 1976–1980. Amman: National Planning Council.

——1976b. Ministry of Labour/Department of Social Affairs Annual Report 1976. Amman: Ministry of Labour/Department of Social Affairs (in Arabic).

——1977a. Symposium on the Municipalities of Irbid, September 25–8, 1977. Amman: Ministry of Municipal and Rural Affairs (in Arabic).

——1978a. Tracer Study of Graduates from Trade and Teacher Training Centres 1971–1976. Amman: National Planning Council (in Arabic).

——1979a. Annual Report of the Ministry of Labour. Amman: Ministry of Labour (in Arabic).

——1979b. Results of Housing and Population Census. Amman: Department of Statistics (in Arabic).

——1980a. Annual Report 1980. Amman: Ministry of Social Development.

——1980b. Symposium of Ministry of Municipal and Rural Affairs and the Environment, Amman, October 13–14, 1980. Amman: Ministry of Municipal and Rural Affairs and the Environment.

——1980c. A Guide to Educational Legislation. Amman: Ministry of Education (in Arabic).

——1981a. The Five Year Plan for Economic and Social Development, 1981–1985. Amman: Ministry of Planning.

——1981b. Annual Report 1981. Amman: Ministry of Social Development (in Arabic).

——1982a. Housing and Population Census: Summary Results for Localities in the East Bank. Amman: Department of Statistics.

——1982b. Annual Report 1982. Amman: Ministry of Social Development (in Arabic).

——1983. Annual Report 1983. Amman: Ministry of Social Development (in Arabic).

——1984. Annual Report 1984. Amman: Ministry of Labour and Social Development (in Arabic).

——1985. General Budget 1985. Amman: Ministry of Finance (in Arabic).

——1986a. Five Year Plan for Economic and Social Development 1986–1990. Amman: Ministry of Planning.

——1986b. The Jordanian Constitution. Amman: Jordanian Houses of Parliament (in Arabic).

——1987. The Jordan Valley: Dynamic Transformation: 1973–1986. A Study Prepared by the Technical International Cooperation Department in association with Louis Berger International. Amman: Jordan Valley Authority.

——1989. Central Bank of Jordan 26th Annual Report 1989. Amman: Department of Research Studies, Central Bank of Jordan.

——1991. Department of Statistics Annual Report 1991. Amman: Department of Statistics.

——1992a. Social Legislation Compendium. Amman: Ministry of Social Development (in Arabic).

——1993a. Economic and Social Development Plan 1993–1997. Amman: Ministry of Planning.

——1993b. Ministry of Energy and Mineral Resources Annual Report 1993. Amman: Ministry of Energy and Mineral Resources.

——1993c. Report on Poverty Study: Situation and Characteristics. Amman: Ministry of Social Development (in Arabic).

——1994a. National Accounts 1952–1992. Amman: Department of Statistics.

——1994b. Annual Report of the Development and Employment Fund 1994. Amman: Development and Employment Fund (DEF) (in Arabic).

——1995a. The General Census of Population and Housing Units 1994: Methodology and Main Results. Amman: Department of Statistics.

——1996. Central Bank of Jordan Yearly Statistical Series (1964–1995). Amman: Department of Research Studies, Central Bank of Jordan.

——1997. National Aid Fund. Amman: National Aid Fund, Published in cooperation with the Ministry of Administrative Development (in Arabic).

——1998a. Conference on Jordanian Social Work. Amman: Ministry of Social Development (in Arabic).

——1998b. Jordan: Economic Review. Amman: Ministry of Planning.

——1998d. Development and Employment Fund Annual Report 1998. Amman: Development and Employment Fund (in Arabic).

——1999a. Economic and Social Development Plan 1999–2003. Amman: Ministry of Planning (in Arabic).

——2000b. Jordan Annual Fertility Survey, 1999. Amman: Department of Statistics in collaboration with the International Programmes Centre, US Census Bureau.

——2000c. Monthly Statistical Series. Vol. 36. No. 7, July 2000. Central Bank of Jordan.

JPRC (Jordan Petroleum Refinery Company). 1996. Annual Report of the Executive Board (1996). Amman: JPRC.

Royal Decree. 1977. Reference No. 3/3/1/24. Amman. 10 November 1977 (in Arabic).

The Official Gazette. 1966. 'Provisional Law No. 101: National Council for Human Resource Planning.' Amman. No. 1965: 2445–7 (in Arabic).

——1985. 'Law No. 37 for 1985: Law of the Queen Alia Jordan Social Welfare Fund.' Amman. 17 August 1985. No. 3336: 1165–7 (in Arabic).

——1994. 'Law No. 3 for 1994: Law of Education.' Amman. 2 April 1994, No. 3958: 608–19 (in Arabic).

——1996. 'Special Issue on the Formation of the Cabinet of H.E. Mr. Abdul Karim Kabariti.' Amman. 5 February 1996. No. 4098: 404–26 (in Arabic).

——1999. 'Law No. 4 for year 1999: An Amended Law to the Queen Alia Jordan Social Welfare Fund Law.' Amman. 16 March 1999. No. 4335: 880–1 (in Arabic).

Other Unpublished Sources

AMIR (Access to Microfinance Improved Implementation of Policy Reform). 1998. 'Microfinance Innovation Program (MIP): MIP Grants Instruction Booklet.'

Benn, Denis. 1997. Development Policy in the Era of Globalisation. Lecture delivered at the International Leadership Conference of the United Nations University's International Leadership Academy: Amman, June 1997.

Bseiso, Samir. 1996. Final Report on Rural Women Groups and Credit in Jordan: Program Evaluation. Prepared for UNIFEM and Queen Alia Fund for Social Development.

CECD. 1992. Consultancy Report to the Queen Alia Fund prepared by the Community Education Development Centre (CEDC). Coventry, United Kingdom.

DFID (Department for International Development). 1999. 'Output to Purpose Review: Report on the Capacity-Building Project for the Zein al-Sharaf Compound for Training and Social Development.' Amman: DFID.

Es-Said, Nimra. 1974. 'The Changing Role of Women in Jordan: A Threat or an Asset?' Paper presented to the research committee on Sex Roles in Society at the VIII World Congress of Sociology, 19–24 August, Toronto, Canada.

EuroCom. 1996. Report on the Second Phase (1996–1998) of the Jordanian-European Information, Training and Technical Assistance Office for NGOs (JETT) by Gessellschaft für europäische Kommunikation e V. (EuroCom).

——1998. Interim Progress Report on JETT by Gessellschaft für europäische Kommunikation e V. (EuroCom).

Ismail, Suad. 1989. Preliminary Recommendations for Evaluating and Developing Women's Programmes at Queen Alia Jordan Social Welfare Fund (in Arabic).

JNCW (Jordanian National Commission for Women). 1999. Compiled Statistics on the Municipal Councils' Election (in Arabic).

JNFW (Jordanian National Forum for Women). 1995. A Background Paper on the Work of Women's Committees in the Governorates (in Arabic).

Masri, Taher al-. 1999. 'Status and Horizons for the Development of the Democratic Process in Jordan.' Keynote Address at the Opening Ceremony of the Conference on the 10th Anniversary of the Launching of the Democratic Process in Jordan, 1989–1999. al-Urdon al-Jadid Research Centre and Konrad Adenauer Foundation, Amman, 6–8 September 1999 (in Arabic).

Muhtasseb, Hani and Yassen Habahba. 1999. 'The Centres of the Jordanian Hashemite Fund in Ma'an Governorate: Present and Future.' Paper presented to the Seminar on the Present and Future of the Non-Governmental Organisations in Ma'an Governorate, 16 May 1999 (in Arabic).

Princess Basma bint Talal. 1978. Speech to the First Meeting of the Board of Directors of the Scientific Organisation for Cultural Studies on Arab Women. Rabat, Morocco, 20–22 July 1978.

Reid, R. 1991. Transcript of presentation at the Roundtable Discussion on the Impact of the Gulf Crisis on Jordan. Amman, 5 January 1991.

Salti, Rebecca. 1979. A Pilot Survey of the Economic and Non-Economic Activities of 300 Jordanian Women Living in Amman.

UNDP. 1997b. Advisory Note for Jordan. Amman: UNDP.

——1998. Scope of Work for Advisory Services: To Assess the Institutional and Programme Capacity of Queen Alia Fund to Deliver Sustainable Micro-finance Services. Report to QAF.

Unpublished Theses

Dajani, Nour. 1984. 'Popular Participation: A Jordanian Attempt.' PhD thesis, Syracuse University.

Kafawin, Mahmoud al-. 1999. 'Exploratory Study on Problems of NGOs in Jordan.' MSc Thesis, University of Swansea.

Kassabeh, Qasem. 1994. 'Community Participation in the Programmes of Social Centres in Jordan: the Experience of Queen Alia Fund.' MA thesis, University of Durham.

Shakhatreh, H.I.A. 1990. 'The Determinants of Female Labor Force Participation in Jordan.' PhD thesis, University of Michigan.

Other Published Sources

JNCW (Jordanian National Commission for Women). 1993. The National Strategy for Women in Jordan. Amman: JNCW.

PBWRC (Princess Basma Women's Resource Centre). 1997. Women in the 1997 Parliamentary Elections: Voters and Candidates. Amman: PBWRC.

ZENID (The Queen Zein al Sharaf Institute for Development). 1999. The Queen Zein al Sharaf Institute for Development: Learning for Social Development. Amman: ZENID.

Books and Articles

Abu-Jaber, Kamel. 1980. The Jordanians and the People of Jordan. Amman: The Royal Scientific Society.

——1982. 'The Dynamics of Change and Development in Jordan.' The Arab Perspective. No. 2: 59–82.

——1991. 'The Hashemite Kingdom of Jordan.' In Tareq Ismael and Jacqueline Ismael (eds) Politics and Government in the Middle East and North Africa. Miami: Florida International University Press.

Adams, Francis; Satya Dev Gupta and Kidane Mengisteab. 1999. 'Globalization and the Developing World: An Introduction.' In Adams, Francis; Satya Dev Gupta and Kidane Mengisteab (eds) *Globalization and the Dilemmas of the State in the South.* London: Macmillan Press Ltd.

AFSC (American Friends Service Committee). 1958. *A Village Development Project in Jordan.* Final Report to the Ford Foundation. Pennsylvania: American Friends Service Committee.

Agrawal, Arun. 1995. 'Dismantling the Divide Between Indigenous and Scientific Knowledge.' *Development and Change.* Vol. 26: 413–39.

Allen, T. and A. Thomas. 1992. *Poverty and Development in the 1990s.* Oxford: Oxford University Press.

Altorki, Soraya and Camillia El-Solh. 1988. 'Introduction'. In Soraya Altorki and Camillia El-Solh (eds) *Arab Women in the Field: Studying Your Own Society.* New York: Syracuse University Press.

Amawi, Abla. 1996. 'USAID in Jordan.' *Middle East Policy.* Vol. 4, No. 4: 77–89.

AMIR (Access to Microfinance Improved Implementation of Policy Reform). 1999. *The AMIR Programme for Sustainable Microfinance Initiative.* Amman: AMIR Program Public Awareness Department (in Arabic).

Archer, Robert. 1994. 'Market and Good Government.' In Andrew Clayton (ed.) *Governance, Democracy and Conditionality – What Role for NGO's?* Oxford: INTRAC.

Avina, Jeffrey. 1993. 'The Evolutionary Life Cycles of Non-Governmental Development Organizations.' *Public Administration and Development*, Vol. 13: 453–74.

Azmeh, Aziz al-. 1994. 'Populism Contra Democracy: Recent Democratist Discourse in the Arab World.' In Ghassan Salamé (ed.) *Democracy Without Democrats? The Renewal of Politics in the Muslim World.* London and New York: I.B. Tauris Publishers.

Baram, A. 1991. 'Baathi Iraq and Hashemite Jordan: From Hostility to Alignment.' *Middle East Journal.* Vol. 45, No. 1: 56–8.

Barham, Nassim. 2002. 'Sectoral Actors in the Jordanian Economy.' In George Joffé (ed.) *Jordan in Transition.* London: Hurst & Company.

BBME (British Bank of the Middle East). 1986. *Jordan. Business Profile Series.* The Hongkong and Shanghai Banking Corporation.

Bebbington, Anthony and Roger Riddell. 1995. 'The Direct Funding of Southern NGOs by Donors: New Agendas and Old Problems.' *Journal of International Development.* Vol. 7, No. 6: 879–983.

Bhatnagar, Bhuvan and Aubrey Williams (eds). 1992. *Participatory Development and the World Bank – Potential Directions for Change.* Washington: World Bank Discussion Papers, No. 183.

Biegel, Renier. 1996. 'Urban Development and the Service and Banking Sector in a Rentier-State.' In Hannoyer, Jean and Seteney Shami (eds) *Amman: The City and Its Society.* Beirut: CERMOC.

Bienefeld, Manfred. 1992. *Rescuing the Dream of Development in the Nineties.* Sussex University. Institute of Development Studies. Paper 10.

Billeh, Victor. 1996. *The Civilized Face of Jordan: Education Report.* Amman: National Centre for Human Resources Development.

Bocco, Ricardo. 1989. 'L'état producteur d'identités locales: Lois electorales et tribus bedouines en Jordanie.' *Le Nomade, L'Oasis et la Ville.* Roundtable Meeting held in Tours, 21–23 September 1989 by Centre d'Étude et de Recherche URBAMA.

——1997. 'Book Reviews.' *Jordanies.* No. 4: 88–94.

Boserup, Ester. 1970. *Woman's Role in Economic Development.* Hants: Gower.

Brand, Laurie. 1992. 'Economic and Political Liberalization in a Rentier Economy: The Case of the Hashemite Kingdom of Jordan.' In Iliya Harik and Denis J. Sullivan (eds) *Privatization and Liberalization in the Middle East.* Bloomington: Indiana University Press.

——1994. *Jordan's Inter-Arab Relations: The Political Economy of Alliance Making.* New York: Columbia University Press.

——1995. 'In the Beginning was the State – The Quest for Civil Society in Jordan.' In Augustus R. Norton (ed.) *Civil Society in the Middle East.* Leiden: E.J. Brill.

——1998. *Women, the State and Political Liberalization: Middle Eastern and North African Experiences.* New York: Columbia University Press.

Brandsma, Judith and Djenan Khayatt. 1996. *Jordan Micro-Credit Mission: Final Report.* Washington: World Bank Private Sector Development Department.

Brett, E. A. 1996. 'The Participatory Principle in Development Projects: The Costs and Benefits of Cooperation.' *Public Administration and Development.* Vol. 16: 5–19.

Brinkerhoff, Derick. 1996. 'Process Perspectives on Policy Change: Highlighting Implementation.' *World Development.* Vol. 24, No. 9: 1395–1401.

Brown, L. David. 1983. *Managing Conflict at Organizational Interface.* Reading, Massachusetts: Addison-Wesley.

Buhbe, Matthes. 1990. 'Jordan's Economy: Some Basic Facts.' In Kamel Abu-Jaber; Matthes Buhbe and Mohammad Smadi (eds) *Income Distribution in Jordan.* Boulder and Oxford: Westview Press and Friedrich Ebert Stiftung.

Buller, Henry, and Susan Wright. 1990. *Rural Development: Problems and Practices.* Hampshire: Gower Publishing Company Ltd.

Burkey, Stan. 1993. *People First: A Guide to Self-Reliant, Participatory Rural Development.* London and New Jersey: Zed Books Ltd.

Cassell, Catherine and Gillian Symon (eds). 1994. *Qualitative Methods in Organizational Research: A Practical Guide.* London and Thousand Oaks, New Delhi: SAGE Publications.

Cernea, Michael. 1988. *Nongovernmental Organizations and Local Development.* World Bank Discussion Papers. Washington: World Bank.

——1991. *Putting People First: Sociological Variables in Rural Development.* New York: Oxford University Press for World Bank.

——1994. 'The Sociologist's Approach to Sustainable Development.' In Ismail Serageldin, and Andrew Steer (eds) *Making Development Sustainable.*

Environmentally Sustainable Development Occasional Paper Series, No. 2. Washington: World Bank.

CGAP (Consultative Group to Assist the Poorest). 1996. 'The Consultative Group to Assist the Poorest: A Micro-Finance Program.' *Focus*, No. 1, February 1996. Washington: CGAP.

Chambers, Robert. 1983. *Rural Development: Putting the Last First.* London: Longman Group Ltd.

——1992. *Rural Appraisal: Rapid, Relaxed and Participatory.* Discussion Paper 311. Brighton: University of Sussex, Institute of Development Studies.

——1997. *Whose Reality Counts?* London: Intermediate Technology Publications.

Chatelus, Michel. 1987. 'Rentier or Producer Economy in the Middle East? The Jordanian Response.' In Bichara Khader and Adnan Bader (eds) *The Economic Development in Jordan.* London: Croom Helm.

Chatty, Dawn and Annika Rabo (eds). 1997. *Organizing Women: Formal and Informal Women's Groups in the Middle East.* Oxford and New York: Berg.

——1996. *Mobile Pastoralists.* New York: Columbia University Press.

Clark, John. 1992. 'Democratization Development: NGOs and the State.' *Development in Practice.* Vol. 2, No. 3: 151–62.

——1995. 'The State, Popular Participation, and the Voluntary Sector.' *World Development.* Vol. 23, No. 4: 593–601.

Clayton, Andrew. 1994. 'Introduction.' In Andrew Clayton (ed.) *Governance, Democracy and Conditionality – What Role for NGOs?* Oxford: INTRAC.

Cohen, J. and Uphoff, N. 1977. *Rural Development Participation: Concepts and Measures for Project Design, Implementation and Evaluation.* Ithaca, New York: Cornell University Press.

Coleman, James. 1988. 'Social Capital in the Creation of Human Capital.' *American Journal of Sociology.* Vol. 94, Supplement: S95–S120.

Cooperative Housing Foundation. 2000. *Southern Jordan Access to Credit Project (SJACP): Group and Individual Loan Program.* No. 2, Vol. 11, February 2000.

Dabbas, Hamed. 1997. 'Centres, Institutions, Organizations, Commissions and Committees Working in the Islamic Field in Jordan.' In Hussein Abu-Ruman (ed.) *Islamic Movements and Organizations in Jordan.* Amman: al-Urdon al-Jadid Research Centre (in Arabic).

Dallas, Roland. 1999. *King Hussein: A Life on the Edge.* London: Profile Books.

Danreuther, Roland. 1999. 'The Political Dimension: Authoritarianism and Democratization.' In Louise Fawcett and Yezid Sayigh (eds) *The Third World Beyond the Cold War: Continuity and Change.* Oxford: Oxford University Press.

Dasgupta, Partha. 1988. 'Trust as a Community.' In D. Gambetta (ed.) *Trust: Making and Breaking Cooperative Relations.* Oxford: Basil Blackwell.

Davies, Rick. 1997. 'Donor Information Demands and NGO Institutional Development.' *Journal of International Development.* Vol. 9, No. 4: 613–20.

Day, Arthur. 1986. *East Bank/West Bank: Jordan and the Prospects for Peace.* New

York: Council on Foreign Relations Books.

Deacon, Bob. 1999. 'Social Policy in a Global Context.' In Andrew Hurrell and Ngaire Woods (eds) *Inequality, Globalization and World Politics*. Oxford: Oxford University Press.

Dejong, Jocelyn. 1996. 'The Urban Context of Health During the Economic Crisis.' In Jean Hannoyer and Seteney Shami (eds) *Amman: The City and its Society*. Beirut: CERMOC.

Dhumale, Rahul and Amela Sapcanin with Judith Brandsma. 1999. *Spinning Off for Sustainable Microfinance: Save the Children Federation into JWDS, Al Majmoua, and Faten: Case Study*. Washington: The World Bank in cooperation with UNDP Regional Bureau for Arab States.

Dhumale, Rahul and Amela Sapcanin. n.d. *An Application of Islamic Banking Principles to Microfinance*. UNDP in cooperation with the World Bank Middle East and North Africa Region.

Dias, Clarence. 1994. 'Governance, Democracy and Conditionality: NGO Positions and Roles.' In Andrew Clayton (ed.) *Governance, Democracy and Conditionality – What Role for NGOs?* Oxford: INTRAC.

Edwards, Michael and David Hulme. 1992. 'Scaling up the Developmental Impact of NGOs: Concepts and Experiences.' In Michael Edwards and David Hulme (eds) *Making a Difference: NGOs and Development in a Changing World*. London: Earthscan.

——1995. 'Policy Arena: NGO Performance and Accountability in the Post-Cold War World.' *Journal of International Development*. Vol. 7, No. 6: 849–56.

Edwards, Michael. 1994. 'International NGOs and Southern Governments in the New World Order.' In Andrew Clayton (ed.) *Governance, Democracy and Conditionality – What Role for NGOs?* Oxford: INTRAC.

Escobar, Arturo. 1984. 'Discourse and Power in Development: Michel Foucault and the Relevance of his Work to the Third World.' *Alternatives*. Vol. 10. No. 3: 377–400.

——1995. *Encountering Development: The Making and Unmaking of the Third World*. Princeton: Princeton University Press.

ESCWA (Economic and Social Commission for Western Asia). 1990. *The Impact of the Gulf Crisis on the Jordanian Economy*. Amman: ESCWA.

——1992. *Proceedings of the Conference on the Capabilities and Needs of Disabled Persons in the ESCWA Region, 20–28 November, 1989*. Amman: United Nations.

Fawcett, Louise and Yezid Sayigh (eds). 1999. *The Third World Beyond the Cold War: Continuity and Change*. New York: Oxford University Press.

Ferguson, James. 1994. *The Anti-Politics Machine – 'Development, Depoliticization, and Bureaucratic Power in Lesotho.'* Minnesota: University Press of Minnesota.

Fisher, William. 1997. 'Doing Good? The Politics and Antipolitics of NGO Practices.' *Annual Review of Anthropology*. Vol. 26: 439–64.

Fowler, Alan. 1988. 'NGOs in Africa: Achieving Comparative Advantage in Relief and Micro-development.' Discussion Paper 249. Brighton: University of Sussex, Institute of Development Studies.

——1996. 'Strengthening Civil Society in Transition Economies – from Concept to Strategy: Mapping an Exit in a Maze of Mirrors.' In Andrew Clayton (ed.) *NGOs, Civil Society and the State: Building Democracy in Transitional Societies.* Oxford: INTRAC.

——1998. 'Authentic NGDO Partnerships in the New Policy Agenda for International Aid: Dead End or Light Ahead?' *Development and Change.* Vol. 29: 137–59.

Francis, Paul. 2001. 'Participatory Development at the World Bank: the Primacy of Process.' In Bill Cooke and Umar Kothari (eds) *Participation: the New Tyranny?* London: Zed Press.

Freire, Paulo. 1985. *The Politics of Education – Culture, Power, and Liberation.* London: Macmillan.

Frischtak. Leila. 1994. *Governance, Capacity and Economic Reform in Developing Countries.* World Bank Technical Paper, No. 24, June 1994. Washington: World Bank.

Garson, Jose. 1996. *Microfinance and Anti-Poverty Strategies: A Donor Perspective.* New York: Policy Series, United Nations Capital Development Fund of the UNDP.

Gledhill, John. 1994. *Power and its Disguises: Anthropological Perspectives on Politics.* London: Pluto.

Goetz, Anne Marie. 1995. 'The Politics of Integrating Gender to State Development Processes.' Occasional Paper. Geneva: United Nations Research Institute for Social Development.

——1996. 'Dis/Organizing Gender: Women Development Agents in State and NGO Poverty-Reduction Programmes in Bangladesh.' In Shirin Rai and Geraldine Lievesley (eds) *Women and the State International Perspectives.* London: Taylor and Francis.

Goetz, Anne Marie and Rin Sen Gupta. 1996. 'Who Takes the Credit: Gender, Power, and Control Over Loan Use in Rural Credit Programmes in Bangladesh.' *World Development.* Vol. 24, No. 1: 45–63.

Guijt, Irene and Meera Kaul Shah (eds). 1998. *The Myth of Community.* London: Intermediate Technology Publications Ltd.

Guijt, Irene and Meera Kaul Shah. 1998. 'Waking Up to Power, Conflict and Process.' In Irene Guijt and Meera Kaul Shah (eds) *The Myth of Community.* London: Intermediate Technology Publications Ltd.

GUVS (General Union of Voluntary Societies). 1996. *History, Programmes and Projects.* Amman: GUVS (in Arabic).

Hamarneh, Mustafa, Rosemary Hollis and Khalil Shikaki. 1997. *Jordanian Palestinian Relations: Where to? Four Scenarios for the Future.* London: Royal Institute of International Affairs.

Hammad, Walid. 1997. 'Islamists and Charitable Work.' In Hussein Abu-Ruman
(ed.) *Islamic Movements and Organizations in Jordan*. Amman: al-Urdon al-
Jadid Research Centre (in Arabic).

Handy, Charles. 1988. *Understanding Voluntary Organizations*. Harmondsworth:
Penguin Books.

Harik, I. 1992. 'Privatization: the Issue, the Prospects, and the Fears.' In D. J. Sullivan and I. Harik (eds) *Privatization and Liberalization in the Middle East*.
Bloomington: Indiana University Press.

Heyer, Judith, Pepe Roberts and Gavin Williams. 1981. 'Rural Development.' In
Judith Heyer, Pepe Roberts and G. Williams (eds) *Rural Development in Tropi-
cal Africa*. London: Macmillan.

Hijab, Nadia. 1988. *Womanpower*. London: Cambridge University Press.

Hobart, Mark. 1993. 'Introduction: The Growth of Ignorance?' In Mark Hobart
(ed.) *An Anthropological Critique of Development: The Growth of Ignorance*.
London: Routledge.

Hoogvelt, Ankie. 2001. *Globalisation and the Postcolonial World: The New Political
Economy of Development*. London: Palgrave.

Hudock, Ann. 1995. 'Sustaining Southern NGOs in Resource-Dependent Environments.' *Journal of International Development*. Vol. 7, No. 4: 653–67.

Hulme, David and Michael Edwards. 1997. 'NGOs, States and Donors: An Overview.' In David Hulme and Michael Edwards (eds) *NGOs, States and Donors:
Too Close for Comfort?* London: Macmillan.

Hulme, David and Michael Edwards (eds). 1997. *NGOs, States and Donors: Too
Close for Comfort?* Basingstoke and London: Macmillan Press Ltd.

Hulme, David. 2000. 'Impact Assessment Methodologies for Microfinance: Theory,
Experience and Better Practice.' *World Development*, Volume 28: 79–98.

Hurrell, Andrew and Ngaire Woods (eds). 1999. *Inequality, Globalization and
World Politics*. Oxford: Oxford University Press.

IMF (International Monetary Fund). 1996. *Building on Progress – Reform and
Growth in the Middle East and North Africa*. Washington: IMF, Middle Eastern
Department.

Johnson, Susan and Ben Rogaly. 1997. *Microfinance and Poverty Reduction*. Oxford:
Oxfam.

Johnston, Charles. 1972. *The Brink of Jordan*. London: Hamish Hamilton.

Jordan Media Group. 1994. *Jordan Israel Peace Treaty*. Amman: JMG, Publication
Number 18.

Joseph, Suad. 1988. 'Feminization, Familism, Self, and Politics: Research as a
Mughtaribi.' In Soraya Altorki and Camillia El-Solh (eds) *Arab Women in the
Field: Studying Your Own Society*. New York: Syracuse University Press.

——1997. 'The Reproduction of Political Process among Women Activities in
Lebanon: "Shopkeepers" and Feminists.' In Dawn Chatty and Annika Rabo
(eds) *Organizing Women: Formal and Informal Women's Groups in the Middle*

East. Oxford and New York: Berg.

Journal of Palestine Studies. 1993. 'Special Document File: The Peace Process.' Vol. 23, No. 1: 104–24.

Jureidini, Paul and R. D. McLaurin. 1984. *Jordan – The Impact of Social Change on the Role of Tribes*. The Washington Papers. Vol. 12. No. 108. New York: Praeger.

Kabeer, Naila. 1994. *Reversed Realities: Gender Hierarchies in Development Thought*. London and New York: Verso.

Kandil, Amani. 1995. *Civil Society in the Arab World*. Washington: CIVICUS.

Kanovsky, Eliyahu. 1995. 'Middle East Economies and Arab-Israeli Peace Agreements.' *Israel Affairs*. Vol. 1, No. 4: 22–39.

——1989. *Jordan's Economy: From Prosperity to Crisis*. Occasional Papers No. 106. The Moshe Dayan Center for Middle Eastern and African Studies, Shiloah Institute, Tel Aviv University.

Khairi, Majdeldin. 1988. 'An Evaluative Study on the Social Development Centres in Jordan.' In Queen Alia Fund Jordan Social Welfare Fund. *Final Report on the Seminar on Evaluation of the Social Development Centres in Jordan*. Amman: QAF (In Arabic).

Khatib, Abdullah al-. 1993. *Voluntary Work and the Disabled in Jordan*. Amman: GUVS (in Arabic).

Khatib, Abdullah et al. 1977. 'Voluntary Social Organizations: Aims, Regulations, Types, Achievements, Hindrances and Development.' In Abdullah Khatib (ed.) *Symposium on Voluntary Social Organizations*. Amman: Ministry of Labour, Department of Social Affairs and General Union of Voluntary Societies (in Arabic).

Khouri, Rami. 1981. *The Jordan Valley: Life and Society Below Sea Level*. London: Longman.

Kingston, Paul. 1994. 'Breaking the Patterns of Mandate: Economic Nationalism and State Formation in Jordan, 1951–57.' In Eugene Rogan and Tariq Tell (eds) *Village, Steppe and State: The Social Origins of Modern Jordan*. London and New York: British Academic Press.

Korten, David. 1980. *Community Organization and Rural Development: A Learning Process Approach*. A Ford Foundation Reprint from *Public Administration Review*.

Krämer, Gudrun. 1994. 'The Integration of the Integrists: A Comparative Study of Egypt, Jordan and Tunisia.' In Ghassan Salamé (ed.) *Democracy Without Democrats? The Renewal of Politics in the Muslim World*. London and New York: I.B. Tauris Publishers.

Lancaster, Carol. 1993. 'Governance and Development: The Views from Washington.' In Mick Moore (ed.) *Good Government?* Brighton: University of Sussex, the Institute of Development Studies (IDS).

Laqueur, Walter and Barry Rubin. 1984. *The Israel-Arab Reader. A Documentary History of the Middle East Conflict*. Rev. ed. 4th ed. New York: Pelican Books.

Lateef, K. Sarwar. 1995. 'The First Half Century: An Overview.' In Sarwar Lateef (ed.) *The Evolving Role of the World Bank – Helping the Challenge of Development.* Washington: World Bank.

Leftwich, Adrian. 1994. 'Governance, the State and the Politics of Development.' *Development and Change.* Vol. 25: 363–86.

——2000. *States of Development: On the Primacy of Politics in Development.* Cambridge: Polity Press.

Lele, Uma and Ijaz Nabi. 1991. 'Concessionary and Commercial Flows.' In Uma Lele and Ijaz Nabi, (eds) *Transition in Development –The Role of Aid and Commercial Flows.* San Francisco, California: International Centre for Economic Growth (ICS) Press: 5–6.

Lewellen, Ted C. 1995. *Dependency and Development: An Introduction to the Third World.* Connecticut and London: Bergin and Garvey.

Lisk, F.A.N. 1981. 'Popular Participation in Basic-Needs Oriented Development Planning.' *Labour and Society*, Vol. 6, No. 1: 3–14.

Long, Norman (ed.). 1989. *Encounters at the Interface: A Perspective on Social Discontinuities in Rural Development.* Wageningen, The Netherlands: Agricultural University.

——1992. 'Introduction.' In Norman Long and Ann Long (eds) *Battlefields of Knowledge: The Interlocking Theory and Practice in Social Research and Development.* London and New York: Routledge.

Majdalani, Rula. 1996. 'The Changing Role of NGOs in Jordan: An Emerging Actor in Development.' *Jordanies.* No. 2: 119–36.

Mallakh, Ragae el- and M. Mihssen Kadhim. 1976. 'Arab Institutionalized Development Aid and Evaluation.' *The Middle East Journal.* Vol. 30, No. 4: 471–84.

Marchand, Marianne and Jane Parpart (eds). 1995. *Feminism Postmodernism Development.* London and New York: Routledge.

Marsden, David. 1994. 'Indigenous Management: Introduction.' In Susan Wright (ed.) *Anthropology of Organizations.* London and New York: Routledge.

Martinussen, John. 1997. *Society, State and Market: A Guide to Competing Theories of Development.* London: Zed Books.

Marzouk, Mohsen. 1997. 'The Associative Phenomenon in the Arab World: Engine of Democratisation or Witness to the Crisis?' In David Hulme and Michael Edwards (eds) *NGOs, States and Donors: Too Close for Comfort?* London: Macmillan Press.

Maynard, Mary. 1994. 'Methods, Practice and Epistemology: The Debate about Feminism and Research.' In Mary Maynard and June Purvis (eds) *Researching Women's Lives from a Feminist Perspective.* London: Taylor and Francis.

Maynard, Mary and June Purvis. 1994. 'Doing Feminist Research.' In Mary Maynard and June Purvis (eds) *Researching Women's Lives from a Feminist Perspective.* London: Taylor and Francis.

Mayoux, Linda. 1995. 'Beyond Naivety: Women, Gender Inequality and Participatory Development.' *Development and Change.* Vol. 26: 235–58.

Mazur, Michael. 1972. 'Economic Development of Jordan.' In Charles Cooper and Sidney Alexander (eds) *Economic Development and Population Growth in the Middle East.* New York: American Elsevier Publishing Company.

——1979. *Economic Growth and Development in Jordan.* Boulder, Colo.: Westview.

McMichael, Philip. 1996. *Development and Social Change: A Global Perspective.* California, London and New Delhi: Pine Forge Press.

Meyer, Carrie. 1992. 'A Step Back as Donors Shift Institution Building from the Public Sector to the "Private" Sector.' *World Development.* Vol. 20, No. 88: 1115–26.

Microfund for Women. 2000. *Newsletter.* January 2000.

Mohan, G. 2000. 'Contested Sovereignty and Democratic Contradictions: The Political Impacts of Adjustment.' In Giles Mohan, Ed Brown, Bob Williams and Alfred B. Zack Williams (eds) *Structural Adjustment: Theory, Practice and Inputs.* London and New York: Routledge.

Moore, Mick. 1993. 'Good Government?' *The Institute of Development Studies.* Vol. 24, No. 1: 1–6.

Morduch, Jonathon. 2000. 'The Microfinance Schism.' *World Development.* Vol. 28, No. 4: 617–29.

Moser, Caroline. 1993. *Gender Planning and Development: Theory, Practice and Training.* London and New York: Routledge.

Oakley, Peter. 1990. 'The Evaluation of Social Development.' In David Marsden and Peter Oakley (eds) *Evaluating Social Development Projects.* Oxford: Oxfam.

——1991. *Projects With People: The Practice of Participation in Rural Development.* Geneva: ILO.

——1995. *People's Participation in Development Projects.* Occasional Papers Series. No. 7 July 1995. Oxford: INTRAC.

OAPEC (Organization of Arab Petroleum Exporting Countries). 1995. *Annual Report 1995.* Kuwait: OAPEC.

Omidian, Patricia. 2000. 'Qualitative Measures and Refugee Research: The Case of Afghan Refugees.' In Frederick L. Ahearn (ed.) *Psychosocial Wellness of Refugees: Issues on Qualitative and Quantitative Research.* Oxford and New York: Berghahn Books.

Otero, Maria and Elisabeth Rhyne (eds). 1994. *The New World of Microenterprise Finance*: *Building Healthy Financial Institutions for the Poor.* West Hartford, Connecticut: Kumarian Press.

Owen, R. 1983. 'Government and Economy in Jordan: Progress, Problems and Prospects.' In P. Seale (ed.) *The Shaping of an Arab Statesman – Sharif Abd al-Hamid Sharaf and the Modern Arab World.* London: Quartet Books.

Patton, Michael. 1990. *Qualitative Evaluation and Research Methods.* London: Sage Publications.

Perera, Jehan. 1995. 'In Unequal Dialogue with Donors: The Experience of the Sarvodaya Shramadana Movement.' *Journal of International Development.* Vol.

7, No. 6: 869–78.

Pfeffer, J. and G. Salancik. 1978. *The External Control of Organizations: A Resource Dependence Perspective.* New York: Harper and Row.

Pieterse, Jan A. 1991. 'Dilemmas of Development Discourse: The Crisis of Developmentalism and the Comparative Method.' *Development and Change.* Vol. 22: 5–29.

Porter, Marilyn. 1994. '"Second-hand Ethnography": Some Problems in Analyzing a Feminist Project.' In Alan Bryman and Robert Burgess (eds) *Analyzing Qualitative Data.* London and New York: Routledge.

Post, Uli and Hans-Joachim Preuss. 1997. 'No Miracle Weapon for Development: The Challenges Facing NGOs in the 21st Century.' *Development and Cooperation (D+C),* No. 6: 4–5.

Pottier, Johan (ed.). 1993. *Practising Development: Social Science Perspectives.* London and New York: Routledge.

Powell, Mike and David Seddon. 1997. 'NGOs and the Development Industry.' *Review of African Economy.* Vol. 71: 3–10.

Pratt, Brian and Adrian Stone. 1994. *Multilateral Agencies and NGOs: A Position Paper.* Occasional Papers Series. No. 1, 1994. Oxford: INTRAC.

PRB (Population Reference Bureau). 1999. *World Population Data Sheet: Demographic Data and Estimates for the Countries and Regions of the World.* Washington: Population Reference Bureau.

Pretty, N. Jules, Irene Guijt, John Thompson and Ian Scoones. 1995. *Participatory Learning and Action: a Trainer's Guide.* London: International Institute for Environment and Development (IIED).

Psacharopoulos, George, and Nguyen Xuan Nguyen. 1997. *The Role of Government and the Private Sector in Fighting Poverty.* World Bank Technical Paper No. 346. Washington: World Bank.

Putnam, Robert. 1993. 'The Prosperous Community – Social Capital and Public Life.' *The American Prospect.* No. 13: 35–42.

Qutaina, Mohammad. 1963. *The Cooperative Movement in the Hashemite Kingdom of Jordan: A detailed report about the establishment of the cooperative movement and its achievements until 21/3/1963.* Amman: The Cooperative Institute (in Arabic).

Rabi, Ahmad al-. 1992. *The Democratic Behaviour with the Jordanian Experience.* Amman: privately published (in Arabic).

Reinharz, Shulamit. 1992. *Feminist Methods in Social Research.* New York and Oxford: Oxford University Press.

Ripert, J. 1990. *Report on a Mission to Jordan.* New York: United Nations.

Robertson, A. F. 1984. *People and the State: An Anthropology of Planned Development.* Cambridge: Cambridge University Press.

Robinson, Glenn. 1997. 'Can Islamists be Democrats? The Case of Jordan.' *Middle East Journal.* Vol. 51, No. 3: 373–87.

Robinson, Mark. 1994. 'Governance, Democracy and Conditionality: NGOs and the New Policy Agenda.' In Andrew Clayton (ed.) *Governance, Democracy and Conditionality: What Role for NGOs?* Oxford: INTRAC.

——1995. 'Introduction.' *IDS Bulletin.* Vol. 26, No. 2: 1–8.

Roy, Ash Narain. 1999. *The Third World in the Age of Globalisation: Requiem or New Agenda?* Delhi: Madhyam Books.

Rubin, H. and I. Rubin. 1995. *Qualitative Interviewing: The Art of Hearing Data.* London: Sage Publications.

Ryan, Curtis R. 1998. 'Peace, Bread and Riots: Jordan and the International Monetary Fund.' *Middle East Policy.* Vol. 6, No. 2: 54–66.

Salibi, Kamal. 1993. *The Modern History of Jordan.* London: I.B. Tauris Publishers.

Salmen, Lawrence. 1987. *Listen to the People: Participant Observer Evaluation of Development Projects.* Oxford: Oxford University Press.

Salzman, Philip. 1999. *The Anthropology of Real Life: Events in Human Experience.* Prospect Heights, Illinois: Waveland Press.

Saqour, Mohammed al-. 1986. *Regional Planning and Development in Rural Communities: A Case Study in Rural Jordan.* Amman: Shuqair and Akasheh (in Arabic).

Saqour, Mohammed al-, Omar al-Sheikh, Issa Ibrahim, Khalid Shuraideh and Fathi al-Nusour. 1989. *Study of Poverty Pockets in Jordan.* Amman: Ministry of Social Development (in Arabic).

Satloff, Robert. 1994. *From Abdullah to Hussein: Jordan in Transition.* New York: Oxford University Press.

Sayigh, Yusif. 1978. *The Economies of the Arab World – Development Since 1945.* London: Croom Helm.

Sayigh, Yezid. 1991. 'Jordan in the 1980s: Legitimacy, Entity and Identity.' In R. Wilson (ed.) *Politics and the Economy in Jordan.* London: Routledge.

Schein, Edgar. 1989. 'What is Culture?' In Peter Frost, Larry Moore, Meryl Reis Louis, Craig Lundberg and Joanne Martin (eds) *Refraining Organizational Structure.* London: Sage Publications.

Schlumberger, Olive. 2002. 'Transition to Development.' In George Joffé (ed.) *Jordan in Transition.* London: Hurst & Company.

Schneider, Harmut and Marie-Hélène Libercier (eds). 1995. *Participatory Development From Advocacy to Action.* Paris: Organization for Economic Co-operation and Development (OECD).

Scudder, Thayer. 1999. 'The Emerging Global Crisis and Development Anthropology: Can We Have an Impact?' *Human Organization.* Vol. 58, No. 4, Winter 1999: 351–64.

Seers, Dudley. 1979. 'The Meaning of Development.' In David Lehmann (ed.) *Development Theory: Four Critical Studies.* London: Frank Cass.

Serageldin, Ismail. 1994. 'Making Development Sustainable.' In Ismail Serageldin and Andrew Steer (eds) *Making Development Sustainable: From Concepts to Action.* Environmentally Sustainable Development Occasional Paper Series, No. 2. Washington: World Bank.

——1996. *Sustainability and the Wealth of Nations – First Steps in an Ongoing Journey.* Environmentally Sustainable Development Studies and Monographs No. 5. Washington: World Bank.

Shami, Seteney. 1988. 'Studying Your Own: The Complexities of a Shared Culture.' In Soraya Altorki and Camillia El-Solh (eds) *Arab Women in the Field: Studying Your Own Society.* New York: Syracuse University Press.

——1997. 'Domesticity Reconfigured: Women in Squatter Areas of Amman.' In Dawn Chatty and Annika Rabo (eds) *Organizing Women: Formal and Informal Women's Groups in Middle East.* Oxford and New York: Berg.

Shryock, Andrew. 1995. '"Tribaliser" la nation, "nationaliser" les tribus: politique de l'histoire chez les Bedouins de la Balqua', en Jordanie.' *Monde Arabe Maghreb-Machrek.* No. 147, January-March, 1995: 121–31.

Singh, N.C. and V. Titi. 1994. 'Adaptive Strategies of the Poor in Arid and Semi-arid Lands: In Search of Sustainable Livelihoods.' Winnipeg: International Institute for Sustainable Development, Working Paper, 31 pp.

Sollis, Peter. 1992. 'Multilateral Agencies, NGOs, and Policy Reform.' *Development in Practice.* Vol. 2, No. 3:163–78.

Srour, Nadia. 1997. *Evaluation of Pre-School Education in the Hashemite Kingdom of Jordan: A Field Study.* Amman: The National Centre for Human Resource Development (in Arabic).

Stewart, Frances and Albert Berry. 1999. 'Globalization, Liberalization, and Inequality: Expectations and Experience.' In Andrew Hurrell and Ngaire Woods (eds) *Inequality, Globalization and World Politics.* Oxford: Oxford University Press.

Stewart, Sheelagh. 1997. 'Happily Ever After in the Market Place: NGO and Uncivil Society.' *Review of African Political Economy,* No. 71: 11–34.

Syam, Majeed. 1999. *Islamic Bank: A Qur'an View of Money, Humankind and Labour in the World Reconstruction.* Amman: privately published (in Arabic).

Thomas, Alan. 1996. 'What is Development Management?' *Journal of International Development.* Vol. 8, No. 1: 95–110.

Tukan, Umayya. 1983. 'The Debate about Development.' In Patrick Seale (ed.) *The Shaping of an Arab Statesman: Sharif Abd al-Hamid Sharaf and the Modern Arab World.* London: Quartet Books Ltd.

UN (United Nations). 1997a. *Implementing Sustainable Development – Experiences and Recommendations from National and Regional Consultations for the Rio +5 Forum.* 1st ed. Compiled and published by the Earth Council for the Fifth Session of the United Nations Commission on Sustainable Development (UN-CSD).

——1997b. *Critical Trends – Global Change and Sustainable Development.* New York: United Nations.

——1997c. 'General Assembly Decides to Convene Two-Day Resumed Session of Economic and Financial Committee to Address "Financing for Development."'

Press Release, GA/9387 UN General Assembly Decision.

——2000. 'Further Actions and Initiatives to Implement the Beijing Declaration for Action.' Unedited final outcome document as adopted by the plenary of the twenty-third special session of the General Assembly 'Women 2000: Gender Equality, Development and Peace for the 21st Century.' June 2000.

UNDP (United Nations Development Programme). 1990. *Human Development Report*. New York: Oxford University Press for the UNDP.

——1991. *Report on Jordan's Economic Trends January– February 1991*. UNDP.

——1993. *Human Development Report*. New York: Oxford University Press for the UNDP.

——1994. *Human Development Report*. New York: Oxford University Press for the UNDP

——1997a. *Human Development Report*. New York: Oxford University Press for the UNDP.

——1997c. *Micro Start: A Guide for Planning, Starting and Managing a Microfinance Programme*. New York: UNDP Private Sector Development Programme.

——1999. 'Microfinance.' *Essentials*. Evaluation Office No. 3, December 1999: 1–12.

——1999 a. *Human Development Report*. New York: Oxford University Press for the UNDP.

UNFPA (United Nations Population Fund). 1997. *The State of the World Population*. New York: UNFPA.

USAID (US Agency for International Development). 1988. *USAID in Jordan: 35 Years of Commitment*. Amman: USAID.

——1995. *Maximising the Outreach of Microenterprise Finance: An Analysis of Successful Microfinance Programmes*. USAID Program and Operations Assessment Report, No. 10, Centre for Development Information and Evaluation, prepared by Robert Christen, Elisabeth Rhyne, Robert Vogel and Cressida McKean. Arlington: USAID.

Van der Heijden, Hendrik. 1987. 'The Reconciliation of NGO Autonomy, Program Integrity and Operational Effectiveness with Accountability to Donors.' *World Development*. Vol. 15, Supplement: 103–12.

Van Ufford, Philip. 1988. 'The Hidden Crisis in Development: Development Bureaucracies in Between Intentions and Outcomes.' In P. Ufford, D. Kruijt and Theodore Downing (eds) *The Hidden Crisis in Development: Development Bureaucracies*. Tokyo: United Nations University, Amsterdam: Free University Press.

Von Pischke, J. D. 1996. *Finance at the Frontier: Debt Capacity and the Role of Credit in the Private Economy*. Washington: Economic Development Institute of the World Bank.

WCED (World Commission on Environment and Development). 1987. *Our Common Future*. Oxford: Oxford University Press.

White, Gordon. 1995. 'Towards a Democratic Development State.' *IDS Bulletin*.

Vol. 26, No. 2: 27–36.

Whitehead, Laurence. 1993. 'Economic Liberalization and Democratization: Explorations of the Linkages.' *World Development.* Vol. 21, No. 8: 1245–61.

Wiktorowicz, Quintan. 1999. 'The Limits of Democracy in the Middle East: The Case of Jordan.' *Middle East Journal.* Vol. 58, No. 4: 606–20.

Wilson, Rodney (ed.). 1991. *Politics and the Economy in Jordan.* London: Routledge.

Woods, Ngaire. 1999. 'Order, Globalization, and Inequality in World Politics.' In Andrew Hurrell and Ngaire Woods (eds) *Inequality, Globalization, and World Politics.* New York: Oxford University Press.

——2000. 'The Political Economy of Globalization.' In Ngaire Woods (ed.) *The Political Economy of Globalization.* London: Macmillan Press Ltd.

World Bank. 1957. *The Economic Development of Jordan.* Baltimore: The John Hopkins Press.

——1990. *World Development Report 1990.* New York: Oxford University Press for the World Bank.

——1991. *World Development Report 1991.* New York: Oxford University Press for the World Bank.

——1992. *Governance and Development.* Washington: World Bank.

——1995a. *Poverty Reduction and The World Bank: Progress in Fiscal 1994.* Washington: World Bank.

——1995b. *Claiming the Future – Choosing Prosperity in the Middle East and North Africa.* Washington: World Bank.

——1997a. *Expanding the Measure of Wealth. Indicators of Environmentally Sustainable Development.* (Environmentally Sustainable Development Studies and Monographs). Washington: World Bank.

——1997b. *World Development Report 1997 – The State in a Changing World.* New York: Oxford University Press for the World Bank.

WPF (World Population Foundation). 1996. *Short-term Consultancy – Birth Spacing Programme: Jordan Report.* Netherlands: WPF.

WWSF (Women's World Summit Foundation). 1999. *Prize for Women's Creativity in Rural Life.* WWSF Global Newsletter No. 8, August 1999. Geneva: Women's World Summit Foundation.

Zaghal, Ali. 1984. 'Social Change in Jordan.' *Middle Eastern Studies.* Vol. 20., No. 4: 53–75.

Zu'bi, S. A. al-. 1991. 'Jordan's Foreign Policy: Regional and International Implications.' In R. Wilson (ed.) *Politics and the Economy in Jordan.* London: Routledge.

Newspapers and Periodicals

The Arab Daily [Amman English Daily Newspaper]. 1999. 'Agreements covering AMIR Program signed.' 21 April 1999: 14.

al-Arab al-Youm [Amman Arabic Daily Newspaper]. 1999. 'The Democratic Experiment in Jordan.' By Mohammad Shar'a. 26 August, 1, 5, 7 September 1999, Vol. 3, No. 830: 6, No. 836: 8, No. 840: 8, No. 842: 8.

——2000. 'Lloyds has received 18 million dollars in al-'Aqaba since 1994.' 24 August 2000: 1.

Baladi [Amman Arabic Quarterly]. 1982. 'The Second National Conference for the Heads of Village and Municipality Councils.' No. 4: 10–14.

——1983. 'An open discussion in Madaba between the municipal council and citizens.' No. 13: 43.

——1988. 'The municipal councils in Jordan between the events, elections, appointments and dissolution.' By Fawzi Khalil. No. 18: 46–51.

ad-Dustour [Amman Arabic Daily Newspaper]. 1990. 'Parliament has begun discussing the draft General Budget.' 28 January 1990: 10–15.

——1994. 'Parliament today ends debate on Budget Law.' 15 January 1994: 10–14.

——1996. 'Economic Supplement.' 27 January 1996: 34.

——1999a. 'In a memo to the prime minister, Dr al-Wahsh asks that no agreements be signed with NGOs except through the Ministry of Development.' 29 September 1999: 3.

——1999b. 'Ramadaniyyat: The goodwill campaign.' 16 December 1999: 3.

——2000a. 'Half a century after establishment, professional associations are expert houses and support for national work.' 5 August 2000: 20.

——2000b. 'Four secretaries-general request raising the liberties' ceiling and drafting a modern electoral law.' 15 August 2000: 20.

——2000c. 'A seminar organized by *ad-Dustour* discusses the issues of foreign funding to research centres.' 20 July 2000: 20.

The Economist. 1995. 'The gift relationship.' 18 March 1995: 19–20.

——1997a. 'Jordan: A not so loyal opposition.' 30 August 1997.

——1997b. 'Jordan: Drifting apart.' 8 November 1997.

Jordan Times [Amman English Daily Newspaper]. 1990. 'Iraq will not invade Saudi Arabia – King.' 6 August 1990: 1, 5.

——1996. 'Tense calm in the south after riots related to increase in bread and fodder prices.' 17 August 1996: 1.

——1997a. 'The Arab state and the loyal opposition: Dancing the validation tango.' By Rami Khouri. 15 July 1997: 6.

——1997b. 'Jordan to host conference on microfinance next week.' 10 March 1997: 8.

——1998a. 'Organized intimidation against foreign funding "postpones" human rights seminar.' 8 September 1998: 1.

——1998b. 'Seminar examines issues of foreign funding to local groups.' 28 September 1998: 3.

——1999. 'Microfinance training programme begins to meet JD 320 million loan demand in Kingdom.' 13 September 1999: 3.

——2000a. 'The old and new worlds of Joe Lieberman, Saad Eddin Ibrahim and Nidal Mansour.' By Rami Khouri. 9 August 2000: 5.

——2000b. 'Foreign funding of NGOs fuels anger.' 12 September 2000: 3.

——2000c. 'Campaign against Mansour heats up: JPA disciplinary council to question journalist on foreign funding.' 7 August 2000: 3.

——2000d. 'Obeidat asks government to investigate NGOs with foreign funders.' 12 June 2000: 3.

——2000e. 'US to continue supporting Jordan.' 27 June 2000: 1.

MEED. 1980a. 'Jordan's five-year plan cuts back on industrial development.' By W. Lee. Vol. 28, No. 34: 4–5.

——1980b. 'Jordan gears itself to Iraq's war effort.' By D. Shirreff. Vol. 24, No. 3: 20–1.

——1997. 'A tale of two countries.' MEED Special Report. 30 May 1997. Vol. 41. No. 22: 9–14.

——1998. 'Making the most of the potential for progress. MEED Jordan special report.' 29 May 1998. Vol. 42. No. 22: 11–13.

al-Mithaq [Amman Arabic Weekly]. 1998. 'Foreign organizations in Jordan and their research funding.' 9 June 1988: 10.

al-Osbou' al-'Arabi [Arabic Weekly]. 1992. 'Islamic organizations in Egypt: The other face of Islam.' No. 1720, 28 September 1992: 33–7.

al-Ra'i [Amman Arabic Daily Newspaper]. 1978. 'In commemoration of Queen Alia's martyrdom, a fund for social work carrying Her Majesty's name: al-Hussein entrusts Princess Basma to chair its board of trustees.' 9 February 1978: 1,12.

——1984. 'The return of parliamentary life to Jordan.' 6 January 1984: 1, 6–7.

——1989a. 'Return of the spirit.' 2 August 1989: 19.

——1989b. 'Candidates ... and the difficult questions.' 14 August 1989: 6.

——1989c. 'Who does not believe in democracy should not participate in elections.' 5 August 1989: 18.

——1989d. 'Who does not believe in democracy should not participate in elections.' 6 August 1989: 16.

——1989e. 'Who does not believe in democracy should not participate in elections.' 7 August 1989: 11.

——1989f. 'Shura and democracy.' 20 August 1989: 17.

——1989g. 'Participating in the dialogue on shura and democracy.' 5 September 1989: 11.

——1989h. 'Popular will ... and public administration.' 5 August 1989: 24.

——1989i. 'Currents in the parliamentary election campaigns.' 5 August 1989: 18.

——1989j. 'In defence of traditionalism and tribalism, in defence of the democratic future.' 9 August 1989: 16.

——1989k. 'Elections and the struggle between various currents.' 14 August 1989: 14.

——1989l. 'Women in the *Badia* and their role in elections.' 20 August 1989: 17.

——1989m. 'Women and elections.' 21 August 1989: 17.

——1989n. 'How will they win the votes of those who lack brains and religion?' 22 August 1989: 12.

——1989o. 'Let's be realistic regarding women's issues.' 5 September 1989: 11.

——1989p. 'Women between equality ... and the wrong equation?' 5 September 1989: 11.

——1989q. 'Politics of a different nature.' 11 September 1989: 13.

——1993. 'The one vote.' By Omar al-Nabulsi. 23 June 1993: 10.

——1998. 'Members of Parliament continue discussing the state general budget for 1998.' 19 January 1998: 32–6.

——1999a. 'The democratic era in the balance.' By Taher Adwan. 18 November 1999: 23.

——1999b. 'In remembrance of Her Majesty Queen Zein al-Sharaf: Umm al-Hussein pioneer of women's movement and political, voluntary and social work.' 26 April 1999: 8.

——2000. 'The Jordanian economy largest sufferer from international sanctions on Iraq.' 22 August 2000: 15.

al-Sabeel [Amman Arabic Weekly]. 1998. 'In a heated seminar by *al-Sabeel*: Foreign funding to national institutions.' 14–20 July 1998: 6–7.

Electronic

CGAP (Consultative Group to Assist the Poorest). 1995. 'The missing links: financial systems that work for the majority.' Focus. No. 3, October 1995. http://www.cgap.org/html/p-focus-notes03.html.

Dawkins Scully, Nan. n.d. Micro-Credit 'No penance for poor women.' The Development GAP website www.igc.org/dgap/micro.html.

Grameen Bank. 2000. 'Breaking the vicious cycle of poverty through microcredit.' http://www.grameen-info.org/bank/bcycle.html.

Jordan. 2000a. Gross Domestic Products. Amman: Department of Statistics. http:///www.dos.gov.jo.

NHF. 1998. Noor al-Hussein Foundation: New Perspectives for Development PORTFOLIO, 1985–1998. CD.

Oxfam, 1997. 'Microfinance policy and the Microcredit Summit.' http://www:oxfam.org.uk/policy/papers/polmicro.htm.

Index